WITHDRAWAL

Through the Schoolhouse Door

Through the Schoolhouse Door

Folklore, Community, Curriculum

Paddy Bowman and Lynne Hamer, Editors

Utah State University Press
Logan, Utah
2011

Utah State University Press
Logan, Utah 84322-3078
www.USUPress.org

The authors of chapters 1 through 8 were grateful recipients of funding from the National Endowment for the Arts Folk and Traditional Arts Program, which made possible the projects so lovingly undertaken and documented in this volume.

Manufactured in the United States of America
Printed on recycled, acid-free paper

ISBN: 978-0-87421-859-6 (paper)
ISBN: 978-0-87421-860-2 (e-book)

Library of Congress Cataloging-in-Publication Data

Through the schoolhouse door : folklore, community, curriculum / Paddy Bowman and Lynne Hamer, editors.
   p. cm.
 Includes bibliographical references.
  ISBN 978-0-87421-859-6 (pbk.) -- ISBN 978-0-87421-860-2 (e-book)
1. Folklore and education--United States. 2. Folklore--Study and teaching--United States. 3. Community and school--United States. I. Bowman, Paddy, 1947- II. Hamer, Lynne M.
  LB1583.8.T47 2011
  398.07--dc23
                        2011032371

For Katie, once my cherished kindergartner,
always my treasured teacher of life's marvels

P.B.

For Julia and Sam, who taught me that I can indeed
tell stories
and who make everyday life joyful

L.H.

Contents

Foreword

How to Begin to Know What You Didn't Know

Bonnie Stone Sunstein

As a longtime teacher, it's hard for me to admit that some of the most permanent teaching and learning happen outside school: "Learn without realizing you're learning." "Teach when the teachable moment presents itself." "The natural classroom of the real world." "A school without walls." Annoying clichés? Perhaps. Idealistic? I'm not so sure. As our schools pressure us to account for *what* students learn, we don't have time to think about *where* and *how* our students learn. Yet we know it is our job to think about *exactly that*. We see learning; we know it happens. Often it's on Mondays or after vacations, when our students arrive with impressive new skills and insights. We delight as they connect their out-of-school knowledge with our curricula; we feel satisfied and smug as we link that learning to our curriculum standards. What we call "community heritage" is simply a part of everything we and our students do. It's invisible, intangible.

For more than twenty years, I taught writing in New England. I read hundreds of students' words about the traditions, crafts, and community activities they learned without realizing they were learning them. I read detailed homages to Canadian pork pie and Greek baklava, peeked through the pages at a whole community's plans for the strawberry festival. I read dialogues about the intricacies of boat building, monologues on the wizardry of net mending. I learned how to build ice-fishing rigs, felt the ruts

---

Bonnie Stone Sunstein, a former high-school teacher, is a professor at the University of Iowa, where she directs undergraduate nonfiction writing and chairs English education.

in spring ski trails, and watched granite being carved into gravestones. I observed grandmothers with wrinkly thighs teaching smooth, slippery babies to swim in lakes as clear today as they were a hundred years ago. On my students' pages, I watched neighbors and relatives spin stories, braid rugs, dry flowers, fiddle, dance, and erect barns with a reverence for the way it's "always been done" and an equal excitement for the latest version that hadn't yet appeared.

I've taught almost another twenty years in Iowa, and still those texts bring New Hampshire back to life when I'm feeling nostalgic or homesick. But here I read about the teenage ritual of cow tipping in pastures at midnight, peace in endless fields of waving prairie grass, or meditations on the ethics of keeping preslaughtered pigs as family pets. I smell chokecherries and fry bread at the entrance to a Sioux grandmother's home, learn about strange textures and awkward finger strategies required to stuff Polish sausages into casings made of animal guts. I indulge in a cultural high as a young man climbs his uncle's silo to get a geometric view of the landscape.

My students teach me their local culture with the words on their pages. I don't know that's what they're doing; they don't know it at the time, either. Students scope a landscape, weave a fabric, tell a story, and chip away at a quarry just as their mentors—and mentors before them—taught. This is community heritage, and wherever we live or teach, we have more of it than we realize. With each time, each product, each performance, each person adds a creative tweak, a dash of knowledge, a dab of contemporary material to make the tradition stronger and more lasting. In each newly tweaked work, there is a unique mixture of disciplines: art, music, science, history, math, physics, biology, critical theory, literature. I think the very best in teaching and learning exists in these scenes. It is private teaching, unremarkable and unmeasurable. It is the folk in folklife.

Out-of-school experience is the great unspoken curriculum. Its main purpose is to conserve culture in an environment as precious as its citizenry. Its student-teacher ratio is often one to one, its final exam is proof the tradition stays alive, and its "outcomes assessment" is the next generation of mentor teachers and apprentice learners. Tradition in this unspoken curriculum—"the way it's always been done"—links itself comfortably and quietly to change, to another curriculum—"the way this version will be this time, in this place, with this stuff." Human knowledge, creation, and transmission constitute a delicate ecosystem.

When you read the chapters in this book, you will learn how to make this kind of learning visible, tangible, and relevant to you and your students. You will get ideas and inspiration—even tips—on how to do your own version. You'll go to Missouri, Pennsylvania, Florida, Louisiana, Wisconsin, New York City, Nebraska, and Ohio, among other places. You'll learn ways to integrate local culture and folk arts across curricula and in professional development for teachers and artists, involve folk artists and parents in education, develop classroom-friendly resources that address educational standards, and recognize and encourage the agency of young people and their community members. The authors will dazzle you with community-heritage projects, each executed with creative aplomb, each recognizing the institutional requirements that make it work.

Ride on a bus with teachers in Wisconsin who used a tragic 1871 fire as a focal point for integrating curriculum and professional development in their Here at Home cultural tour project. Listen to an Ojibwe Woodland flute maker at a hotel, wafting music across the shores of Lake Superior as he shows teachers how the local environment contributed to the shaping of his flute, the making of his music. Meet a Hmong seamstress, a basket maker. Visit a bison ranch, fishing families, and Mexicans making altars for the Day of the Dead.

Peek inside folklorists' careers as teachers and collaborators of teachers; keep them company as they gather local knowledge in unfamiliar places and devise ways to connect teachers and students to their personal and community traditions. Open a trunk and view cultural artifacts from Mexicans who have settled in Nebraska; then imagine or even make your own trunk. Enter Folkvine.org on your computer and browse a spinning display of postcards to view folk artists at work around Florida. See how four years, seven grants, ten artists, four tour guides, and countless podcasts, events, articles, and presentations link students and faculty with the local arts: signage from a produce stand, Hawaiian quilts, a family of clown shoemakers, model circuses, a painter of parallel universes, a Puerto Rican mask maker, a sculptor who uses roadkill bones, a Peruvian carved-box maker, bobbin lace makers, a Jewish *katuba* maker, and a group of fourth graders designing an Internet game with avatars.

Or go to Louisiana and enter an enormous statewide effort for conducting fieldwork and creating community projects linked to educational content standards. For one chapter, you can join a huge team of teachers, students, museum people, Web developers, artists, and scholars working for more than ten years with National Endowment for the Arts funding to create a thousand Web pages and four online databases.

In a time of increasing public pressures and dwindling grant funds, the challenges are daunting, but the results of these projects are remarkable. The chapters offer common threads: teacher-initiated curricular plans, careful attention to state standards, integration of local arts and artists, and discovery of self and community. The authors help us make connections among the sociological, linguistic, economic, ecological, atmospheric, pedagogical, artistic, and performative features that we find inside local cultures; they even help us learn where to look for those links. They interrogate the term *folklore* and offer us an opportunity to define *folk arts* and *folklife* for ourselves or anyone who asks us. Each chapter offers a different model that echoes the twenty-first-century initiatives for social justice and experiential learning that we meet these days in our schools: creative partnerships among universities, K–12 schools, communities, museums, historical societies, churches, service clubs, local artisans, and more.

But as new as these projects may seem, this book echoes the very oldest of educational traditions. I like to think of "experiential," "pragmatic," "constructivist" learning—whatever we want to call it—as its own subculture, rich with example, tradition, and a long line of mentors who are our tradition bearers, beginning with ancient folk wisdom whose records have survived.

In translation Confucius uses the term *rites* to mean the everyday rituals, the routines that we use—knowingly or unknowingly—during our daily lives. And understanding those rituals—in short, "knowing what you know and how you know it"—leads to a satisfied and healthy society. "Respectfulness, without the Rites," said Confucius, "becomes laborious bustle; carefulness, without the Rites, becomes timidity; boldness, without the Rites, becomes insubordination; straightforwardness, without the Rites, becomes rudeness" (1997, 7:2). In short, the most human learning involves understanding what you've done in terms of knowing what you know. And that takes thought and articulation.

As a pupil of Plato, Aristotle understood the value of learning when it connects with experience and reflection: "Anything that we have to learn to do we learn by the actual doing of it. . . . We become just by doing just acts, temperate by doing temperate ones, brave by doing brave ones" (1976, 91).

In short—as the approaches and projects in this book remind us—one of our most precious pedagogical legacies is knowing how to help our students begin to know what they didn't know—in relationship to the cultures that surround them—and then designing ways to articulate it. Social critic Raymond Williams (1958) pointed out that we learn to see things by describing them to others: an approach he called "public pedagogy," which took education out of schools and into other public places. Public pedagogy "projects us beyond the schools to a host of other institutions that educate: families, churches, libraries, museums, publishers, benevolent societies, youth groups, agricultural fairs, radio networks, military organizations, and research institutes" (Cremin 1976, 27-28).

Philosopher Soren Kierkegaard reminds us that life must be understood backwards: "But then one forgets the other principle," he wrote, "that it must be lived forwards" ([1843] 1996, 161). We read our surroundings, our "stuff," our sayings and stories and rituals as if we were reading texts. We "read the world," as Brazilian literacy educator Paulo Freire reminds us, to "read the word" ([1973] 2000; Freire and Macedo 1987). But we don't always know we're doing it. We give out and take in our cultural texts regularly. We share what we learn, and in doing so, we tailor it anew each time.

And in the personal tailoring, we make meaning of our surroundings. Philosopher Maxine Greene writes, "For those authentically concerned about 'the birth of meaning,' about breaking through the surfaces, about teaching others to 'read' their own worlds, art forms must be conceived of as ever-present possibility. . . . They ought to be, if transformative teaching is our concern, a central part of curriculum, wherever it is devised" (1988, 131). Transformative teaching indeed. And the ironic point of such transformation is understanding what's already there. This book invites us to think of our teaching, our students, and shows us by example many ways to plumb—and sustain—our local resources.

Whenever I read my students' writing, I discover again and again that teaching and learning happen best when the student looks back at any experience and makes personal sense of it. "Metacognition," contemporary educationists like to call it. "Reflective practice," say others. "Understanding backward." However long your career, this book will remind you—as it has reminded me—that we're always—student by student, project by project— beginning to make meaning of what we know we didn't know and, in the process, learning how we knew it.

Introduction

Through the Schoolhouse Door

Lynne Hamer and Paddy Bowman

THE KNOWLEDGE, AESTHETICS, SKILLS, AND BELIEFS THAT YOUNG people, educators, and staff members bring through the schoolhouse door each day accompany them in almost invisible backpacks that too often go unopened. Likewise, the culture unique to each classroom and school may be as overlooked as water is to goldfish. While experts in educational research and leadership continue to call for improved home-school relations, the opportunities for developing such relationships remain severely constrained. Even before the strictures wrought by the education wars of the past decade, school-community connections were not as deep as folklorists working in K–12 education could envision. Today what folklorists regard as natural resources freely available in any school and in any community are unlikely to be tapped.

In this volume, readers will see ways in which folklore connects home, community, and school. We address two audiences: first, folklorists seeking to go *in* through schoolhouse doors to work with students, teachers, and parents to bring family and community culture into schools; and second, teachers and teacher educators wanting to take their curriculum as well as students *out* through schoolhouse doors into the community to make their work culturally relevant and socially useful.

The pressures of national and state standards, high-stakes testing, narrowed curricula, and scripted teaching should prompt us all—community members, teachers, administrators, parents, and guardians—to come together to find sustainable, grounded solutions. Instead they distract us further from local ways of knowing—the bedrock of folklore, and the bedrock

1

of family and community. Educational equity demands cultural equity. Educational reform cannot happen without taking both school and community culture into serious consideration. To this end, the chapters of this book demonstrate the usefulness of what folklorists call *traditional knowledge* and formal educators call *intrinsic knowledge*. They show by example the potential for rich learning when partnering among teachers, community members, and folklorists helps to reach all students, support students' participation in their local communities, and deepen students' agency and understanding of the wider world and the diversity of people and knowledge in it.

But First, What Is Folklore?

Folklore has been defined many ways for many purposes. In 1846 William Thoms suggested "a good Saxon compound, Folklore—*the Lore of the People.*" Folklore thus replaced the term *popular antiquities*, which had been used for the leisured gentlemanly collection of relics and oral materials and preservation of antiquarian architecture, which Thoms and other scholars feared were disappearing in industrializing England (Bronner 2002, 9). Today the term *folklore* can refer to items of verbal, material, or behavioral culture or to the process of collecting and documenting (the fieldwork process), also sometimes called *folkloristics*.

Jan Brunvand, in his classic book, *The Study of American Folklore* (1978), emphasizes three aspects of the definition of folklore that are particularly useful in considering the relationship between folklore and education. First, Brunvand states, "Folklore is the traditional, unofficial, non-institutional part of culture. It encompasses all knowledge, understandings, values, attitudes, assumptions, feelings, and beliefs transmitted in traditional forms by word of mouth or by customary examples" (1978, 8–9). "Unofficial" and "non-institutional" tell us that folklore does not include official pacing guides, textbooks, or standardized tests in school, but it does encompass just about everything else—positive and negative—from jump-rope rhymes and cruel taunts on the playground, to Roy G. Biv (a children's color-spectrum mnemonic), to the stories that teachers tell about childhood memories, favorite books, classroom disasters, and a grandfather's recipe for meatloaf topped with peanut butter.

Second, Brunvand describes the forms of folklore, providing a framework for what folklorists focus on as significant and worthy of attention: "Folklore manifests itself in many oral and verbal forms ('mentifacts'), in kinesiological forms (customary behavior, or 'sociofacts'), and in material forms ('artifacts'), but folklore itself is the whole traditional complex of thought, content and process—which ultimately can never be fixed or recorded in its entirety; it lives on in its performance or communication, as people interact with one another" (1978, 9). Thus, as folklorists we look at children's jokes and riddles as art forms, and we delight in the turns of speech of parents and teachers (oral/verbal). We are intrigued by the ways that students greet each other and take leave and by the contents of their lunch boxes, the ways that they arrange their contents on the table and divide desirable contents among friends (customary behavior). We take seriously the artistry of "cootie catchers" and paper airplanes, as well as the teacher's arrangement (and the students' rearrangement) of the story corner (artifacts). But in looking at all these things, we are most interested in the ways that students, teachers, and others are constantly enacting and recreating them—always a bit differently than before.

Third, Brunvand distinguishes the categories of elite, normative, and folk. "In general, the elite and normative traditions are transmitted mainly in print or by other formal means, while the folk tradition relies on oral or customary circulation" (1978, 10). Thus, in a classroom, if we consider the oral/verbal forms, *The Catcher in the Rye* and *Romeo and Juliet* are elite culture; Harry Potter or the Goosebumps series is normative culture (popular or mass); and "knock, knock—who's there?" is folk. These categories are fluid. "Snow White" was a folktale told in many variations until the Grimms collected it and wrote one authoritative version, which became elite. Disney turned it normative or popular. And each time children act out or play the story, it is back to folk. (Those interested in learning more about the discipline of folklore can link to highly readable introductions to the field by selecting About Us on the Web site of Local Learning: The National Network for Folk Arts in Education [http://www.locallearningnetwork.org].)

In education the distinction among elite, normative, and folk parallels the differentiation among formal, nonformal, and informal (Coombs and Ahmed 1974). Formal education takes place in schools, academies, and other official institutions that exist to socialize individuals into roles in society. Nonformal education occurs in community groups, religious associations, and other grassroots organizations. Informal education happens through interactions with family, friends, and neighbors outside specific institutional structures; it is not regulated and does not result in certification or a degree. Whereas schools and teacher-education programs are squarely in the arena of formal education, the traditions and practices that folklorists study—and help bring into schools—occupy the realms of nonformal and informal education. In this volume, we refer to teachers and theorists who practice and study mostly in schools as "formal educators" or simply "teachers," and to parents, community elders, peers, and neighbors from whom children and others learn at home, in afterschool programs, in religious institutions, or in any other nonschool setting as "tradition bearers," "indigenous teachers," "cultural experts," and "community members."

As connoisseurs of occupational folklore and traditionally honed skills, folklorists working in education appreciate the artistry that teachers must develop to be effective in K–12 classrooms. The formal training of educators prepares them to teach various subjects and grade levels, but much of the craft of excellent teaching flows through informal channels. Managing classroom discipline, balancing students' needs and abilities, and engaging and inspiring young people usually come to both novice and expert teachers through the folkloristic process of observing peers and years of learning on the job, as well as memories of favorite teachers and crucial learning experiences. The learning between teachers and folklorists is similarly reciprocal. Working with teachers improves folklorists' presentation strategies and teaching, even in higher education. Listening to teachers and administrators helps us as folklorists to understand K–12 education better, the tough realities that educators face daily, and, ultimately, community culture. Collaboration is essential if folklorists are to advocate successfully to integrate folklore and folklorists' methods into K–12 curricula and to teach teachers in schools of education, summer institutes, and other professional-development opportunities.

Folklore and Education: A Brief History

At the turn of the twentieth century, proponents of social efficiency in the progressive educational movement worked to wrest control of schools from their communities. As documented by David Tyack in *The One Best System,* "community control of schools became anathema to many of the reformers of 1900" (1974, 14), who attacked the rural school "problem" while simultaneously grieving disappearing ways of life and later extended their onslaught to neighborhood control of urban schools. Prior to this time, Tyack notes,

Schooling . . . was only a small and, to many, an incidental part of
the total education the community provided. The child acquired his
values and skills from his family and from neighbors of all ages and
conditions. The major vocational curriculum was work on the farm or
in the craftsman's shop or the corner store; civic and moral instruction
came mostly in church or home or around the village where people
met to gossip or talk politics. A child growing up in such a community could see work-family-religion-recreation-school as an organically
related system of human relationships. (1974, 14–15)

Social efficiency proponents erased individual and community traditions
in their desire to standardize—supposedly to equalize—educational opportunity. Still more reformers tackled the urban immigrant "problem," and
European, Asian, and Latino immigrants, as well as African Americans of
the Great Migration, learned through formal schooling to be ashamed of
their differences, as did rural people the reformers perceived as deficient—
for example, poor whites of the upland south and Cajuns and Creoles of
southwestern Louisiana, not to mention Native Americans forced to attend
boarding schools far from home. Tyack compellingly narrates the rise of this
supposedly "best system" and its critique that reinforced social stratification,
rather than challenging it, culminating in demands for a return to community control of schools, beginning in the 1960s and continuing today.

Offering an alternative to this prevailing system, early twentieth-
century child-centered democratic-progressive educational reformers began
to examine the tension between people and schools and question the ways that
schools damaged family and community culture. Folklorist Jan Rosenberg
has noted, "Folk arts in education/folk artists in the schools was progres-
sively guided" (2004, 1) and cites educational historian Lawrence Cremin
as characterizing democratic progressivism as based in the belief that "culture could be democratized without being vulgarized, the faith that everyone could share not only in the benefits of the new sciences, but in the
pursuit of the arts as well" (1964, viii–ix). Some progressive educators/
social reformers created successful folkloristic projects. At Hull House,
Jane Addams organized exhibits displaying elite art borrowed from museums next to local workers' pieces documenting their homelands as well
as their current predicaments. At the Bureau of Educational Experiments
(later Bank Street College of Education), which she founded in 1916, Lucy
Sprague Mitchell took New York City students to explore the folk culture
of their neighborhoods.

During the 1930s and 1940s pioneer folklorist-in-education Dorothy Howard (who taught in public schools and colleges in New York, New Jersey, and Maryland and for whom the annual American Folklore Society Folklore and Education Section prize for outstanding contributions to the field is named) created curricula and pedagogical approaches to make folklore accessible to schoolteachers—including methods to bring the playground, which she called the "uncovered schoolroom," into the classroom by using jump-rope rhymes, bouncing balls, and rolling marbles as entry points to the metaphor and rhyme of poetry (Rosenberg 2011; Howard 1950). In New Jersey, teacher Rachel Davis DuBois, as part of the intercultural educational movement responding in the 1920s to widespread prejudice and later as founder of the Workshop for Cultural Democracy, brought folklore into the school in her Woodbury Plan, creating an ongoing series of social encounters among members of different ethnic groups to help students develop new values and positive emotional responses to difference (Rosenberg, 2011; Howard, 1950).

In *Democracy and Education* (1916), philosopher John Dewey described democracy as beginning at home and in neighborly communities, and a democratic culture as characterized by trust, tolerance, and humor, as well as recognition of the inherent value of each individual. When related to the institution of schooling, we can see this as uniting informal and nonformal education (through family, friends, work, neighborhood, and religious and spiritual communities) with formal education (institutions that exist primarily for schooling).

The democratic-progressive educational movement continued full force through the 1930s and was paralleled by the development of public-sector folklore with the establishment in 1928 of the first national archive for traditional culture in the United States: the Archive of American Folk Song at the Library of Congress (later to become part of the American Folklife Center and renamed the Archive of Folk Culture). Seven years later, in 1935, the Works Progress Administration's Federal Writers Project began hiring writers and folklorists to document many regional cultures, both urban and rural. During the same period, Alan Lomax became arguably the first folklorist to develop a folklore and education initiative with his *American School of the Air* (later *Wellsprings of Music*), which aired on CBS Radio from 1939 to 1941 (Rosenberg, personal email communication with the authors, 22 April 2011; Szwed 2010). Concurrently, in his treatise "American Education and Culture" ([1929] 1964), John Dewey called for active learning and intergenerational interaction; study and use of culture that is actively being formed, rather than veneration of European culture; and schools as places where new culture is created, rather than old culture perpetuated.

Thus, the 1930s were a crucial decade for establishing institutions intended to collect and preserve traditional, community-based ways of life that seemed in danger of disappearing, as well as deepening the critique of the social-efficiency aspect of progressivism, by then in firm control of the nation's schooling, which had been largely designed to sort the professional class from the working class and to educate each for its proper place in society (Cremin 1964). The definition of folklore was part of this critique because it was set apart from—and in contest to—commercial (popular) and academic (elite) culture increasingly controlled by centralized, capitalist authority. In 1938 the progressive scholar-activist Benjamin Botkin, national folklore editor of the Depression-era Federal Writers Project, usefully defined folklore as a body of traditional belief, custom, and expression passed down by word of mouth and observation outside commercial and academic communications (Botkin 1938). This definition highlights the expression and authority of folklore as independent of both popular and elite culture as perpetuated through the mass media and educational institutions—and thus as a crucial resource for contesting the classist sorting and labeling inherent in formal schooling during that time and since.

In the same era, Carter G. Woodson penned his classic critique of "the so-called modern education . . . worked out in conformity to the needs of those who have enslaved and oppressed weaker people" ([1933] 2011, 5). Woodson explained cogently the process and purpose of deculturalization or "education under outsiders' control" (23), which he saw as the central accomplishment of formal schooling, for African Americans and other people of color. "If you control a man's thinking you do not have to worry about his action. When you determine what a man shall think you do not have to concern yourself about what he will do. If you make a person feel that he/she is inferior, you do not have to compel him/her to accept an inferior status, he/she will seek for it" ([1933] 2011, 125). Woodson called for subordinated people to "do for themselves" and become "autodidacts"—to rely on the informal and nonformal educational opportunities in their communities and of their making.

Working parallel to both Botkin and Woodson, George S. Counts and his colleagues founded the social-reconstructionist approach (as opposed to the prevalent child-centered one based in Dewey's work) as well as the interdisciplinary Department of Social Foundations of Education at Columbia

Teachers College in the 1930s. As his *Dare the Schools Build a New Social Order?* ([1932] 1978) lays out, the goal of social reconstructionists of that time was to use schools as microcosms to build a society based on cooperation, rather than exploitation, with the goal that students take these inculcated beliefs and experiences into the macrosociety. Also at Teachers College, Harold Rugg developed a highly influential series of social-studies textbooks that—after selling five million copies—were censored as anticapitalist and driven off the market; *The Child-Centered School* (Rugg and Shumaker 1928) had major influence on progressive educators by introducing a social-reconstructionist approach: the call to "build a new social order" á la Counts, to adopt progressivism, and to align this emphasis with the child-centeredness already established by Dewey and others as a central feature of democratic education.

Midcentury examples of the use of folklore in K–12 curricula and classroom practice do not measure up to the authentic, child-centered approaches of democratic progressives such as John Dewey, Lucy Sprague Mitchell, Dorothy Howard, and Rachel DuBois. The intercultural, community-centered approaches that would bring real citizens into schools were for the most part eclipsed by textbook publishers and the mass media, which appropriated sterilized folk legends and fairy tales, already sanitized by anthologists such as the Brothers Grimm and Hans Christian Andersen. Such popularized lore still colors the general public's perceptions about folklore (Dorson and Carpenter 1978). Johnny Appleseed, Pecos Bill, Paul Bunyan, Snow White, Cinderella, and a canon of "folk songs" such as "She'll Be Coming 'Round the Mountain" and "Old MacDonald Had a Farm," peopled children's readers, music books, cartoons, movies, comic books, and even social-studies texts, masquerading as democratic culture. Although some were charming cultural expressions in their own right, and even entered back into individuals' vital folk traditions, they were limited to a carefully selected and sanitized version of America that left out most Americans and their living, authentic traditions.

Skip forward to the civil-rights era of the 1960s, and we see folklorists working in tandem with those challenging the "one best system" and working to reclaim community influence—to insert nonformal and informal education, which had previously balanced formal education, back into the formal educational system that had gained control over most aspects of life and chances for success through social mobility in the larger society. Educational psychologists and sociologists had created a new theory of "cultural deprivation" to replace biological determinism as a way of explaining why some groups of people tended to be less successful in dominant-culture schooling than others did. Folklorists made biting critiques of cultural-deprivation theory (Abrahams 1971; Abrahams and Troike 1972; Dundes 1969). Cultural deprivation is now recognized as just one more part of a system that blamed poor people for their poverty, manufacturing the idea that some groups have limited or no positive cultural resources (Ryan 1976). Folklorists pointed out that groups marginalized on the basis of race, ethnicity, or socioeconomic status were not culturally deprived; rather, they were ignored, and their cultural knowledge was silenced—part of the legacy of deculturalization imposed through formal schooling to keep immigrant and colonized groups powerless (Spring 2009).

Drawing upon empirical studies, folklorists explained the dynamic between marginalized cultural groups and dominant-culture schools, becoming among the first to elucidate the nature of cultural incompatibilities between home and school (Baker 1977; Cazden and Hymes 1978; Haring and Foreman 1975). And in efforts to promote the value of uniting the informal learning of home and community with the formal teaching of schools, folklorists began producing arguments, data, and materials to provide "bridges to the curriculum" to help connect students' worlds of home and school (Danielson 1976; Stekert 1969).

Out of this period of social change came a renaissance of folkloristic, ethnographic approaches to K–12 education. The confluence of the civil-rights, women's, Chicano, and antiwar movements met the swell of heritage fervor attendant to the U.S. Bicentennial of 1976, and folklore in education has since been here to stay in various guises. A landmark was established when Eliot Wigginton and his high-school English students at Rabun Gap-Nacoochee School in northeastern Georgia published the first *Foxfire* magazine in 1966. Recalling Dewey's concepts about experiential education and students' home communities, Wigginton led a national constructivist educational movement that eventually faltered but remains alive in the public imagination (Puckett 1989; Foxfire Fund 2011).

In addition to a return to democratic-progressive philosophies of education, a new infrastructure and funding source influenced the development of what is now called FAIE (Folk Arts in Education): the National Endowment for the Arts (NEA). Among recipients of its first round of grants in October 1965 was the National Folk Festival (Bauerlein and Grantham 2008, 20). Arts-education grants began in 1967 with the Laboratory Theatre Project to train high-school students in classical drama with professional theater companies in three cities (Bauerlein and Grantham 2008, 23–25). A decade later, this support for elite arts education was extended to folk arts. In the bicentennial year, Folk Artists in the Schools (FAIS) grants began to bring folk artists into classrooms to demonstrate and teach. These "tradition bearers visited classes to teach their traditionally learned skills, teachers received information about the person and the art form as well as guidance for facilitating classroom activities beyond the visit, and folklorists mediated the communication and the residency" (Rosenberg, personal communication with the authors, 22 April 2011). Beginning in 1976, a Special Projects office that supported folk arts gave several FAIS grants each year, usually underwriting short- or long-term folk-artist residencies. NEA officially established the Folk and Traditional Arts Program in 1979 with Bess Lomax Hawes as director.

FAIS support evolved through the 1980s into Folk Arts in Education (FAIE) and to include professional development for teachers and folk artists, production of a wide array of standards-based curriculum materials, in-school and out-of-school projects, folk-artist and folklorist residencies, and the founding of Local Learning, the national FAIE service organization, in 1993. The 1980s and '90s saw a burgeoning of folkloristic materials and methods manuals for teachers, including Marsha MacDowell's seminal *Folk Arts in Education: A Resource Handbook* (1987). These and other materials were first catalogued in Paddy Bowman and Peter Bartis's *A Teacher's Guide to Folklife Resources for K–12 Classrooms* (1994), now updated in MacDowell and LuAnne Kozma's revised manual, *Folk Arts in Education: A Resource Handbook II* (2008, 27–31).

Folklorists working primarily for local, state, and regional government cultural agencies and museums were deeply influenced by Barbara Kirshenblatt-Gimblett's argument for the utility of "an accessible aesthetic" through bringing what she calls "indigenous teachers" from students' home communities into schools (1983, 11). Nancy Groce and Janis Benincasa's "Folk Artists in Staten Island Schools: Developing a Workable Model for Larger Communities" (1987), along with Mary Hufford's *A Tree Smells like Peanut Butter: Folk Artists in a City School* (1979), elucidate the FAIE approach. Rita Zorn Moonsammy's *Passing It On: Folk Artists and Education in Cumberland County, New Jersey* (1992) remains a classic example of the power of indigenous teachers in the classroom. Excellent folklore collections and guides for teachers to involve their students in collecting lore span genres and geographies. Early examples include Sylvia Grider's *Children's Folklore: A Manual for Teachers*

(1988), Betty Belanus's *Folklore in the Classroom* (1985), and Elizabeth Radin Simons's *Student Worlds, Student Words: Teaching Writing through Folklore* (1990), and Debora Kodish and William Westerman's "Negotiating Pitfalls and Possibilities: Presenting Folk Arts in the School" ([1996] 2011).

Home-School Disconnects

The schoolhouse door is a revolving one: students, teachers, and administrators bring their home and community culture into schools, and they work and learn within a web of school and classroom folk culture. Shirley Brice Heath described this profoundly in a study that revolutionized literacy research in education, *Ways with Words* (1983), in which she traced lack of success among poor white and black students, coming from their two different communities, in school, where their middle-class white teachers had very different "ways with words." Teachers' home culture, she argues, is considered objectively normal and thus right in school—because the teachers are in charge. Thus, when students' cultures are different, they are too often considered wrong.

Here is where distinctions among elite, normative, and folk culture are critical: success in school is based on showing proficiency in elite culture (nowadays too often through multiple-choice identification of elite facts on standardized tests). However, success is first based on an ability to function within the school's and teachers' culture, which is normative. When students bring their home "ways with words," nonverbal communication, and behaviors into class, this is folk culture. If the folk and the normative collide, the elite goals will probably not be achieved. *Ways with Words* alerted the educational-research world that there is no normal but only dominant culture versus nondominant culture—and that we as teachers must be aware of the differences among all children and their families to teach effectively.

Heath's thesis was similarly demonstrated in higher education in an essay, "Narrative and Story-Telling Rights" (1978), by educator Courtney Cazden and folklorist Dell Hymes, in which they examined what happened in their adult-education classes when nontraditional students brought their working-class culture into the classroom. As might be predicted, if the instructor did not recognize the value of the student's culture in the classroom and build from it, the student did not succeed.

Folklorists' concrete efforts have occurred parallel to—and sometimes informed by—a deepening critique by educational theorists of the continuing tendency toward deculturalization in the formal school system.

bell hooks's inspirational *Teaching to Transgress* (1994) exposes the nearly comprehensive requirement that university students abandon working-class home culture to succeed and describes her ways of keeping that home culture alive and bringing it with her into the academy. Lisa Delpit's classic *Other People's Children* ([1995] 2006) captures the dilemma of removing schooling from local communities' control. Delpit describes the different facets of cultural estrangement between teacher and students and depicts the efforts of nondominant-culture teachers to bridge the disconnects. Delpit's work reveals that if the "one best system" relies on outside expertise, the intimate relationship between teacher and child is destroyed. Using empirical data, Gloria Ladson-Billings describes "successful teachers of African American students" as those who "honor and respect the students' home culture" ([1999] 2009, 157). hooks sums up the need for school reform based on the recognition of knowledge and skills outside the one best system in *Teaching Community: A Pedagogy of Hope* (2003), in which she calls for an "insurrection of subjugated knowledges" (4), echoing Dewey's 1929 argument by emphasizing that schools should be places where people learn something new to them, not just venerated culture, and noting that educators need to find and make spaces for teaching and learning outside the norm.

Current FAIE Approaches

Today FAIE programs are housed not only in schools but also in museums, local arts agencies, and community organizations with the shared aim of humanistic understanding of individuals and social groups through engaging students in documenting and analyzing local culture. Much FAIE work takes place in cyberspace. Local Learning, with its goal to "prepare young people, their teachers, and their families to discover, research, and draw on traditional culture and local knowledge to enrich education and create stronger communities" (2010), is a central clearinghouse. In advocating for the full inclusion of folk and traditional arts and artists in the nation's education, Local Learning, funded by the NEA Folk and Traditional Arts Program, provides resources, tools, lessons, and virtual folk-artist residencies to help users find local traditions and materials that connect to the classroom and students' lives.

Analysis of recent FAIE publications and programs reveals five prevalent goals (Hamer 2000), all of which appear as themes in the chapters of this book. First, FAIE programs help students and teachers identify and value their own and familiar individuals' folk groups and their vernacular, everyday artistic expressions. Typically this is described as helping young people see that people can be creative artists and masters outside the mass media of popular culture or the elite and official cultural institutions, such as schools, universities, museums, and concert halls.

Second, this recognition, plus the folklorist's outsider perspective, helps students see the importance of familiar heroes and local events, especially since many programs focus on students' families and neighbors in the context of history, politics, and economics. Common activities include visits to local cultural centers and workplaces with students prompted to identify traditional culture and analyze its relationship to a sense of place, the dominant culture, and their own lives.

Third, FAIE programs engage teachers and students in critically observing differences, as well as intersections, between elite and popular culture and the folk culture of their communities, thus helping students recognize their "cultural capital" and agency as equally authoritative as what is promulgated by schools and the media.

Fourth, FAIE recenters authority outside institutions. A central—although usually unstated—purpose of all FAIE curricula is challenging the exclusive legitimacy of official knowledge and thus challenging institutions to include truly heterogeneous authorities and bring into the classroom community knowledge as authoritative and community people as teachers. Peggy Bulger stated this most pointedly, observing, "The premise of folklorists working in the schools seems highly irrational if we admit that we are bringing an informal-anti-institutional form of knowledge (folklore) into the institution that is designed specifically to perpetuate institutions. We advocate the folk process which is directly counter to the educational theory and practice that has shaped our American schools" (1991, 17).

Finally, because FAIE projects are based on students' participation in real learning situations inside and outside the classroom, the work is inherently collaborative as well as interdisciplinary, connecting students in classrooms with people and organizations in larger community settings and involving young people in creating knowledge by using and developing primary sources.

The Chapters

In chapter 1, Paddy Bowman, director of Local Learning and adjunct professor for Lesley University, narrates her journey as a folklorist learning to be a folklorist in education. Her experience is highly instructive to folklorists thinking of taking a similar plunge, but she also explains clearly why teacher education needs folklorists, a position that will be provocative and perhaps compelling to our colleagues in colleges of education. As we travel with her, we see what valuing nonprofessional, everyday artistic expressions looks like, as well as the value of promoting local and family discovery and knowledge. The second part of Bowman's narrative allows us to grasp the key to folkloristic approaches for democratic education. As she describes basic fieldwork methods that allow teachers to cross socioeconomic boundaries successfully to learn about their students' nonformal and informal learning environments and build relationships with their indigenous teachers, we see the transformative potential of a folkloristic approach to education. She notes that folklorists see traditional cultural expressions as intriguing texts that reveal clues to personal, community, regional, and national identity as well as to history, economics, religion, and geography. She also sees in them not only connections to all the arts, sciences, and humanities, but also to the essential cores of these institutionally canonized fields.

Louisiana Division of the Arts Folklife Program director Maida Owens relays in chapter 2 how she launched a groundbreaking online FAIE guide by searching for an audience for digitized scholarly articles and photographs documenting traditional culture of the state. Owens describes the ways that she came to collaborate with many others, including Eileen Engel, a highly experienced educator, to develop *Louisiana Voices: An Educator's Guide to Exploring Our Communities and Traditions.* Chapter 2 thus epitomizes the partnership between folklorists and teachers. By probing K–12 educators for advice on publicizing the digital collections, Owens learned that they wanted scaffolding to help them and their students understand folklore and its relevance. Thus began the thoughtful, in-depth process that produced the extensive public-domain Web site. Owens describes how this guide came to focus on fieldwork. In doing so, she also explains how FAIE can facilitate students' recognizing their cultural capital and agency and working as legitimate researchers documenting valuable primary sources for their communities.

In chapter 3, an interorganizational team demonstrates the value of collaboration across boundaries to create interdisciplinary professional development and curricula organized around themes in local culture. We join Anne Pryor, folk and traditional arts specialist at the Wisconsin Arts Board; Debbie Kmetz, program officer at the Wisconsin Humanities Council; Ruth Olson, associate director of the Center for the Study of Upper Midwestern Cultures at the University of Wisconsin-Madison; and Steven A. Ackerman, professor in the Department of Atmospheric and Oceanic Sciences at the University of Wisconsin-Madison, for their Here at Home bus tours with teachers across their state. Teachers learn on the ground from local people and landscapes how they can use history and culture to integrate language arts, history, science, geography, weather, economy, land use, and material arts around the local. This team presents an exciting professional-development model and shows how teachers returned to their classrooms to create curricular materials and pedagogical approaches that bring local knowledge and community members as teachers into the classroom and the ways that they continue to stay involved through a statewide network.

Amanda Dargan, education director of New York City's City Lore, draws on her experience in K–12 arts-education programs in chapter 4 to describe vividly how artists who usually practice and perform outside formal institutions—in home and community settings—enrich classroom arts residencies in a variety of models. The FAIE approaches that she has developed clarify the goal of valuing the worth and importance of artists who are in students' families and neighborhoods and recentering cultural authority outside the classroom—by bringing it in. Dargan emphasizes the education that students receive in recognizing both the universal and the particular, the overlap between similarity and difference, and the variations that reveal boundaries, history, and culture. She also describes the ways that exploration of traditional arts and artists in teaching artists' residencies can inspire students' creativity in visual art, theater, dance, music, and writing, and can be woven into any subject area through sustained thematic inquiry. City Lore has indeed constructed revolving doors on schoolhouses: artists not only come in, but students sometimes follow them out to document neighborhood culture and become experts to one degree or another in the arts of their communities.

In chapter 5, Lisa L. Higgins, the director of the Missouri Folk Arts Program, and Chicago folklorist and educator Sue Eleuterio combine the live performances of folk artists in rural classrooms with close attention to Missouri's K–12 academic standards. They emphasize the basics of FAIE that cut across materials and approaches in the field and itemize the particular skills that students learn: observing, listening, interviewing, organizing, and performing. They remind us that when students learn from authentic performances learned for their communities and have that as part of their assessment, authentic education occurs. They describe partnerships with local arts agencies that helped their residencies succeed, and we witness how warmly rural students and communities embraced diverse and unfamiliar art forms and artists. Most important in their chapter are the lessons that every community has art; students live next door to artists; and students can become active, valued partners with those artists in the shared goal of strengthening their communities.

Nebraska folklorist Gwen Meister joins forces with classroom teacher Patricia Kurtenbach in chapter 6 to demonstrate the ways that they make local and family knowledge available to teachers and students across their state by packing it into traveling culture trunks. Authenticity is the watchword in this chapter. Rather than presenting a romanticized, outsider's view of ethnic cultures, Meister emphasizes the folklorist's approach of focusing on culture in actual use by real individuals. Through the contents of the trunks, students can relate their personal traditional culture and history to those of familiar and unfamiliar individuals and groups and their vernacular, everyday artistic expressions. Thus, the trunks' contents reflect the folkways that are the stuff of informal and nonformal learning. Kurtenbach's contribution is framing these trunks in a way that makes them relevant to the state's learning standards, and, in so doing, she bridges the gap between the goals and purposes of democratic-progressive educators and the social-efficiency system still in place.

In chapter 7, professor emerita of philosophy and humanities Kristin Congdon and elementary art teacher Karen Branen document collaborating with faculty and students from the University of Central Florida, as well as folk artists and their communities, on a complex multimedia project that makes thick cultural description available via cyberspace. The vibrant Folkvine Web site deeply contextualizes artists' lives and environments in a variety of platforms within a virtual vintage visitors' center. On one level, straightforward documentation of folk artists through an outsider folklorist's perspective helps students and community members recognize the value of their local artists; on another it prompts students to differentiate critically the similarities and differences among elite, popular, and folk art. Weaving through it all, we see Congdon and Branen's students participating in real learning with authentic outcomes: a community resource with components suitable for various age groups and interests built through collaboration with artists, students, and community members—an example of the sort of engaged pedagogy that schools across the nation are seeking.

Independent folklorist Lisa Rathje turns our attention in chapter 8 to the energetic creativity of youth as they use, critique, reject, and recreate traditions from their communities and classmates, skipping easily among the realms of folk, normative/popular, and elite learning. The students' work is part of the Institute for Cultural Partnerships' program The Art of Many Voices, an arts-residency and mentoring program in Harrisburg, Pennsylvania, collaboratively designed by folklorists, community artists, and teachers to increase the academic achievement of at-risk teens. The work provides alternative opportunities for youth to earn the credits necessary to graduate, either in the formal education setting of a classroom or the non-formal one of an afterschool program. Through the program, students recognize and value individuals' (including their own) verbal traditions, learn ethnographic skills while conducting research, and work with established community members and artists to produce exhibits and performances for public audiences. By merging these typical FAIE goals with the mentorship that students receive to value academic achievement, the program addresses crucial issues in schooling, community organizing, and educational reform.

Finally, in chapter 9, associate professor of education Lynne Hamer describes a collaboration among a university, community center, and local public school system that demonstrates the potential of a folkloristic approach to educational reform. The Padua Alliance for Education and Empowerment began with an idea to base a graduate research course, Qualitative Research I, at a community center and have the graduate students work as a research team with community members. Taking graduate students into the community was followed by bringing undergraduate coursework there and encouraging community members—many of whom might not have gone to the university otherwise—to become undergraduate students. On the surface, the Padua Alliance has nothing to do with folklore; however, underneath it is based in that by-now-old valuing of artistic expression by ordinary individuals in everyday life, as well as elevating the importance of local heroes, issues, and events above the study of canonized texts. Above all, the main interests in chapter 9 are recentering authority outside institutions and involving students in collaborative work with people in their communities.

This volume thus assembles experiences of folklorists who have been engaged in K–12 education for more than two decades, grounded in work of the past century, to illuminate the potential value of folklorists and educators joining forces at every level—from elementary classrooms to the academy—in schools, universities, and community organizations. As such its audience is both folklorists who wish to deploy folklore's materials and methods to address the challenges of formal schooling and teachers whose goal is to understand themselves, their students, and their communities so that they can develop culturally vibrant and socially transformative pedagogy. Let the schoolhouse door be opened!

1

"I Didn't Know What I Didn't Know"
Reciprocal Pedagogy

Paddy Bowman

Ask someone to tell you the most important thing he or she has learned, and you will be told a story. Deep learning takes the form of a story. The most important stories in education often aren't the ones we are told—they are the ones we live. To be deeply changed requires a quest with our emotions and desires engaged, so a powerful education is necessarily an adventure that can be narrated.

—Michael Umphrey, *The Power of Community-Centered Education*, 15

THIS CHAPTER CHRONICLES THE ARC OF MY DEVELOPMENT as a teacher educator. Documenting my teaching comes from the natural habit of a folklorist. I take notes and photographs and hang onto teachers' assignments, evaluations, and artwork. My original chapter concept took me to thick files in my informal archive. I planned to appraise teachers' assignments accumulating since 1994 to illustrate the powerful promise of folklore and fieldwork for K–12 educators' understanding the deep connection between traditional culture and formal pedagogy. My research revealed more than I had anticipated—one of the gifts of writing, of course. Reviewing teachers' work and my field notes exposed how much I had needed to learn about teaching teachers. This personal account describes how and why I came to love working in education and believe so strongly that folklorists in academic and

Paddy Bowman is the director of Local Learning: The National Network for Folk Arts in Education and an adjunct faculty member of the Lesley University master's program, Integrated Teaching through the Arts.

public programs gain from such engagement. I have learned firsthand the transformational impact of teachers and students learning from and with each other—"emotions and desires engaged"—an event that is powerful enough to be narrated. I call this *reciprocal pedagogy* to highlight the deep collaborative relationship that good teaching involves, whether within the traditional or the academic sphere.

In her 1994 presidential address to the American Folklore Society, Sylvia Grider chose folklore and teaching as her theme, urging folklorists to take teaching seriously because "teaching is so fundamental to the function and process of folklore that tradition cannot exist without it" (1995, 179). Both folklorists and educators are intimately concerned with the transmission of knowledge, but we are engaged with different realms of knowledge and methods of transmission. Finding ways to meld these ways of knowing profits folklorists as well as teachers. I hope that my journey inspires other folklorists to engage in education and with educators and students as teacher, collaborator, and fieldworker. Perhaps my evolution as an educator who began by modeling her graduate-school pedagogy for K–12 teachers may serve as a cautionary tale, allowing others to avoid mistakes that I made.

I also hope that educators will learn more about the perspectives of folklorists and the potential educational gifts of our discipline, for example, culturally authentic resources and ethnographic fieldwork methods. Such research can shift perspective and suspend judgment, which in turn can positively influence the teacher-pupil connection for the dozens of new students whom teachers face each year. "Through modeling and encouraging the development of fieldworker skills and attitudes, teachers foster an environment in which children are enabled to be both the resource and the analyst for the study of expressive human behavior. The student and teacher are placed in a cooperative relationship" (Haut 1994, 56). Finally, as Grider said, "The act of teaching is the connection between the formulaic classroom exercise and the age-old process of tradition. In both instances, the precious materials that provide essential cultural continuity are transmitted from the masters to the neophytes, from one generation to the next, in what we hope will be an unbroken chain but which, in reality, is only a frayed and tangled thread" (1995, 179). Again folklorists and educators are bound by their love of knowledge and its transmission.

Since 1993 I have had the satisfaction of coordinating a network funded by the National Endowment for the Arts Folk and Traditional Arts Program to advocate for the inclusion of folk arts and artists in the nation's education. Now called Local Learning, we began as the National Task Force on Folk Arts in Education after a roundtable that the Folk and Traditional Arts Program convened to assess the state of the field of Folk Arts in Education (FAIE) and bring FAIE advocates together with Arts in Education (AIE) leaders. My position as director keeps me in touch with folklorists, folk artists, and educators who work in many settings. I gather and disseminate information on FAIE resources and training opportunities, provide technical assistance, coedit a national newsletter called *CARTS* (Cultural Arts Resources for Teachers and Students), and manage locallearningnetwork. org, our new Web site first launched in 1996 as CARTS.org.

The network's founding coincided with the inception of the Arts Education Partnership (AEP)—a national coalition of almost 150 organizations.[1] I have served on the AEP steering committee since its beginning and often work with AIE colleagues and projects. Articulating the differences between these related fields is an ongoing conversation in which I point to the emphasis on ethnography and learning within traditional folk groups in everyday life as FAIE hallmarks. In addition, I develop FAIE curriculum, lead workshops, and direct teacher institutes around the country. Since 2004 I have been teaching in the more formal structure of a university master's degree program for teachers. It is in this role that I have come to appreciate— and communicate—better the "so what" of our field in the context of social foundations of education. I have not stopped learning about teaching since I first stepped onto this path by accident, not by intent.

The Thrill of It All

Two time zones away from home, I stand in a roomy school library where the hands on the wall clock point to five o'clock and survey a new cohort of graduate education students. A typical class of eighteen teachers—mostly women, mostly white—gaze expectantly from their chairs around tables crowded with large drinks, cracker boxes, candy bags, spiral notebooks, and laptop computers. Containers brimming with art supplies spill onto the floor. Even after teaching all week, somehow they are ready for class on this Friday evening. Outside dusk is well under way. By the time we adjourn at ten o'clock, I will have learned a great deal about my students and this place that is brand new to me. Although the teachers have been together in a master's program for almost two years, and many are teaching where they grew up, they, too, will learn new information about one another and their community throughout the weekend.

I have spent the day bustling around in search of local businesses where my students can document occupational culture on Saturday morning. My day of hasty fieldwork has involved plenty of U-turns, but my introduction to this small city has given me clues about neighborhood boundaries, the economy, architectural styles, arts facilities, new immigrants, established residents, and a list of sites to check out further: a mural in progress, a small Asian market, a community garden. A phone call to a folklorist in the state capital prior to this visit did not turn up much because she had never conducted fieldwork in this region, but by the time I leave Sunday night, I will have a notebook filled with field notes and my students' lore that I will later share with her.

My peripatetic pedagogy delights me time and again as I engage in similar routines in new towns—more than twenty in the past seven years. I relish my discoveries about a place and my students. They start to see their community differently through my outsider's eyes, and we weave a trusting learning environment, which will allow me to choose appropriate ways to take them across new cultural boundaries when I return in a month to finish the course. In the meantime, they have a lot to digest, plus assignments to complete, on top of their classroom teaching, and I will return to my regular work back East.

Everything I've Learned Began with Kindergarten

My initial desire to investigate folklore in K–12 education sprang from my daughter's enrollment in kindergarten in Alexandria, Virginia, in 1988. Her teacher was new to northern Virginia and public schools and did not connect well with students and families. I volunteered in the class in the hope that I might deepen her cultural understanding and engagement with students, parents, and the neighborhood. I trekked to the Smithsonian Center for Folklife and Cultural Heritage and the American Folklife Center at the Library of Congress to review FAIE resources and shared them with the teacher. Soon she urged me to "teach the children about folklore," so I developed a unit for the young students on cowboy culture. This caught the notice of the district social-studies curriculum specialist, who got excited about folklore in the classroom and hired me to conduct a workshop for the school system's annual in-service training day. I thought that I knew all about workshops. I considered myself a serious scholar who knew her way around libraries and MLA citation formats. This would be Folklore 101 in two hours.

My early attempts to teach teachers replicated my graduate-school experience. I wrote lengthy definitions on a chalkboard to support my lecture. Not only did I write "folklore" and "fieldwork" on the board, but I wrote LOTS more terms along the lines of "emic," "etic," "liminality," and "variant." As twenty teachers settled into desks, I straightened my pages of notes on the podium and began lecturing. Occasionally I referred to the chalkboard and underlined a word to drive home a point. Eyelids began drooping. Teachers were napping. In my class! As I began sharing examples of my personal folklore to illustrate genres, however, people woke up and started chortling. The more they laughed, the more stories I told. I became a stand-up comic. Lesson learned: one must engage teachers, not merely inform them.

When I repeated my floor show at a parent-teacher workshop, evaluations brought me up short: "Ask others about their traditions." "Speaker needs to use hands-on activities." I felt defeated. There was no time in my already-truncated Folklore 101 lecture to elicit examples from participants. And how could I deliver complex theory and scholarly definitions through "hands-on activities"?

In 1995 Elizabeth Simons, author of the notable book about folklore for teachers, *Student Worlds, Student Words: Teaching Writing through Folklore* (1990), reiterated the admonition to make my teaching interactive and involve participants. I had asked her help designing a syllabus for a three-week graduate education course called the Multicultural Folklife Institute, which the University of Virginia Northern Virginia Center had invited me to teach with funding from the Virginia Foundation for the Humanities (VFH). "I know you," Liz said. "You're great at talking, but you have to let others talk." I addressed this by inviting a host of colleagues from the area to give the lectures. I would share glories of my discipline, and teachers would see how vital folklore and fieldwork were to their classroom practice.

Except for Liz's book, my reading list featured nothing about K–12 education. I was teaching Folklore 101 again. I had turned to Liz because of her excellent demonstration during the first American Folklore Society (AFS) education workshop, cosponsored by the National Task Force on Folk Arts in Education and the AFS Folklore and Education Section in Milwaukee in 1994. Liz had modeled impressive in-depth activities, evoking naming traditions and memories of childhood play through writing.

I decided to adapt these to open my course. Liz had also introduced me to the National Writing Project, for which she was a trainer, so I had become familiar with the process-method teaching of writing and the current trend of dialogue journaling with teachers.[2] To make room for everything else that I had packed into the three-week syllabus, I chose to journal with teachers about their nightly folklore reading assignments to track their comprehension. Each day we heard from scholars and watched folklore documentaries. We occasionally ate in local Vietnamese and Salvadoran restaurants and visited the Smithsonian Folklife Festival, where teachers went behind the scenes to learn from program curators and participants. During the second week, teachers practiced interviewing, audio and video recording, and photography in preparation for individual fieldwork projects to present on the last day of class in the third week. I had failed to realize that it would be their fieldwork that would finally be transformative.

Breaking the Folklore 101 Mold

A turning point came when journaling began to feel like psychotherapy. Diligent teachers sat up night after night reading lengthy articles after a full day of class, and I sat awake responding to their journal entries. These intimate midnight dialogues exposed teachers' discoveries, but instead of the revelations about folklore and the classroom that I had anticipated, the teachers related personally to scholars' writing. For instance, Victor Turner's ritual theories inspired often-moving descriptions of their own liminal experiences, such as becoming a novice, pregnancies, miscarriages, betrothals, divorces, and a year of chemotherapy. I had witnessed the power of teachers applying folkloristic theory to personal-experience narrative, but I wanted to divert attention and make connections to their students, classrooms, and communities. To avoid becoming the accidental therapist, during class I began to frame readings with questions and brought discussion out of journals and into the classroom to make way for integrating folklore theory into classroom practices.

An anonymous class notebook also offered feedback on my pedagogy. Despite generally positive comments, my oversights emerged. One teacher admonished, "Ask us to draw instead of write. People can tell the stories of their drawings instead of reading their writing." Someone reacted to yet another guest scholar by writing, "Now that you know that most teachers in graduate classes come prepared to work, I think you might put more emphasis on our project presentations. The guest speakers are good, but we want to hear from each other." Tellingly, someone advised me to move the fieldwork earlier: "This is the heart of the course; we should be doing it at the front end." Another wrote, "Venn diagrams are good for comparing and contrasting information." Note to self: ask a teacher how to use a Venn diagram.

Phase two of my education about teaching began. Tackling individual fieldwork projects challenged the teachers, dramatically deepening their understanding of folklore. I did not line up places or people for them to document, and later I realized that—despite their initial anxiety—their choices were wholly organic to their personal interests or curricula. They eased themselves over their discomfort, but at the same time, they stretched themselves. For example, a former radio journalist who had become a middle-school media instructor eschewed audio to photograph neighborhood taverns in black and white. Others selected neighbors or places they had always wondered about or returned to the Smithsonian Folklife Festival to seek out specific artists about whom they were curious. Teachers were also designing curriculum units—a course requirement—and brainstorming some classroom applications in our group discussions. The course was starting to accomplish what I had anticipated.

I also learned of these teachers' preconceptions about folklore. Like the general public, most viewed folklore as antiquated or "other." In the class notebook, someone wrote,

> When I mentioned to my friends that I was going to be in this course, they all chuckled and asked if I would be wearing gauze skirts and love beads and playing the guitar. I honestly wasn't sure. The course outline certainly helped me fine-tune my preconceived notions, but even those notions were redefined after our first class. The most significant realization that I walked away with is this: we live folklore every day, and I am starting to view my stories differently and am discovering how my students' stories of their lives will play an important role in the classroom.

Such observations reveal the challenges with which most American folklorists are familiar. People often see our discipline as marginal as well as static. By evoking teachers' folklore and supporting their fieldwork, I was witnessing successes, yet I wanted to motivate more transference from folklore to classroom. I was leaving connections too implicit, assuming that teachers would build the bridge from the course to curriculum.

Learning from Teachers

VFH funded this institute from 1995 to 1997, and each year teachers taught me more about teaching: their own and mine. Looking back, I realize that, up until this point, I had been trying to turn teachers into folklorists. Emphasizing theory and documentation got in the way of teachers' applying folklore. Touting the inherent multidisciplinary nature of folklore and fieldwork, I was failing to take advantage of teachers' knowledge of their disciplines and teaching itself. During the third year, a fourth-grade teacher concisely articulated my shortcomings during a class discussion about curriculum development. She said, "Now I can see why all this stuff is so cool, but what does it have to do with my fourth-graders?" Insert light bulb. I wanted to reply, "Don't you *see* what it has to do with your students?," but she was a prize pupil, married to a folklorist and eager to try out fieldwork with her students. With her simple question, she challenged my assumptions and teaching strategies of the previous three years. If she could not see the bridge from folklore to her curriculum, I was in trouble. I asked what she absolutely had to teach her students in the coming year. She promptly replied, "Reading, writing, graphing, fractions, mapping, Virginia history."

Like her the others did not care primarily about improving the quality of their photography or audio recording. Rather, they cared about improving their teaching and negotiating curriculum demands effectively. On the spot, I revamped the syllabus to allow the class to discuss fully what each teacher had to teach and how to integrate folklore and fieldwork practices and applications into their required curricula. Serendipity crept into my curriculum. She was to become my favorite companion, revealing new pedagogical insights and unplanned opportunities for teachers to encounter challenges to their cultural assumptions about people, places, and pedagogy.

As I learned to turn over more class time to teachers, they demonstrated the artfulness of good teaching that I had been overlooking, demonstrated by a shift as what they gained from reading the work of folklorists began to relate to their teaching instead of their inner lives. Assigned to lead a discussion of class readings, their take on a text was usually shared through an activity, and I began adapting their applications to my teaching and keeping markers, colored pencils, paper, index cards, and glue sticks at hand. Each successive course enhanced my understanding of and regard for teachers' ability to take what they needed and weave it into lesson plans. I was discovering the culture of K–12 teaching, which includes ripping curriculum resources apart to lift and reshape what is individually meaningful. Each educator inevitably generates a unique spin.

Despite my previous overemphasis on folklore, rather than folklore and education, teachers had indeed been learning important lessons. Thus, in embracing their curricular and pedagogical skills, I needed to avoid throwing out what had worked. Fieldwork was the crucible. This was the place where they struggled hardest and overcame shyness, equipment failures, language barriers, and overexposed film. Recognizing her mistakes as well as her persistence, a soft-spoken art specialist prefaced her fieldwork presentation by saying, "I'll be more understanding of my students' failures in the future." Heads nodded. Fieldwork not only produced insights and inspired pride in workmanship, but it also provided time and space for teachers and interviewees to develop a bond, the key to all good fieldwork—and good teaching!

A third-grade teacher described her deepening relationship with a woman who worked at her mother's nursing home—a Rwandan refugee she was interviewing—this way: "My fieldwork assignment made changes in me, the interviewer, and the person I interviewed. She began to see I was truly interested in her and her culture; she was not just my mother's aide. She was also a mother, and I learned how valuable time with her boys was. I also learned how deeply she respects elders, and thus why she is an excellent caregiver." A high-school English teacher wrote that when she went to interview a walking-cane carver and his wife without her camera, he questioned her oversight, only half joking, "You have to get an A. We don't want to waste our time with a B interview." A middle-school music teacher, who lived in Prince George's County, Maryland, but had been born in New Orleans, met a distant cousin who was playing with the Treme Brass Band of New Orleans at the Smithsonian Folklife Festival and invited the group home to supper. The next day she told the class, "Now I grasp why students' musical tastes should matter more to me. I didn't want to hear their rap, but meeting the Treme Brass Band was like going home. I'll start the year by asking them what music they love."

These human connections emanating from basic fieldwork assignments were making my course come alive for teachers, but the constraints of integrating these independent fieldwork projects and providing time for teachers to work their magic reshaping the projects into curriculum challenged me. Collaboration with other folklorists working in education would help me solve this problem and became the next step in honing my new craft as an educator.

Learning from Folklorists

In addition to learning from teachers and teaching, I find ongoing professional and intellectual nourishment among folklorists, learning all the time from generous, imaginative colleagues. For example, Bonnie Sunstein and Elizabeth Chiseri-Strater's workshops and their book, *Field Working: Reading and Writing Research* (2002), improved my course portfolio approach and gave me strategies for teaching point of view and cultural assumptions more effectively. Like Liz Simons, these folklorists are comprehensively engaged with teachers, and folklore deeply informs their instruction of English teachers.

Working from 1997 to 2000 with Maida Owens, director of the Louisiana Division of the Arts Folklife program, and a team of teachers and folklorists on Louisiana Voices (see chapter 2) also influenced my approach significantly.[3] Genres such as family and occupational folklore, oral narratives, music, material culture, or rites of passage had to dovetail with what and how teachers must teach. Educators on the planning team deeply appreciated the richness of the content that folklorists study and the potential of fieldwork methods for the classroom. After a couple of years, we added a half day of fieldwork to the usual presentations by folklorists and folk artists during summer institutes for teams of teachers to document local occupations, accompanied by a folklorist. Teachers returned exuberant from a bakery, a pipeline company, an ironworking shop, and a saddlery, full of discoveries about occupational culture and curriculum connections.

The success of this team approach solved my dilemma of how to teach fieldwork in a short time frame. By emphasizing individual projects that might produce archival-quality documentation, I had been trying to get teachers to become "junior folklorists." Another lesson hammered home: teachers are experts, masters of their pedagogical craft. I saw that my disciplinary snobbery had been condescending, a sort of ethnocentrism that put my field at the center. Teamwork allowed teachers to play to their strengths, go into the community with less anxiety, and discover powerful surprises about the value of the local. The team approach became an organizing principle for my syllabus. Although I line up occupational sites, teachers go on their own so that they will not look to me as the fieldwork expert. Team members choose roles such as interviewer, photographer, sketch artist, audio or video recorder, and note taker. This process produces various types of media that teachers can use to create presentations that tell the stories of these occupations during training and gives them resources to take back to the classroom later.

Lesley University graduate students illustrate their occupational-culture documentation of a quilt shop in Boise with a quilt poster. They made squares alternating interview quotes and photographs for an Art and Culture in Community course in 2006.

Publication of the *Teacher's Guide to Local Culture* and the *Kids' Guide to Local Culture*, by Mark Wagler, Ruth Olson, and Anne Pryor (2004), was another milestone. These straightforward guides—written in fresh language aimed at fourth-graders but adaptable for all ages and settings—have proven very successful at helping teachers quickly understand and connect folklore and fieldwork to their teaching. The guides encapsulate coauthor Wagler's many years of experience as an elementary teacher—experience that underpins deceptively uncomplicated guides that inspire inquiry. I have used the guides regularly and witnessed how—without prompting—teachers try out activities and bring to class their students' work, such as personal relationship webs, drawings of their homes, and family rule surveys. In fact, teachers recommended that I use them as textbooks for my courses.

On top of my academic training and project-based work with these and many other folklorists, involvement with two extensive initiatives deepened my awareness of regional traditions and master folk artists nationwide, allowing me to share rich genres and resources with teachers in many parts of the country. As education director for Nick Spitzer's public-radio program *Folk Masters* from 1994 to 1997, I helped develop units for students on musicians from Hawai'i to Florida who appeared on the show. Then, as lead writer for the *Masters of Traditional Arts Education Guide*, I worked with Alan Govenar of Documentary Arts and a group of school-library media specialists to design themes and lessons to make the vast amount of media on the NEA's *National Heritage Fellowships 1982–2007* DVD-ROM navigable for educators and students (National Endowment for the Arts 2007). Through these experiences, I can reference publications, recordings, films, and exhibits about specific regional traditions and artists in my teaching. Folklorists may know about the decoy carvers, basket weavers, and polka musicians in their regions, but too often teachers and students do not.

I continue to learn from folklorists in the academy and public programs, and they keep me up to date on new fieldwork and resources. And I continue to share their archival-quality scholarship with teachers, so they can in turn use and share information with students and colleagues. The repertoire of excellent folklore materials available—often for free—to teachers, students, and the general public is extensive. I also encourage teachers to establish contact with local folklorists to learn even more about local culture, events, and resources. If I do not know about an area or a cultural group, I know where to go for help, and through Locallearningnetwork. org and many other sources (see the appendix), the FAIE field has made it possible for teachers to do the same. Thus, there are almost always materials appropriate for wherever I am teaching, reinforcing to teachers the vital work of folklorists. Invariably educators are surprised and grateful to discover that folklorists have documented a local tradition and produced these materials.

Enter Improvisation

My early attempts at teaching what I mistook to be Folklore 101 have evolved into a richer, more improvisatory course. Freeing myself from a pure folklore syllabus; collaborating with teachers, artists, and folklorists; and building on teachers' classroom applications over the years have made my syllabus more three dimensional, a bricolage. As I travel, I still use academic publications, films, and recordings related to the local culture, but by

An Art and Culture in Community class field trip took my Lesley University graduate students from Marietta, Georgia, to the NAMES Project Foundation in Atlanta,
where they viewed sections of the world's largest work of folk art—the AIDS
Memorial Quilt—and also interviewed the curator.

emphasizing hands-on experiences and serendipity over lectures and theory,
teachers and I can collaborate on choreographing learning opportunities
relevant to them. This approach challenges many teachers, who often prefer
a set timetable and concrete assignments over open-endedness. It requires
significant work to identify potential field-trip sites, community members,
community-based artists, and resources. Discoveries often come in the midst
of a course, so I put generic field trips on the syllabus to leave possibilities
open. I have a solid structure so we always have meaningful things to do in
class, but the best course experiences arise from my trusting serendipity and
adjusting in midstream.

I start with teachers sharing their stories and traditions, and we build an
environment of trust, which means that later they are willing to take risks.
They become cocreators of the syllabus because I adjust it to meet needs
that may be articulated during class discussions or take advantage of local
events, people, or places that challenge the class. I seek to model methods

that teachers can also use to teach and assess their students. I take copious notes and photographs and pay attention to class culture, students' folklore shared in class, seating patterns, side conversations, and generalizations. Are any teachers behaving or talking insensitively about a peer, a cultural group, or a student? What are their concerns? How can I stretch them? What can I learn from them? I am always asking myself how I can best instill knowledge and tools that teachers can incorporate into their individual repertoires, build upon, and return to time and time again. Shifting one's point of view a bit can be only a temporary blip or revelatory. When we experience something by crossing a new threshold, we are more likely to remember it, to incorporate it; knowledge has a better chance of becoming embodied. Thus, a class field trip to a museum or cultural center becomes a group learning experience that we analyze in the context of the classroom and community. Even if teachers have been to a site before, as participant observers they examine it more deeply on class field trips. I give them scaffolding, such as worksheets on observing and analyzing events or exhibits, to help position themselves as researchers and to listen, look, take notes, sketch, photograph, and ask questions mindfully. Becoming a participant observer in a family-owned shoe store prompted a Georgia teacher to write, "I've shopped here since I was a little girl, but I didn't ever think about the store as a sort of museum."

No longer Folklore 101, my course has become teacher driven because I want to honor the expertise of my students and at the same time push them to think more deeply about traditional culture and equity and their relationship to education. Thus, I must gauge cultural awareness, political engagement, and local school culture and adjust as I go. I usually do not know ahead of time my students' subjects and grade levels, local issues affecting schools, student demographics, or which cultural institutions teachers frequent. I have to do my own fieldwork and interpretation quickly and fit my course plans into their lived contexts. In some places, teachers have never been to the fine-arts museum, much less a community arts center. Again I seek to take them somewhere they may have overlooked or never visited. Not every community has Atlanta's NAMES Project Foundation, home base for the AIDS Memorial Quilt, or Boise's Basque Museum and Cultural Center, but every community has traditional culture treasures that can induce teachers to regard community—and therefore students and even teaching—with more awareness of multiple points of view and insider cultural knowledge.

The Importance of Grounding

Preparing educators to address local social issues and cross boundaries that they may have overlooked or regarded as intimidating is important. Teachers often live at the socioeconomic center of local culture, but some of their students may live at the margins. Situating them in the local takes more than theory and goodwill. It necessitates guiding them to center themselves in their cultural traditions, consider insider/outsider points of view, and practice basic ethnographic skills in preparation for their entering local communities. The importance of this hit home when an education professor in Virginia consulted me after a failed assignment. She had sent teachers in her graduate program into unfamiliar neighborhoods where their students lived with the goal of teaching them about community. Groups were given only a map and the charge to talk to people. When they returned, they complained about inaccessibility and feeling uncomfortable. Gated communities in the rich neighborhoods, strip malls where "no one spoke English," or housing projects where they felt intimidated put the teachers off. They had found exactly what they expected because they were not prepared to experience their visits differently—as teacher researchers—than they had as citizens passing through. They needed tools to "read" the neighborhoods, personal introduction to some insiders, and the basic ethics of interviewing. With appropriate grounding, they could have overcome their assumptions about their students and the places where they live and returned to class excited by having glimpsed what it means to be an insider in these neighborhoods. As the folklorist Judith Haut wrote in an early article on folklore and pluralistic education, ". . . there are advantages to acting like a fieldworker, i.e., suspending judgment while observing, asking question, and in other ways obtaining information to help answer or resolve puzzling issues" (1994, 53).

The education professor's failed assignment reinforced my appreciation of the essential components of a folkloristic methodology and how it can help teachers negotiate entry into and develop understanding of the very real social-justice issues connected to the characteristics and cultures of the neighborhoods where their students live: the profound differences between the economically poor and rich, juxtaposed with the wealth of culture available in both environments. This approach can help educators identify their assumptions and biases about students and communities.

My strategy has evolved to introduce people to folklore and fieldwork through sharing their often-overlooked personal traditions and practicing

Photo by Paddy Bowman.

Educators with Local Learning's Let's Go Arlington summer institute prepare to document the Roots of Virginia Culture program at the 2008 Smithsonian Folklife Festival on the National Mall in Washington, DC.

interviews through low-stress classroom exercises. Once teachers discover the power of the ethnographic lens and analysis, they then hone documentation skills. Changes in media and technology since my early work with teachers have dramatically lowered documentation and presentation hurdles. Teachers come to class with digital cameras and recorders, already knowing how to download and edit photographs and sound and video files, and their students of all ages use technology glibly. Tools are meaningless without content, however, and folklore provides relevant, authentic, local content. A folkloristic approach also gives teachers tools that allow K–12 students to understand themselves more fully, polish inquiry skills, and contribute to the wider community, including the school community. A first-grade teacher in Alexandria, Virginia, described why she reorganized her school year to focus on all students, not just high performers: "Children who are advanced in reading and writing are considered the source for all information. They are like information gods. Calling upon their folklife allows all students to be experts."

Photo by Paddy Bowman.

A San Diego cohort's July 2011 creation of *Who is the Voice of Education?* for the famed Chicano Park murals was the first public art installation by an Art and Culture in Community class. One of the original artist-activists, Mario Torero (left), helped my students promote student, family, and community voices in education.

Art and Culture in Community

Over a decade of learning and growing as a teacher educator, I grew to love working with teachers more than any other part of my work as a folklorist specializing in K–12 education. In 2004, when I joined the faculty of Lesley University's Integrated Teaching through the Arts master's program for teachers, I found a berth that consistently allows me to marry my passion for folklore and fieldwork with teaching K–12 educators. I am among an extensive cadre of adjunct faculty members who teach in the twenty-four states where Lesley offers this degree. My course, Art and Culture in Community, falls next to last in a two-year program, so when I meet them, the teachers have studied visual art, poetry, music, drama, storytelling, and dance, as well as technology and integrated arts-curriculum theory. Social justice and experiential learning are also central to Lesley University's mission.[4] It is this course that sparked a teacher's observation, "I didn't know

A high-school art teacher made a book box that she called "The Fieldworker" for her Art and Culture in Community course portfolio.

what I didn't know," which I hear in variations that continue to tell me that I am on track; that insight also seemed appropriate for this chapter's title.

The core of the course is occupational-culture fieldwork, done in teams during two-hour sessions at local businesses where I have found people willing to be interviewed. A discussion about the occupational culture of teaching—substitute teacher behavior, classroom décor, and discipline, for example—introduces the topic. As scaffolding the teams receive an occupational-culture survey, a fieldwork rubric, and release forms adapted from *Louisiana Voices*. Team members quickly choose documentation roles and head out with their cameras and recorders. Scouting local occupations adds to my teaching load, but my research satisfies my folklorist's curiosity. Before they depart, I ask students to inventory their assumptions about what they will find, and afterward they free-write about the experience to capture their reflections while they are fresh. Later, they reference these notes for final assignments.

Throughout the course, teachers keep a portfolio for all class work, notes, recordings, sketches, photographs, and artifacts. They find unique ways of storing and cataloging their work. They come across containers during fieldwork, at home, or in the classroom: a Victoria's Secret shopping bag, a thrift-shop suitcase, a son's old Spiderman backpack. Approaches may be personal or strictly classroom related. Usually they fall somewhere in between. Adapting strategies from Bonnie Sunstein and Elizabeth Chiseri-Strater (2002, 465–73) allows students to hang onto their portfolios and attendant two- and three-dimensional contents and turn in a final assignment requiring them to organize and analyze everything in their portfolios to create an annotated table of contents. They must also write a synthesis on the process of keeping and analyzing their portfolios. An elementary music specialist in Macon, Georgia, relayed her new way of seeing the world in her portfolio synthesis this way:

> Have you ever tried to take a picture with the lens cap still on the camera? If you have, then you know you cannot see the image of the picture you want to capture. I think this is a good description of how this class has made me "take off the lens cap" so I can see more clearly. When I first heard we were going on fieldtrips around the community, I thought this will be fun, but I have been there before. What is the point? But after going and being aware of my purpose and delving more deeply into the aesthetics and learning about the people working at the store, I began to see a bigger and brighter picture. When I was told I was going to the music store, my immediate reaction was BORING! I let my own prejudices as an outsider cloud my enthusiasm for what I might discover. . . . If I do not dig deeper, I will miss the true treasures that lie within my community. I now feel more equipped with knowledge and tools so I can continue to be an ethnographer wherever I go. I will adjust my lens so I can zoom in to find connections to what I observe.

What seemed natural to me—paying attention to a locally owned music store that survives in the struggling downtown of a small southern city— seemed extraordinary to the team of four teachers who ventured there on their occupational fieldwork assignment. The lens-cap metaphor is apt; revealing her preconceptions let me know that this teacher felt safe as well as challenged and that her view of her students as well as her community will differ in the future.

Learning on and from the Margins

Exploring the margins raises the learning stakes. Taking risks deepens learning. Steve Seidel of Harvard University's Project Zero described this as an essential pedagogical feature during a 2008 Arts Education Partnership forum presentation: "Powerful learning experiences put you off balance, challenge you, make you uncomfortable."[5] A folkloristic approach takes teachers into the vernacular classroom and introduces them to what folklorist Barbara Kirshenblatt-Gimblett terms "indigenous teachers" in the community ([1983] 2010, 11). They are likely to encounter a certain amount of discomfort and confront their cultural assumptions about places and people. A high-school Spanish teacher wrote after her visit to a Lao Buddhist temple in Fauquier County, Virginia, "You're stepping into another world and out of your shoes." Another Virginia teacher used this analogy: "This class has been like an immersion into a new country that we've been interested in from the sidelines but hadn't had a chance to visit." Teachers express surprise that people of different backgrounds share many of their traditions, and they also confront their personal biases and others' prejudices. These kinds of observations let me know that teachers are meeting my course goals. After a class lunch at a Mexican restaurant in Boise, a teacher wrote, "I have become more conscious of places, people, or artwork that may reinforce stereotypes. I find myself questioning representations of culture, attempting to ascertain whether there is a sense of caricature about its representation. I am more aware now of the perpetuated stereotypes in our community and the hidden prejudice toward the various ethnicities here." A teacher from Guam, who teaches on an Idaho military base, described encountering and uncovering her ethnocentrism:

> After attending a social gathering with my Chamorro friends, I realized that my friends and I are extremely ethnocentric. I know we like to stick together, but we are an extremely hospitable group of people.

It is part of our culture to be hospitable. However, at this one function, I noticed how all the Chamorro locals gravitated to one side of
the party while the white group of people gravitated to the other side.
It is hard for an "outsider" to understand the jargon, gestures, and
conversation if they had never been on the island before. I am more
aware of this ethnocentrism, and I am working hard to include everyone, no matter what skin color or heritage a person may be from.

This realization expresses the kind of learning that I believe the study of
folklore encompasses and illustrates the reasons that I continue to find
teaching teachers inspirational.

What, Exactly, Are We Learning?

From my courses, I find that teachers typically learn what they want their
students to learn: look and listen carefully, ask good questions, find the
main idea, synthesize and re-present information, use and create primary
sources, connect self and curriculum, be aware of assumptions and points
of view, recognize multiple forms of diversity, seek the authentic, investigate context, recognize that process can trump product, call upon intrinsic
knowledge, and behave ethically. They also become more self-aware and
curious about their students and develop lessons that elicit students' cultural expertise. It is of course affirming for young people to have a voice
in the classroom and see themselves in the curriculum, the community,
culture, and history. It is also satisfying for community members to find
that their traditions are interesting to others and for parents to have opportunities to connect with their children through the curriculum. Teachers
often tell me that middle-class students believe that they "have no culture,"
that only students from minority groups or other countries "have folklore,"
so the realization that everyone has it and adapts and transmits traditional
knowledge affects all students' self-identity positively.

Interrelated Realms of Knowledge

Focused on required academic subjects in a high-stakes testing environment,
teachers are aware of popular culture but are not necessarily media literate.
Too often they overlook the value of traditional ways of teaching, learning,
and knowing. The interrelatedness of folk, popular, and academic knowledge is well represented in three overlapping circles—a Venn diagram, that
mysterious teaching tool that I discovered during my first graduate course.

Many times I feel as though I am introducing teachers to an undersea world of knowledge, where they have been floating without realizing what lies beneath, when I display this diagram. Then, as they begin to consider their traditional culture, my students start to grasp the important folk knowledge that underpins their lives, their work, and their communities.

The indigenous-teacher concept reinforces the importance of traditional pedagogy for educators (Kirshenblatt-Gimblett [1983] 2010). When people are asked to list things learned outside a formal academic setting, it is not an algebra formula that heads the list. It is instead the lesson of patience that came with learning from a brother how to drive a stick shift or the lesson of compassion learned by caring for a grandparent. Indigenous-teacher conversations evoke someone's past as well as character. We spend meaningful time talking about how this kind of traditional pedagogy teaches us what matters most. Our values are embedded and passed along through such learning and teaching, and recovering memory of indigenous teaching is extremely useful in developing the relevance of folklore to teachers' lives and practices. A teacher from rural South Carolina reinforced, for example, what she learned from her grandmother, from whom she inherited a green thumb and a lot of knowledge about gardening: "If you don't know what you're doing, take it to an older person." But we also learn from young people, and many teachers describe their students as teachers, especially in relation to new media. A Washington state middle-school teacher wrote,

When we listed things we have learned outside the classroom, the variety of experiences that emerged and the long lists of my classmates were impressive. Many of our most deeply felt experiences were learned outside the classroom. The applications of sharing such experiences could be a powerful teaching tool, especially when we combine this with ethnographic fieldwork. Academia, then, has a "real-life," emotionally grounded context, which is fertile ground for learning. Durable learning must have an emotional component.

Thus, my teaching of teachers is fieldwork. I learn about communities and from class participants, who represent different generations as well as diverse places since some are newcomers. K–12 educators have this same opportunity; by tapping into student and community traditional knowledge, they can situate learning in a broader context that includes students as teachers and creators as well as carriers of culture. By sharing their folklore in stories and drawings, teachers stay in my memory bank. I may not always

Teachers, artists, and community scholars in the 2009 Arts and Gullah Culture Integration Institute, directed by Paddy Bowman, visit an African American graveyard on a field trip to the Seabrook community near Beaufort, South Carolina.

remember their names, but I will not forget the sixty-seven-year-old nun who, as a child, was an ace with her pocketknife and played mumblety-peg with her brothers, a clutch of Mississippi teachers who dressed their little brothers in girls' clothing, a cousins' board-game night that has lasted into adulthood, hide-and-seek in cornfields and the streets of the Lower East Side, and a make-believe beauty pageant that Miss Venezuela always won.

It still surprises me when something that catches my eye as soon as I drive into town—what's with the countless coffee huts, signs for freshly boiled peanuts, a Korean Baptist church, Spanish graffiti?—has escaped the notice of many people in my class. The Colorado teacher who wrote, "I didn't know what I didn't know," also noted, "I saw my community through your eyes, and it was a new place." Teachers ask, "Why does it take an outsider to introduce us to our own community?" This is part of the power of ethnography. By learning to suspend themselves as outsiders and look through an ethnographic lens, teachers focus on culturally significant phenomena that can extend to their students as well as themselves.

As I continue to learn about the importance of teachers' revelations about local culture, they demonstrate that hands-on experiences open up for them the promise of fieldwork for students of any age and subject. Because they learn more deeply by doing, teachers lead me to experiment with more interactive ways of teaching folklore and fieldwork. I turn more time over to them to lead discussions and critique folklore and educational resources.

They report through interactive applications pertinent to their teaching in ways that I could never conceive. They act out vignettes, write and perform poetry, put on radio dramas, sing, dance, and produce sophisticated multimedia presentations. I assign teams to lead class discussions of readings, which now include more education texts. This change brings scholars' work to life and more deeply imprints knowledge on sometimes-unwilling readers.

Presentation as Performance

I watch the faces of the teachers who have been in my folk-arts track on the last day of the 2008 Explorations in Puerto Rican Culture Institute in Springfield, Massachusetts, and I am entranced. Unlike the other classes presenting final projects that day, we have no drums, no murals, no dancers, yet our presentation turns out to be powerful. We sit in a semicircle of chairs before the teachers and artists who fill the banked seats of an auditorium. Behind us a slide show loops, displaying photographs from our fieldwork at a local Puerto Rican–owned *supermercado*. A low sound bed of Puerto Rican music provides the appropriate grocery store Muzak. I introduce our presentation by describing ways that folklorists look for art in daily life and summarize the steps that prepared the group for fieldwork. I sketch the scaffolding the team used and my charge that teachers inventory their assumptions about the market beforehand. This is the first time that I have accompanied a team. I find it important for teachers to figure things out on their own instead of looking to me, but this team was shorthanded, so I was privy to their excitement and discoveries during—as well as after—the fieldwork. Faced with a technology glitch, we abandon our elaborate media presentation and opt to play ourselves instead. Now I am the folklorist interviewing teachers about their fieldwork and its implications for their teaching.

I begin by asking a fifth-grade teacher born in Peru what her assumptions were. She confesses that she was nervous about going to "the North Side," but when she got lost, she did something she normally would not do. She asked a group of teenaged boys dressed in gang colors how to find the store. They got excited and started telling her in Spanish how best to get to her destination. As she got out of her car in the parking lot, she heard a child yelling, "Oh, Missy, oh, Missy," and suddenly one of her students was hugging her and saying, "Mami, come and meet my teacher." The boy's delight in seeing her at his family's grocery was more than evident. She publicly acknowledges her negative assumptions about the neighborhood

Photo by Paddy Bowman.

Teachers in the folk arts strand of the 2008 Explorations in Puerto Rican Culture Institute in Springfield, Massachusetts, focused an inspired final presentation on their documentation of a local *supermercado*.

and promises to take fifth-grade teachers at her school on their own field trip to the market: "This is our students' neighborhood, and we should get to know it." She describes the atmosphere of the store as "like a party" with colorfully packaged goods adorning shelves, music playing in the background, and people greeting and talking with each other in every aisle.

The sociability strikes a middle-school math teacher: "When I was a kid, going to the grocery store was not something you wanted to do. My parents were old-school French Canadians, and there was no touching anything, no asking them to buy you anything. At this market, families were enjoying being together and shopping; kids were having fun." He compares the meat department—and its two lively butchers—with the deli at the big suburban supermarket where his family shops: "At the counter, you take a number, and people are tapping their feet, they're impatient, and no one is talking. Here everyone was talking to each other—the butchers, us. When I asked the man who bought the frozen pig's head, which we used to eat and called *tête de cochon*, how he was going to cook it, everyone chimed in. Everybody's talking."

An elementary ELL (English language learning) specialist says, "It was like walking through the Plaza del Mercado de Rio Piedras [in San Juan, Puerto Rico], where there is something everyone needs. As we met other members of the group, it was strange how we would stop and talk about different dishes and foods, how articles are used in different cultures." She also calls the market "a time machine" because so many products took her back to her grandmother's kitchen. Enraptured by labels that bespoke home, the Island, or loved ones, teachers started noticing how many different Latino products graced the shelves. "This is food for Mexicans, Venezuelans, Guatemalans. Puerto Ricans don't eat this," they noted about many products. A cashier confirmed that in the past four years, the clientele has diversified. "I didn't know Goya made so many different things," comments a technology educator. The time-machine analogy puts the market in the past, present, and future of a community.

When asked about going to a store that she has known all her life with colleagues from different parts of her city, our final presenter beams: "I was so happy to have people coming to my neighborhood for a change, to see that it's not some scary place. For once I was the insider. I didn't have to go downtown to the art museum. I was home, and I loved having the others come here." The audience breaks into applause. Each teacher's synopsis of his or her experience at the *supermercado* differed but was compelling. A few photos and personal experience narratives taught others the power of place and influenced their understanding of what it means to be Puerto Rican in their city.

What Am I Leaving Behind?

Teachers with whom I work do not plumb the multiple theories and complex cultural interpretations of folklore. Rather, they employ the scaffolding of the ethnographic standpoint of folklore, learning new perspectives on themselves and their students and altering their concept of community. Ideally this deepens their empathy, improves their teaching, and translates into action. Unlike some FAIE colleagues who remain engaged with teachers over time, I usually do not see the ways that my work with teachers plays out in their classrooms. A sustained relationship with a group of teachers takes time and ongoing funding. Occasional communications relay success stories: "Thought you might want to read my students' stories." "I passed my National Board certification thanks to the course." "Parents have become more involved in the classroom." When I leave a group whom I have come to know well and have learned from and with, I remember what a Montana classroom teacher concluded:

> Before I interviewed the saddle maker, I assumed he would be a cowboy with basic education. I was very impressed with his history, knowledge, dedication, and experiences in his field. After our fieldwork, one thing occurred to me. All these folk groups were leaving something behind. They were producers, not just users, and they all eagerly shared whatever skill they had with others. This realization made me ask myself, "What effect do I have on others, and what am I leaving behind?" I realized I was passing on traditions and behaviors to my children and my students through some of the things we were learning in our course.

I return to Michael Umphrey's quote that introduced my story. Writing this chapter required me to examine the most important things that I have learned from teaching teachers. Only now—as I write this retrospective, which began as a paean to what teachers learn about themselves and their communities through studying folklore and fieldwork—do I take stock of what a dunce I was in the beginning and what gifts of learning I continue to receive from all with whom I work and those in their communities whom I encounter. Like the work of any folklorist with the folk, I find the reciprocity of learning an essential component in my development as an educator. What I learn from teachers about their folklore and teaching makes my course unique to place and time. Although teachers often describe their discoveries as "I didn't know what I didn't know"—about themselves, their communities, or their students—taking stock reveals how much I didn't know what I didn't know about teachers and teaching. As the evolution of my teaching continues, I grow and learn from each experience. Work stays fresh because every place differs, every group creates its own culture, and teachers surprise me with what they make of folklore and fieldwork. From comedian to therapist, learner to teacher, I wear different hats from the continuum of my development as an educator even as I acquire new ones. As Umphrey describes deep learning, "The most important stories in education often aren't the ones we are told—they are the ones we live" (2007, 15).

Notes

1.   The Arts Education Partnership came together around the development of the National Standards for Arts Education (Consortium of National Arts Education Associations.

The National Standards for Arts Education. Reston, VA: Music Educators National Conference, 1994. Available online at http://www.artsedge.kennedy-center.org/educators/standards.aspx). AEP is supported by the National Endowment for the Arts and U. S. Department of Education in cooperation with the Council of Chief State School Officers and the National Assembly of State Arts Agencies (see http://www.aep-arts.org).

2. The National Writing Project (NWP) has many chapters nationwide, and NWP approaches to the teaching of writing have influenced thousands of educators. Get more information at http://www.nwp.org

3. *Louisiana Voices: An Educator's Guide to Exploring Our Communities and Traditions,* available online at http://www.louisianavoices.org

4. "Lesley University prepares women and men for lives and careers that make a difference. A Lesley education empowers students with the knowledge, skills, and practical experiences they need to succeed as leaders in their professions and their communities. Members of the Lesley community believe in the power of individuals—working collaboratively—to bring about constructive change. A Lesley education fosters ethical judgment and engaged citizenship, and produces graduates who are equipped and committed to help shape a more just and humane world. The Lesley community shares a commitment to active teaching and learning, creativity, critical inquiry, and individual development across the lifespan. Through innovative programs and pedagogy, high quality instruction, scholarship, advocacy, and outreach, Lesley identifies and meets new educational challenges, extends educational opportunities, and serves the evolving needs of students and a diverse society." Available online at http://www.lesley.edu/about/mission.html (accessed 11 November 2010).

5. Steve Seidel, "The Qualities of Quality in Arts Education," Arts Education Partnership forum workshop, 18 January 2008, Irvine, CA.

2

A Tale of Discovery
Folklorists and Educators Collaborate to Create and Implement the Louisiana Voices Educator's Guide

Maida Owens with Eileen Engel

In 1997 THE LOUISIANA DIVISION OF THE ARTS Folklife Program had digitized a cornucopia of photographs and essays documenting traditional culture and folk artists from every parish in the state. With release of an extensive oral narrative collection in *Swapping Stories: Folktales from Louisiana* (Lindahl, Owens, and Harvison 1997) and launch of an auxiliary Web site, introducing educators to our rich collections seemed a natural step. But how to do it? This chapter chronicles the development of the extensive Louisiana Voices project—a tale, yes, of discovery, with interludes of reflection, frustration, alteration, and joy.

An initiative of the Louisiana Division of the Arts Folklife Program from 1997 until 2007, the Louisiana Voices Folklife in Education Program developed complementary resources, *Louisiana Voices: An Educator's Guide to Exploring Our Communities and Traditions*, an online public-domain resource (http://www.louisianavoices.org), and the Folklife in Louisiana Web site (http://www.louisianafolklife.org). The goal was to provide frameworks for the study of culture and an academically sound basis for both multicultural and technological education. The program offered professional-development opportunities for educators to learn to use the guide

Maida Owens, a cultural anthropologist who specializes in Louisiana's traditional cultures, has been director of the Louisiana Division of the Arts Folklife Program since 1988.
Eileen Engel is an award-winning teacher and education program manager who works to bring innovative programs to teachers and students.

and incorporate information about Louisiana folklife into their classrooms. From its inception, the program involved intensive collaboration between folklorists and educators to create both resources and professional-development strategies.

The guide focuses not only on teaching students about their own and others' folk traditions but also on ways to conduct fieldwork and produce their own documentation. "Unit II Classroom Applications of Fieldwork Basics" provides instruction on teaching students to do fieldwork and interviews and then present their results while also addressing state education content standards and offering assessment strategies. The guide includes many themes, and the project offered many tactics to implement them. This chapter describes the process of conceiving and creating the guide and training educators, as well as the collaborations that made Louisiana Voices more classroom ready.

Why Folklife? Why Louisiana Voices?

The impetus for Louisiana Voices was to make folklife resources and methods available in classrooms and show educators ways to use them to enrich student learning. We argued that teaching folklife provides a means to connect with every student since everyone—regardless of age, gender, socioeconomic class, or ethnic heritage—and every community has folk traditions—expressive customs currently practiced within a group that are passed along by word of mouth, imitation, and observation over time and through space. A folk group shares similar values, goals, experiences, and interests. Within these folk groups, those who create, enact, and represent the group's values are called *tradition bearers* or *folk artists*. Since each of us belongs to various folk groups at the same time, each student has multiple ways to connect to others.

The interdisciplinary study of traditional arts and community-based research in classrooms validates students' heritages and traditions while fostering critical-inquiry skills, developing primary research skills, and relating curriculum and classroom to students' lives and communities because they participate as experts about their folk groups and cultural traditions. Louisiana Voices provides K–12 teachers and other educators with tools for teaching folklife, including extensive teaching materials, research strategies, student activities, concepts, and high-quality content about Louisiana's cultural groups and their folk traditions. Although much of the content is specific to Louisiana, it is highly adaptable for any region.

Incorporating folklife into the classroom educates, motivates, engages, and fosters students' creative expression and, at the same time, connects them to their communities and state. When studying folklife, students acquire new perspectives about themselves, their culture, and the culture of others; these activities introduce multicultural heritage and multiple points of view to students in a positive manner. Furthermore, by seeing the continuation of folk expressions in their communities, students can connect the past with the present. By conducting fieldwork, they use and create primary sources, an important and rich opportunity. Folklife provides a readily accessible subject and methods in which students can be the experts.

The Educator's Guide

The heart of Louisiana Voices is *Louisiana Voices: An Educator's Guide to Exploring Our Communities and Traditions* (available at http://www.louisianavoices.org). It offers rich, extensive teaching resources for conducting fieldwork and studying Louisiana folk and traditional arts and culture and pinpoints the Louisiana education content standards that each lesson addresses. Every lesson addresses social studies and English language arts standards, and some also address visual-arts, music, foreign-language, mathematics, or science content standards. Because the lessons align with standards, they accentuate and augment existing curricula, rather than creating extra work for teachers. They simply offer new ways to teach what teachers are already required to cover. The lessons target fourth and eighth grades but can be adapted to any grade level. In addition to introducing students to Louisiana folklife, their community traditions, and fieldwork, the units include extensive technological applications and authentic assessment strategies, as well as Internet referrals that link students to high-quality folklife videos, music, stories, bibliographies, and Web sites. Thus, the units provide a fascinating blend of high tech and low tech, marrying the traditional and the technological.

Before Louisiana Voices

Before the creation of Louisiana Voices, only a few teachers who had the time and motivation to research a folklife topic and create a lesson used information and materials on Louisiana's folk cultures. Some of these highly motivated teachers were assisted by one of the many folklorists in the state, but generally they worked independently. Although Louisiana has numerous folklorists, none focused on integrating folklore into education. As a result, K–12 educational efforts were sporadic. In addition, folklorists' research was not readily accessible to teachers. Yes, some of it had been published in books and lesser-known journals, but much had not—particularly the research gathered by the Louisiana Division of the Arts Folklife Program. Furthermore, K–12 textbooks, even Louisiana history books, included minimal to no information about the state's folk cultures. So it is not surprising that little folklore—either content or methods—was taught in Louisiana classrooms.

The NEA Challenge

In 1997, when the National Endowment for the Arts announced the Folk Arts Infrastructure Initiative as a challenge to state arts agencies to expand and deepen their folk-arts programs, the Louisiana Folklife Program was already well developed with a nineteen-year history of continuous support in the Louisiana Division of the Arts (LDOA), a state agency within the Louisiana Department of Culture, Recreation, and Tourism (LDCRT). We had developed effective strategies to document folk artists and twenty different folk cultural groups in the state and had used many approaches to present them to the public. These included producing a statewide exhibit, regional surveys, books, an annual festival, and recordings. In addition, LDOA supported folklife through several grant programs, most notably project assistance, apprenticeships, and fellowships. We also had three regional folklorists stationed at universities. The most glaring omission was that we had not focused on folk arts in education. So, in response to this NEA challenge, LDOA initiated the Louisiana Voices Folklife in Education Program and development of a companion Web site, Folklife in Louisiana (http://www.louisianafolklife.org).

Over the next ten years, LDOA and NEA invested more than half a million dollars in this effort. The end result is two interconnected Web sites that consist of more than a thousand web pages and four online databases. The Folklife in Louisiana Web site includes essays, photographs, a bibliographical database, video and audio clips, and links to related online resources that feature the research of many folklorists, cultural anthropologists, and ethnomusicologists. The Louisiana Voices Educator's Guide consists of nine units with forty-three lessons that include student worksheets, assessment strategies, technology connections, and links to folklife resources about Louisiana and elsewhere.

The process of creating Louisiana Voices was collaborative at each phase. The initial step was to develop the lessons and post them online. I directed the effort and negotiated the concerns of educators and other folklorists and then worked with writers and technologists to develop the final product. The educators included classroom teachers, curriculum writers, and Louisiana Department of Education (LDOE) educational-technology specialists. The folklorists included academics with experience teaching at the university level, public folklorists, and graduate students who had some K–12 classroom experience. The technologists consisted of Web design contractors and the LDCRT Webmaster, Greg Wirth. Notably the lead Web designer, Diane Wanek, saw this as an opportunity to produce a signature product and delivered far more than what she was contracted to do. Over the years, the team members fluctuated with some only involved at that early creative phase, some coming in for certain tasks or phases, and some connected throughout the project. Significantly, no one was both an experienced folklorist and master educator, much less a skilled and creative Web designer, so collaboration was required every step of the way.

The core team throughout the years consisted of Paddy Bowman as lead folklorist and writer, Sylvia Bienvenu as educator, and me, a cultural anthropologist, as project director. An additional thirty-seven cultural researchers and educators were involved. (Thus, when I use "we" in this article, I refer to the team members involved at that time.) Other writers included Jane Vidrine, a folklorist, musician, and classroom teacher who worked on the music unit, and Jocelyn Donlon, a folklorist and writer who worked on the music unit and rewrote the "Defining Terms" unit and "Fieldwork Basics" unit. In the fall of 2004, Eileen Engel, a former educator and education-program specialist, became project manager. Her past experience included working in educational system change, transforming classroom learning by training large numbers of teachers to use new methods, teaching every K–12 grade except third, and serving as a museum educator facilitating a curriculum network for teachers. She was charged with getting the lessons used in Louisiana classrooms. Later in this article, excerpts from her extensive field notes provide insight into this process.

Other Contributors

Many, many more people contributed in various ways. Because we did not have the expertise in the state to develop completely new resources, we drew on the work of other folklore-in-education programs and incorporated their resources, strategies, or activities with permission. These included CARTS (Cultural Arts Resources for Teachers and Students), the *Folkwriting, A Teacher's Guide to Kentucky Folklife,* Michigan Folkpatterns, Montana Heritage Project, Oregon Folklife Program, *Wisconsin Folks,* Lucy Long's *To Dance Irish: An Educational Resource Guide* (1999), Bea Roeder's folklife bingo, and Frank Stasio's interviewing scripts in the fieldwork unit.

Because Louisiana Voices was developed over such a long time, some of these projects were progressing parallel to our program, and we ended up borrowing back and forth from each other. Most notable is *Folkwriting,* an initiative of the South Georgia Folklife Project. Laurie Kay Sommers adapted some Louisiana Voices activities that were then incorporated back into our project. In other cases, we simply linked to resources in other online programs. Because the lessons and activities in the Louisiana Voices Educator's Guide are public domain (but the resources on the Folklife in Louisiana Web site that they link to are not), they can be found in many other resources as well.

Another key partner was LDOE. When we first started, technology education was an LDOE priority. We eagerly jumped on that bandwagon since we knew that we wanted the lessons to be delivered online. This turned out to be very strategic since the new Louisiana Center for Educational Technology (LCET) was starting a major initiative to incorporate technology into classrooms. We met with Carol Whelan and Sheila Talamo one month after they were hired at LCET. They had expertise, strategies, and funding and were in the process of selecting content to instruct teachers how to use technology in their classrooms. After seeing the amount of Louisiana-specific content we already had developed and that we were willing partners with at least some money, they changed plans and adopted Louisiana folklife as their content. They also introduced us to Sylvia Bienvenu, a master teacher, curriculum writer, assessment designer, and educational technologist. LCET and Bienvenu became key partners in the development of the Louisiana Voices core strategies.

Development of the Units

In the summer of 1998, Paddy Bowman led a group of folklorists and educators in an intensive, three-day planning session to identify appropriate unit themes and ways to reach teachers. After considering many different strategies, the team decided that the units should focus on folklore genres. I was actually surprised that the educators wanted units that clearly taught folklore since I feared that most of them would feel that this was simply something else to teach. I was hoping that the team would come up with something that a folklorist would not propose—something clever to sneak into the classroom. Instead, the educators proposed an overview of folklore genres in seven units—exactly what most folklorists would have suggested. The first two units were initially background information for the other units. "Unit I Defining Terms" provides definitions of basic folklore terms in addition to activities to help students understand folklore concepts. The second, originally called "Unit II Fieldwork Basics," contains an overview of the issues involved in conducting fieldwork, activities and suggestions, and necessary forms. For these sections, we drew upon a number of existing resources since many folklorists had already developed these types of units, yet we did have to create some additions, including an appropriate example of double-column note taking during interviews. I could not find an appropriate example, so I interviewed my daughter about making fortune-tellers (cootie catchers) in grade school for "Sample Fieldnotes: Teen Memories of Grade School Traditions."

One goal is first to make students aware that everyone has folklore, so the third unit is key to the success of Louisiana Voices. "Unit III Discovering the Obvious: Our Lives as the 'Folk'" focuses on children's lore and family and school traditions to help students recognize that they, too, have folklore. This is the best way to introduce students to folklife because they find where their traditional arts and folklife exist in daily life. Then they can more easily study others' cultural expressions and find commonalities as well as differences with greater understanding and tolerance. Nina Asher, associate professor at Louisiana State University's College of Education, who specializes in multicultural education, noted that by focusing first on the student's own folklore, folklorists had identified a strategy to teach multiculturalism without objectifying "the other," a major issue that multicultural education attempts to address. The next unit, "Unit IV The State of Our Lives: Being a Louisiana Neighbor," introduces students to the state's cultural groups and regions by using cultural geography and the concept of sense of place. This unit heavily links to folklorists' research on the Folklife in Louisiana Web site.

The remaining five units each explore a folklore genre using Louisiana examples. "Unit V Oral Traditions: Swapping Stories" covers a wide variety of oral traditions—from local and historical legends to personal-experience narratives—drawing heavily on *Swapping Stories: Folktales from Louisiana*, a publication, video, and Web site produced by the Louisiana Folklife Program. "Unit VI Louisiana's Musical Landscape" explores traditional music, dance, and movement; addresses listening skills; and relates music to social studies, economics, language arts, musical legends, career education, and visual arts, as well as school-based music studies. "Unit VII Material Culture—The Stuff of Life" introduces the concept of material culture and provides ways of looking at artifacts, art, teaching, and learning. Students examine the aesthetics of everyday life, such as vernacular architecture, gardens and yards, needlework, crafts, hairstyles, foodways, body ornamentation, clothing, and costumes. They consider questions of utility and beauty and the importance of context to artifacts. "Unit VIII The Worlds of Work and Play" encourages students' interaction with adults in the community through documenting occupations. Students also investigate ways that adults enjoy life and share community through recreation, hobbies, celebrations, oral narratives, and other traditions. "Unit IX The Seasonal Round and the Cycle of Life" also encourages students' interaction with adults and covers seasonal customs, beliefs, traditions, celebrations, and holidays. The foodways and occupational lessons emphasize fieldwork since every community and student can readily identify tradition bearers for a class project.

The Writing Process: Negotiating Collaboration

A recurring struggle in the early phase was determining whether an educator or a folklorist should be the lead writer. I was surprised that the educators consistently wanted the folklorists to offer approaches, activities, and content. A process evolved in which a folklorist identified the lesson goals and proposed activities and sometimes worksheets and then an educator responded to the folklorist's work.

Paddy Bowman ended up being the lead writer for most units, but that was not the original plan. Initially we had seven writers working at the same time who were to submit a first draft in four months. When the time was up, it became clear that writing units was much more specialized and difficult than we had anticipated. Gradually the other folklorist writers withdrew, really through no fault of their own. It was evident that this was a much more challenging task than we had realized. We also came to appreciate that curriculum writing is a specialized field and just because people had classroom experience did not mean they could provide what we needed.

We developed a process to create the units. Bowman delivered a draft to me, and I checked it for style and format. I then identified or developed folklife resources to support the lessons. This could be as simple as inserting examples and adding links to existing resources or creating new ones. Examples include selecting photographs of crafts for the material-culture lessons, maps for the cultural-geography lesson, Louisiana examples for the folklife bingo activity, or appropriate tales for the narrative lessons. I then sent the units to other folklorists who had expertise in that genre for review and incorporated their suggestions. Next, I sent the lesson to Sylvia Bienvenu, who developed the final lesson format, identified the content standards that the lesson addressed, added technology connections, and designed assessment strategies specific to the activities. In an e-mail written in 2008, Bienvenu describes her strategies when working on the Louisiana Voices lessons:

> When I first began working on the Louisiana Voices lesson plans, my primary focus was adding the Louisiana Content Standards to each lesson. These standards had just recently been developed and the Louisiana Department of Education was searching for ways to integrate them into education at all levels in the state. . . . So, from the start, I approached the Louisiana Voices lesson plans from this viewpoint. After finding content standards that *could* be used in a lesson, I often found myself revising the lesson to incorporate steps that would lead students to *think* in the way described in the standard. Quite often I found that the most expedient way to assure this was to develop a worksheet that caused this to happen. For instance, in Unit III Lesson 3, the Standard ELA-7-M2 "Problem solving by using reasoning skills, life experiences, accumulated knowledge, and relevant available information," prompted me to develop the "That's the Context" worksheet that requires intense investigation and gathering information from family members to discover the history of an object and possible hidden meanings. Then the lesson progresses to sharing the information in class to discover themes and categories that objects fall into, as a means of accomplishing the standard CL-1-D2 "Identifying cultural practices that give rise to commonly held generalizations and/or stereotypes."

After receiving the lesson from Bienvenu, I checked it again for style and format and general editing before sending it to Web specialists to post. For some lessons, the process had to be repeated before the unit was considered finished. Then I worked with the Web designer on the overall Web-site strategies.

The easiest unit to produce was the third one since it is basically the teaching progression that Bowman learned from Elizabeth Radin Simons (1990) and both had been using in teacher institutes across the country. These were highly refined activities that Simons and Bowman had piloted with countless teachers, so only a few Louisiana-specific resources were needed. No other units were so easy, and some were a struggle because we were going into new territory. Also we were developing units for genres that we did not already have well-developed folklife resources to support. Jane Vidrine, a musician, folklorist, and new teacher, and Jocelyn Donlon, a folklorist and writer, together developed the core strategy for the music and dance unit while I commissioned essays, musician bios, and play lists and acquired rights to post music samples online. When the music unit was completed, we thought we were finished.

Classroom Ready?

One of the frequent comments—or complaints—about Louisiana Voices is that the lessons try to do too much and are not classroom ready. We realize this and actually intended it. We wanted to create a resource for teachers of different subjects and grades. We knew we did not have the resources to develop and test lessons for every grade and subject, so we compromised and created a guide that offers suggestions and options. So, yes, every teacher will likely have to adapt every lesson, but that is the strength of the guide. Every teacher can modify every lesson. And it turned out that we did, too. When Eileen Engel joined the team, she adapted some lessons and made them more classroom ready to satisfy her goal to get Louisiana Voices into more schools.

Revising the fieldwork unit—which did not directly teach students how to do fieldwork by itemizing the skills they needed—became important. Originally it was conceived as background information, along with the first unit, for the other sections and did not identify the education-content standards addressed or offer assessment strategies. During the initial planning phase, the educators said that the material in these two units was too important and should not be considered just background information, so they became Units I and II, even though they were not structured as lessons like the others. They remained that way until the other seven units were completed six years later.

Teachers Start to Respond

Because development of the guide took so many years, we started offering professional-development opportunities for teachers before all the units had been completed. Some teachers attended almost anything we offered and subsequently gave thoughtful feedback. A recurrent theme was the difficulty of teaching students how to do fieldwork. It became apparent that "Unit II Fieldwork Basics" did not fully articulate all the steps. We expected teachers to learn about folklore and how to do fieldwork much as most folklorists had been taught in graduate school—by simply doing it. But whereas as folklorists we had been attracted to fieldwork and this type of professional training and research, the teachers had not. I gradually accepted that we were expecting the teachers to intuit too much and learn our profession too quickly. I asked Jocelyn Donlon to address the issues, and she proposed five sequential lessons that teach students to plan fieldwork research collaboratively and, step by step, to set goals, choose methods and technology, identify subjects, design research instruments, and develop project schedules and checklists. The new unit emphasized the importance of testing equipment and practicing interviewing in steps. The final lesson focused on making use of the fieldwork results.

Sylvia Bienvenu was invaluable in this process. Reflecting on this part of our collaboration, she made an important observation in her 2008 e-mail:

> When I received lesson plans from the folklorists, I was often reminded of our family discussions about family recipes handed down from parents or grandparents. They never seemed to come out quite like when Mama or Grandma made them. And the reason, we concluded, was that they were such masters and worked so intuitively that many of the little details were not written into the recipe. Important things like how long to cook it, the correct sequence for adding ingredients, even standard measurements that we found crucial but were just measures of common sense and lots of experience for them. . . . This insight became my guiding light, because I realized that the folklorists were the masters of collecting and recording folklore, but had omitted "ingredients and steps" that had to be made clear to the rest of us who had not had their vast experience. I tried to fill in this missing information and put it in sequential steps that efficient learning required.

Gradually Bienvenu drew out of us more and more details about the process that experienced fieldworkers have internalized. She asked us to articulate the difference between interviewing and fieldwork. This was especially important since many teachers would likely end up using online resources without having a folklorist to consult. As a result, the fieldwork unit is significantly longer and more involved than those that folklorists produced for other projects. As with many of the lessons, we realize that most teachers will not be able to implement the entire process, but it is there to inform them so they can adapt it for their specific needs and students.

Assistance with developing lists of possible interview questions was another thing that teachers needed. Folklorists tend to be highly intuitive individuals, and their advanced training and experience enable them to develop interview questions easily. They fluently adapt questions to the context during an interview and highly value this ability and the organic process of designing a research project. But in our workshops, we kept seeing teachers struggle to develop what most folklorists consider obvious. This became clear to me during one specific workshop when teachers were to interview each other about their names. I was struck that some could not think of any questions to ask about their partner's name! After that I decided that we had to suggest questions. Some folklorists on the team resisted this since they felt that coming up with the questions is an important step in the fieldwork process that fosters critical thinking. They feared that teachers and students would just use the list of questions without considering their specific context. That certainly is a concern, but developing questions is still an advanced skill. The educators were adamant that teachers needed more guidance about doing it. We created some questions and adapted lists from other folklore-in-education projects, such as Lucy Long's Irish dance guide (1999). Altogether we developed seventeen worksheets concerning questions.

Another challenge was devising an assessment strategy for teachers to evaluate student fieldwork. Bienvenu insisted that teachers needed a tool to assess their students' products and process—a rubric. Again she pulled the information out of the folklorists and devised the fieldwork rubric, which distills the key steps and elements of fieldwork (see figure 1).

So after intensive collaboration between folklorists and educators, "Fieldwork Basics" became "Unit II Classroom Applications of Fieldwork Basics." We did not eliminate the original unit but retained it because it is useful for projects not based in K–12 classrooms and serves as a convenient introduction for educators considering using the full unit.

Louisiana Voices Folklife in Education Project
www.louisianavoices.org

Fieldwork Rubric

Name _____ Title/Topic _____ Date _____

Task You are a folk researcher who has been directed to conduct fieldwork to research some aspect of folklife.
You will be assessed on your ability to prepare carefully, practice needed skills, conduct fieldwork productively and accurately, process and archive materials properly, and present your findings.

Performance Element	Accomplished Points	Developing Points	Beginning Points	Total Points
Preparing	• Correctly identifies who to interview and what to collect and/or study. • Chooses appropriate method of documentation and prepares needed materials and tools.	• Identifies inappropriate interviewee or irrelevant terms to study or collect. • Method of documentation is not most appropriate; prepares some materials and tools.	• Incorrectly identifies who to interview, what to collect and/or study. • Chooses inappropriate method of documentation fails to prepare materials and tools.	
Practicing	• Sufficiently practices using the equipment that will be used. • Practices interviewing interviewees. • Completes items in the **Before** section of the **Interview Checklist**.	• Practices using the equipment a little, mastery not attained. • Practices interviewing interviewees a little. • Omits some items in **Before** section of the **Interview Checklist**.	• Fails to practice using the equipment. • Fails to practice interviewing interviewees. • Omits most items in the **Before** section of the **Interview Checklist**.	
Conducting Fieldwork	• Collects appropriate notebooks, forms, surveys and/or checklists. • Asks meaningful questions, records accurately • Takes high-quality photographs; labels prints, slides, diskettes • Tape records at appropriate volume, with no interfering noises. • Completes items in the **During** section of the **Interview Checklist**.	• Collects most of fieldwork tools. • Asks mostly meaningful questions, recording mostly accurate. • Takes a large amount of high-quality photographs, labels them adequately. • Tape recordings lacking in quality, some interferences. • Omits some items in the **During** section of the **Interview Checklist**.	• Collects inappropriate or inadequate fieldwork tools. • Omits questions, records inaccurately. • Takes insufficient photographs, labels them inadequately. • Tape recordings of poor quality. • Omits most items in the **During** section of the **Interview Checklist**.	
Processing Fieldwork Materials	• Completes **Tape Log** and **Photo Log**. • Labels materials carefully, files permission slips with materials • Transcribes tapes accurately; proofs and edits transcriptions. • Archives recorded materials where they will be protected. • Completes items in the **After** section of the **Interview Checklist**.	• **Tape Log** and/or **Photo Log**, incomplete. • Labels some materials inaccurately, files most permission slips. • Transcribes some tapes inaccurately, proofs and edits most transcriptions. • Archives most recorded materials where they will be protected. • Omits some items in the **After** section of the **Interview Checklist**.	• **Tape Log** and/or **Photo Log**, incomplete. • Labels most materials inaccurately, files few permission slips. • Transcribes most tapes inaccurately, proofs and edits few transcriptions. • Archives few recorded materials where they will be protected • Omits most items in the **After** section of the **Interview Checklist**.	
Presenting Findings	• Chooses appropriate medium for presenting findings. • Conveys a message through creative presentation.	• Chooses appropriate medium for presenting findings. • Conveys a message through mundane presentation.	• Chooses inappropriate medium for presenting findings. • Fails to convey a message through creative presentation.	

Figure 1. Louisiana Voices Unit II Fieldwork Rubric found at http://www.louisianavoices.org/ pdfs/ Unit2/FieldworkRubric.

Professional Development for Educators

The second component of the Louisiana Voices program was offering educators experiential opportunities to learn to integrate the lessons into their classroom teaching with fieldwork a priority. Although Louisiana Voices was relatively well funded as an arts or folklife project, it was never sufficiently underwritten as a statewide education initiative. Our professional-development approaches changed over the years depending on available funds and partners. We partnered with LDOE on various statewide initiatives, including training in-service and university educators and K–12 principals; enhancing afterschool initiatives; and restructuring English language-arts education. In their technology education efforts, LDOE used folklife content, and presenters participated in many of their workshops. We offered a full-day seminar for district administrators and LDOE staff and did presentations to state teacher conferences, university colleges of education classes, and informal groups, such as museum educators and librarians. Learn and Serve offered Louisiana Voices grants that included service learning for students. The Louisiana Serve Commission manages the state's Learn and Serve America K-12 service learning grants, which promote experiential learning in community service projects.

In the first four years, we offered five-day summer institutes, an intensive, but expensive, model favored by many comparable initiatives. From 1999 to 2002, we spent twenty-five thousand dollars in one week each year to assemble twenty-five teachers and seven to eight faculty folklorists and folk and teaching artists. Everyone described the week as transformative. Guest faculty included leading voices in folk arts in education, as well as many Louisiana folklorists. As a result, the institutes also served as professional development for Louisiana Voices staff and many folklorists in the state.

Decreasing funds forced us to reevaluate the summer institute model, so we experimented with and learned from other formats. We knew that teachers needed to be taught in teams, so we tried a one-school-at-a-time program that focused on getting teachers from a single school trained together so they could then support each other when implementing collaborative lessons, but it quickly became evident that we did not have the financial or staff resources for that model.

In 2002 we surveyed teachers who had attended our institutes to determine how they were using the Louisiana Voices resources in their classrooms and were disappointed to learn that few were implementing them. The survey showed that once back in the classroom, teachers' overwhelming enthusiasm for the program met with reality, including school and district requirements, time allotments, and difficulty translating the experience for their students. Additional emphasis on supporting the teacher once back in the classroom was necessary for the activities to be used more often. We also had difficulty engaging teachers during the academic year, even though that was part of their agreement when they attended the institute. When we shared our findings with our LDOE cohorts, they were not surprised. They explained that research shows that professional development without follow-up during the academic year results in poor implementation.

As a result, we narrowed our target audience and focused on teachers who had already attended summer institutes. We made exceptions and accepted motivated teachers who approached us, but our priority was to deepen our connections with fewer teachers. Most of our offerings were one-day workshops during the academic year or summer that built on each other. The most successful was held on Martin Luther King Day in January 2004. Seventy-five teachers applied for twenty-five openings for Not Just Entertainment: How to Design Activities around Visiting Folk Artists. Teachers practiced interviewing each other, and then one teacher interviewed a folk artist in front of the others. This was followed by Practical Fieldworking: The "How To" Workshop for Producing Student Fieldwork Experiences and Process, Product, and Publicity: Getting Projects Done. These three workshops covered the fieldwork unit. We repeated this series in the summer.

We also experimented with two other formats. Folklorist Susan Roach offered a three-week, university for-credit graduate class at Louisiana Tech University to seventeen teachers. Louisiana Voices provided workshop pre-senters, folk artists, fieldwork expenses, and a teacher stipend of $250. And with a National Endowment for the Humanities focus grant, we offered a series of four weekend seminars to thirteen teachers. They came as three teams from three schools with the hope that they could support each other back in the classroom to implement the lessons, and it worked. Of all the formats, this seminar series was by far the most successful. Every teacher implemented lessons during that academic year. But it was still expensive: twenty-five thousand dollars. Without another NEH grant, we were unable to offer this series again. Funds continued to dwindle.

Our most intensive partnership occurred in 2003 and 2004 with Shana Walton at Tulane University's Deep South Regional Humanities Center called Lessons in Folklife and Technology for English Language Arts (LiFT-ELA), a professional-development opportunity that consisted of a ten-day summer institute followed by ten days during the academic year for thirty-two teachers in the greater New Orleans area. Walton describes the project:

> The goal was not only to improve teacher skills in teaching student reading skills and to heighten student (and teacher) motivation, but also to raise the English Language Arts test scores at specific schools. LiFT-ELA was funded by the Louisiana Systemic Initiative Program (LaSIP) as part of a challenge to Louisiana universities to offer cre-ative approaches to improve English Language Arts teaching at low performing schools based on test scores. With $170,000 the first year and $260,000 the second, this was a rare opportunity to use Louisiana Voices strategies with the recommended LDOE professional develop-ment model. (2004a)

Of the ten teachers that went on to fully implement, half were fourth grade teachers whose students faced Louisiana's comprehensive LEAP test. . . . Four saw their students perform better than other fourth graders at their schools who were not in the project. The teacher whose students did not outperform their peers . . . had an ability-grouped class of special education students and students who were a grade level behind in work performance. (2004b)

The Lift-ELA summer institute featured presentations from folklorists, other cultural documenters, and folk artists. The teachers divided into teams and conducted fieldwork around New Orleans on occupations that included musicians, grocery-store owners, snowball and lunch-stand operators, a plasterer, and a parasol maker. Their research produced fieldwork folders containing data sheets, interview audiotapes, CDs, release forms, drawings, interview topic summaries, still-photography logs, interview transcripts, and lesson plans. The academic year follow-up consisted of an additional ten days of work and staff observation. Cherice Harrison-Nelson, an Orleans Parish educator who had received the Louisiana Endowment for the Humanities Teacher of the Year award, headed the follow-up work, which included observing the teachers instructing their students in the activities. At the end of the next school year, each teacher created a binder containing lesson plans and examples of classroom work. This clearly was the ideal model but also expensive. Without comparable funding, we could not continue this approach, even though the project showed that the Louisiana Voices strategies increased English-language-arts test scores for the students of participating teachers.

New Leadership for Professional Development

In 2004 experienced teacher Eileen Engel joined the team. In six months, she had more teachers actively using Louisiana Voices than we had had over the preceding five years. With a master teacher at the helm of professional development, the project was off to a new start. At this point in the tale of Louisiana Voices, Engel's insights are especially valuable. Her words deserve their own space because they convey an insider's account of an important role: bridging the world of formal folklore practice to K–12 educators.

W W W W W W W W

An Educator's Tale

Eileen Engels

Before I interviewed for the Louisiana Voices position, I spent a number of hours online looking at the activities in the Educators Guide. My experience in both teaching and education program management with an emphasis on system reform had taught me what to look for in activities that worked in the classroom and provided learning opportunities for students. I was delighted to see that the Louisiana Voices activities were excellent examples of best practice in materials development. I knew teachers, their students, families, and schools would find them innovative and worthy of effort. But I also knew from experience how difficult it is for teachers to translate a summer workshop experience—no matter how great—into a change in their teaching strategy. There are numerous challenges that await the teacher who tries to bring new activities into a classroom. These obstacles include district, school, and state requirements, as well as time and resource constraints, to mention just a few. For teachers to surmount these obstacles, they needed units that were ready to go with just a few variations for their particular classroom. Small incentives could go a long way in helping them try out new things, too.

After I came on board, the Louisiana Voices team emphasized reorganizing already-created activities to make them more user friendly, partnering with other teacher-education programs to leverage resources, providing theme- and event-based activities, developing a cadre of teachers who use the activities with their students, and designing site-based workshops.

The first step involved taking a fresh look at the extensive online activities. The guide presented so much information that it was a challenge to put together a personalized unit for an individual class, a common practice with teachers. The foodways materials, which emphasized fieldwork activities, afforded the best opportunity for redesign. The activities involved having students interview someone preparing a dish that is traditional in the family. The student filled out recipe and interview sheets and often took pictures of the event with a disposable camera. Back in the classroom, more activities offered students further enrichment after the interview. A classroom cookbook was a possible product. The original lessons provided background on Louisiana food, its origin and culture, ways to introduce and carry out the activities, resource lists, and a complete handout section for teachers to print out and use immediately. However, it was spread over several lessons.

After spending a few hours compiling and editing the lessons into one comprehensive unit and repackaging it with a new cover, the section was ready to go straight into the classroom. We posted the new version, "Louisiana's Many Food Traditions," online and offered a hundred dollars to any teacher who would try it out, send us classroom products, and fill out an evaluation form. Some were offered funds for bringing in a guest folk artist. Within a few months, teachers working with more than two hundred students tested the activities and sent us information that we used to enhance the materials. They requested more assessment strategies, which we included in the revised foodways unit.

Just as the unit's popularity was ready to spread throughout the state, Hurricanes Katrina and Rita hit Louisiana. To assist with recovery from the effects of two of the nation's largest natural disasters, we offered teachers a coping strategy that also reinforced our focus on fieldwork. We distilled the fieldwork unit and drew upon materials developed for the In the Wake of the Hurricanes Research Coalition. The resulting "In the Wake of the Hurricanes" unit for teachers of grades five through twelve had students interview each other, community members, and family members about their storm experiences. Students learned the basics of interviewing and then employed their new skills in discussions with evacuees and emergency, rescue, and assistance personnel. Again we gave a hundred dollars to teachers who used the activities.

Interestingly the teachers who responded lived in coastal areas that were less affected but had received displaced students. Teachers in the most profoundly impacted areas or those more removed from the coast did not use the unit. The experience was too fresh for some of them, although one produced a wonderful story/quilt project. Teachers creatively employed the activities in their classrooms and designed innovative products, including mathematical sheets on evacuation costs, audio- and video-taped interviews, and an impressive poetry anthology entitled "Making Lemonade." Another original teacher worked with a quilter and had her students— many of whom had lost their homes in Katrina—write a short story and then create a picture that was made into a quilt square. The quilt was presented to city officials.

To involve teachers statewide and create a cadre of additional teachers and students working on the units, a curriculum network began. Louisiana Voices staff invited all teachers who had attended any program to participate and kept contact with those most likely to implement the lessons in their classrooms. They were invited to become part of the network through the e-mail Listserv, which includes more than a thousand educators. Interested teachers signed up and received more information. They completed the units and sent in products or pictures of them and evaluation forms. For their efforts, they received a hundred dollars and some money to cover material costs. The curriculum network proved to be a highly successful, inexpensive method of dissemination.

❦ ❦ ❦ ❦ ❦ ❦ ❦ ❦

The Value of Expertise and Experience

Engel's strategies and expertise were clearly instrumental in the advances that Louisiana Voices made in such a short time. Actually the curriculum network was the same idea that Louisiana Voices staff had tried since the beginning, but now we had a master teacher who understood teachers, knew how to connect with them, and truly could create a network of educators. Engel invited teachers to extraordinary events. She had huge response to the one-day foodways workshops she offered, at least partly because she fed them throughout the day. Through it all, she was modeling for the teachers how engaging and effective the lessons could be—even when they were surveying food vendors at the New Orleans Jazz & Heritage Festival. The teachers went back to the classroom and adapted these strategies with their students. Engel attracted teachers by treating them as colleagues. The result was that more teachers were using Louisiana Voices lessons for significantly less money than the cost of one summer institute. Within a few months, hundreds of students learned more about their traditional culture.

Strategies to Institutionalize Louisiana Voices

After years of operating on federal grants and state matching funds, I realized that we needed to institutionalize the program. The resources had been developed and would remain online, but offering professional-development opportunities required ongoing funds. Partnering with the Louisiana State Museum to produce the Heritage Education Day was a strategy to broaden our network by connecting with other educational programs within LDCRT and build a case for institutionalizing our program.

We collaborated with the Division of Archaeology and the Division of Historic Preservation to design a Heritage Education Program. Through a strategic planning process led by Eileen Engel, we crafted a plan to implement the professional-development component of all three programs and administer grants. Archaeologists, folklorists, and architectural historians currently on staff would then serve as resource support to educators who determined the educational strategies. This project has not been funded to date, but if priorities shift again in the future, this plan will be ready to implement.

The Impact and Future of Louisiana Voices

Although the curriculum network and Louisiana Voices classroom strategies are still effective, priorities changed within the Louisiana Division of the Arts with new leadership. In 2008 funding for Louisiana Voices ended with exhaustion of the last federal funds. I provide minimal Web site maintenance, but my program cannot support the curriculum network. In 2007, when the LDOE asked us to add grade-level expectations to each lesson, we did not have the ability to do it since this would require addressing every content standard at every grade level.

As of 2011, Louisiana Voices consists of only a Web site and e-mail list, yet its impact continues. Because Louisiana Voices is public domain and, thus, people do not have to inform us that they are using the resources, we actually do not know the full influence of the project. Although the Louisiana Voices Web site is for the most part static, we continue to add folklorists' research to the Folklife in Louisiana Web site. Louisiana Voices also continues to be a model for initiatives in other states. At least seven U.S. states and one in India have used Louisiana Voices extensively. Also academic folklorists often use Louisiana Voices activities to enhance their teaching strategies. In 2000 Louisiana Voices received the Dorothy Howard Folklore and Education Prize for the best project from the American Folklore Society Folklore and Education Section.

The Web sites generate queries from around the world. Because they are so large and link to so many other sites, they frequently come up high in Web searches. Thus, the Folklife Program routinely gets queries from writers, researchers, students, and curious people worldwide. In 2007, when the LDOE rewrote the social-studies curriculum, it directed the contracted writers to use the Louisiana Voices and Folklife in Louisiana Web sites as resources. Some of the most exciting queries come from textbook publishers. Making the lessons public domain means the materials are readily available for textbook writers. Since publishers have to get permission to use photographs from the Web site, we are aware of this, but they are also incorporating information about Louisiana's traditional cultures into their textbooks. One of the most commonly used textbooks for history classes—Anne Campbell's *Louisiana: The History of an American State* (2007)—includes significantly more information about traditional cultures, including chapters on "Louisiana's Culture" and "Louisiana's People." This is a major advance since the textbook used for many years—Edwin Davis's *Louisiana: The Pelican State* (1985)—included only one paragraph about Louisiana's people.

When we were searching for ways to institutionalize Louisiana Voices, we discussed tactics with Sheila Talamo at LDOE. A consistent supporter, she said that most projects like Louisiana Voices last about three years, run out of money, and fade away. We have managed to last longer than that. In addition, because this is a Web-based project, its impact continues, even though the funding has faded away. I still get queries from around the world about the lessons and resources, and for anyone wanting to delve deeper, all materials generated by the Louisiana Voices Folklife in Education Program and Tulane University's LiFT-ELA project, including some student work, are archived.

3

Here at Home
Learning Local-Culture Pedagogy through Cultural Tours

Anne Pryor, Debbie Kmetz, Ruth Olson, and Steven A. Ackerman

HAVE YOU HEARD OF THE CHICAGO FIRE? MOST people have, along with the legend of how Mrs. O'Leary's cow started it. The story is untrue; the fire is not.

Although the fire in Chicago may be the best known fire of the era, it was neither the largest nor the most deadly. The Chicago fire was but one of a series in 1871 that ravaged the upper Midwest, the largest of which occurred in Wisconsin on October 8. This fire swept along the shorelines of Green Bay, burning more than 1.28 million acres. An estimated thirteen hundred people lost their lives, and seventy-five hundred were made homeless (Wells 1968). It is the most destructive fire in American history, although it has been mostly forgotten because it occurred on the same day as the Chicago fire. About twelve hundred people died in the Wisconsin town of Peshtigo, so the conflagration is referred to as the Peshtigo fire—at least on the western shore of Green Bay. On the eastern and southern shores, the

Anne Pryor, a cofounder of Wisconsin Teachers of Local Culture, serves as the folk and traditional arts specialist at the Wisconsin Arts Board.

Debbie Kmetz, former coordinator of Wisconsin Teachers of Local Culture, is now a program officer at the Wisconsin Humanities Council.

Ruth Olson, a cofounder of Wisconsin Teachers of Local Culture, is the associate director of the Center for the Study of Upper Midwestern Cultures at the University of Wisconsin-Madison.

Steven A. Ackerman is a professor in the Department of Atmospheric and Oceanic Sciences at the University of Wisconsin-Madison and the director of the Cooperative Institute for Meteorological Satellite Studies.

fire storm is known as the Great Fire of 1871. The fire resulted from a combination of wind, topography, ignition sources, and the land practices of the region's settlers. It permanently altered the landscape and the local economy of southern Door County. It consumed shingle factories and sawmills that were never rebuilt, while fostering farming by clearing the forest and tree stumps and thus opening the land to crops.

In June 2006 and again in 2007, the coauthors of this chapter and a busload of K–12 teachers traveled through the region scorched by the great fire, talked with descendants of the survivors, and discussed its causes. This interaction was part of Here at Home: A Wisconsin Cultural Tour for K–12 Teachers, an eight-day professional-development adventure offered by Wisconsin Teachers of Local Culture (WTLC). We found that people in this place know the fire: it is part of who they are. We used this historic event to model ways that teachers can apply such a focal point to take an integrated approach to a variety of subjects (for example, weather, geography, economics, and land use). We wanted the teachers to know that using this local incident can help students strengthen their connection to the region and culture in which they live. Because not every town has such a historic event that defines part of its heritage, the tour modeled how teachers can identify local culture anywhere and incorporate it into their classrooms.

The main purpose of this chapter is to consider cultural tours as a professional-development model, identifying elements that can be replicated in other offerings that folklorists provide to K–12 teachers. Its sections discuss the underlying philosophy of the Here at Home tours, their structure and content, the community of educators that came together during the experience, and the teachers' subsequent pedagogical interpretations of the tour. It examines the tour goals—for teachers to gain insights about the value of local culture and then apply those insights to their communities and curricula—and proposes reasons we were successful in reaching them.

WTLC, a joint project of the Wisconsin Arts Board and the Center for the Study of Upper Midwestern Cultures at the University of Wisconsin (UW)-Madison, is the sponsor of the Here at Home tours.[1] WTLC is a statewide network of local-culture educators that includes classroom teachers, administrators, museum educators, librarians, and cultural-resource specialists.[2] This network helps teachers incorporate local culture into their classes by providing support in curriculum development, teaching, resource identification, and communication. By uncovering the connections between local culture and the curriculum, WTLC assists teachers in

Place-based learning: Meeting artist Juan Flores and experiencing his Milwaukee murals led one teacher to bring him to her school for a local-culture residency.

creating integrated lessons that are linked with academic standards and allow broad contextualization of specific local knowledge.

WTLC's cultural tours are based on the premise that resources and content for teaching exist all around us: in the local environment and landscapes, in family stories, in local music and artistic expressions, in community history, in occupations and recreational pursuits, and in contemporary social issues. We believe the most authentic learning occurs when the outside world is reflected in the classroom, when students have the opportunity to consider and build on prior experience and knowledge in specific and meaningful ways. The endorsement of this type of learning hardly originated with us; in 1900 John Dewey warned in *The School and Society* that schools wasted children's ability to apply their everyday experiences to institutional learning, and that, likewise, they often could not use their formal learning in daily life: "That is the isolation of the school—its isolation from life. When the child gets into the schoolroom he has to put out of his mind a large part of the ideas, interests, and activities that predominate in his home and neighborhood. So the school, being unable to utilize this everyday experience, sets painfully to work . . . to arouse in the child an interest in school studies" ([1900] 1990, 75).

Current proponents of place- and community-based education continue to fight against the tide of American educational policies that isolate learning from life, adhering to standards rather than place, and are bound by ever-increasing stress on accountability measured through testing. Gregory Smith and David Sobel observe, "The theory of human learning encountered in most contemporary reform efforts appears to be dominated by the belief that fear of failure and institutional censure will lead teachers to do a better job and students to apply themselves to their studies" (2010, 33). Rather, Smith and Sobel suggest, we need to give our teachers and their students reasons to invest in learning by restoring community-school connections, building social capital, exercising real competencies, and creating authentic learning experiences. At least since the 1960s, folklorists have been contributing actively to place- and community-based education—by describing multiple folk groups within the so-called homogeneous mainstream, examining differences between school and home, finding ways to create meaningful experiences within and without the classroom, foregrounding collaboration through fieldwork and related methods, and showing ways that folklore can connect schools and communities (Hamer 2000). We benefited from this long-standing and well-articulated argument for the value of local culture as we designed the Here at Home tours.

More than Folklore

Over the years, the team that launched the WTLC network frequently puzzled about how to get schools to recognize the value of folklore in education. Too often, that term "folklore" got in the way. Teachers and administrators equated it with narrative pummeled into the most digestible forms of children's literature and delivered through entertainment-style storytelling. In schools folklore often was presented as romantic, antiquated, and stereotyped "food, festivals, and folktales." How could we get educators to see the immediacy—the concrete experiences of the present—that make the study of folklore so compelling? How could we help them see that the methods of folklore—learning to interview dynamically, documenting thoroughly—offered ways for students truly to engage in learning? Studying folklore, we knew, not only encouraged students to gather, select, and process information to create meaningful knowledge that they could own, it was also a way for students to appreciate and possess their own culture (Wagler 2006). We wanted people to realize that folklore is rooted in experience, not in static and processed literary productions. We needed teachers and their students to understand the excitement and challenge that result from studying the local.

Photo by Debbie Kmetz.

Experiential learning: Dozens of bison surround teachers as they learn about reclaiming land and culture at Bison Prairie I, a working ranch of the Ho-Chunk Nation near Muscoda, Wisconsin.

A number of teachers in our state did, in fact, use local resources in their teaching. Some biology classes, for example, worked with students to help them understand the environment where they lived. A number of teachers collected oral histories of elders in their communities. Still others worked with parents, neighbors, and community members to bring local arts into their schools. These efforts to make use of the local captured some aspects of community, but, we thought, we could all learn from each other (Wagler 2002). We wanted to bring together these champions of the local, and so WTLC was born.

Science education has long included a real awareness of a hands-on approach in which students increase their investment in learning because they can ask the questions, touch the materials, and interpret the data (Wagler and Beeth 2002). Similarly *hands-on culture* needs to access more than words. Not only do teachers often introduce interviewing without the disciplinary rigor of fact checking required for real oral history, they disconnect historical information from the contemporary lives of the people being interviewed. If one takes the perspective that one is "only doing oral history," one gets only words. But the power of studying local culture is that talk is contextualized. When talk is situated in the thick mix of materials and activities, students experience hands-on culture.

Exploration of the local means an ecological focus in the largest sense of that word. Rather than being just interdisciplinary—as folklorists view themselves, with one foot in the humanities and another in the social sciences—we need to be multidisciplinary. To get a truly meaningful picture of a place, local culture must be viewed through many disciplinary lenses: environmental studies, architecture, economics, the arts, literature, linguistics, and more. The word "culture" needs to be a tool that teachers and students use to see the interconnectedness—the ecology—of all dimensions of local place (Wagler 2000).

Our vision for WTLC was that folklore was one of several disciplines that needed to be represented in our professional-development opportunities. The Here at Home cultural tours gained power with every diverse voice added. Every academic scholar—whether trained in history, music, geology, atmospheric science, or geography—enriched what the teachers learned on the tour. Even so, for K–12 study of local culture, folklore has a special standing. Folklore has centrality because it is so accessible: more than any other discipline, it studies everyday life—the ordinary worlds that students inhabit. Folklore's emphasis on expressive culture engages students.

The teachers on our cultural tours experienced such engagement many times. When Frank Montano, Ojibwe Woodland flute maker and musician, talked and played his flute on the deck of the Hotel Chequamegon on the shore of Lake Superior, the teachers encountered the uniting of many cultural elements: hearing about the wood harvested for the flute, learning how Montano gained the skills to make flutes, understanding why loons or other iconic figures are featured on the flute and emanate through its playing, and experiencing the music floating over the lake and expanding across the water in this traditional homeland for the Ojibwe. Their immersion in Montano's world helped the teachers see the past within the present; it allowed them to connect elements from nature, social structures, and history and situate them in place. These teachers owned the immediacy of experience.

Contextualized Knowledge

Two of the most important elements about cultural tours are that they offer contextualized knowledge and ask participants to compare, reference, and measure what they already know against what they are hearing about a local place. Cultural tours energize learning and make knowledge particular to place (Pryor 2004). Students who do not feel a connection to history are more likely to recognize its relevance when they see its impact on their communities. That relevance is amplified when history is just one aspect of a more complete experience. Studying local culture forefronts the kind of history that impinges on the present and is a bridge to more distant history.

When Here at Home visited the Hmong blacksmith shop in La Crosse in 2006 and again in 2007, we had the opportunity to talk individually with some of the elders who use the shop as a senior center. Basket and *paj ntaub* makers came to meet the teachers and show their work. Many of the elders spoke only a little English, but they managed quite eloquently to share with us the ways that they had come to the United States, how much their lives had changed through the war and their forced immigration to this country, and how important maintaining their traditions was to them. WTLC faculty member Ruth Olson sat with one woman who told how she had lost most of her family, including her mother and aunts, and had had to learn to sew as best she could on her own. Olson wrote,

> Her unique sewing style, which I had taken as artistic innovation, instead revealed how war disrupts the staying power of tradition. I could not help but reflect on how remarkable it was that I was sitting in a concrete block building in La Crosse, Wisconsin, listening to a powerfully intimate story about life half a world and half a century away, impressing on me the lasting effects of economic entwinements and multinational conflicts that are indeed part of my history as an American.

That is another property of cultural tours. Everybody learns. Any teacher who signs up for such a demanding experience is likely to be an adventurer, open to new experiences. Any scholar or community member who agrees to participate in such an enterprise is bound to be extraordinary as well. The energy that such people generate when they are brought into each other's presence is palpable. As organizers we have benefited beyond anything we expected through recognizing the respect that educators still receive as guides for young lives, developing relationships as participants exchange ideas and insights, and witnessing the transformative power of knowledge as teachers catch fire in their local places. The Here at Home tours allowed us to do some of the typical work that folklorists in education do: we modeled interviewing skills, the importance of building on prior research, and the ethics of asking permission for documenting cultural activities in photographs and recordings. But we also presented a model of the ways that different disciplines can work together to create a partnership of perspectives. Presenting material holistically allowed different types of teachers (elementary, art, consumer-education, social-studies, and science, among others) to reach in and find something applicable to their teaching. We found that focusing the cultural tours on a theme, rather than on a discipline, made them much more powerful experiences for all of us.

Our First Here at Home Tour

On Friday, 23 June 2006, twenty-six teachers and one new School of Education graduate embarked on an eight-day trip around Wisconsin that would take them to places ranging from the Ho-Chunk Nation's bison ranch near Muscoda to the Slovan Country Inn and dance hall in Kewaunee County. Here at Home also offered participants opportunities to meet a fourth-generation member of a Lake Superior fishing family and tour his fish-processing plant; watch a contract logger at work in the Chequamegon National Forest; and speak with Rosa Zamora, whose Day of the Dead altars have served as a catalyst for continuing that Mexican tradition in Milwaukee's Walker's Point neighborhood.

The tour—presented again in 2007 with much of the same itinerary—sought to introduce teachers to Wisconsin's many cultural traditions by taking them directly to local communities and providing opportunities to meet residents, take part in discussions, observe customs, travel through the landscape, participate in community events, and receive hospitality. The tour offered experiences that reached beyond simple introductions. For example, in Lac du Flambeau, Jerome "Brooks" Big John, accompanied by a son and a nephew, spoke to the teachers about his skills and experiences as an Ojibwe decoy maker and also about the area's cultural and civil-rights struggles during the spearfishing controversy of the late 1980s and early 1990s.

Our planning for the tour relied on some of WTLC's earliest efforts, in which folklorists Ruth Olson and Anne Pryor worked closely with folklorist and fourth/fifth-grade teacher Mark Wagler to develop a series of cultural

Photo by Anne Pryor.

Ethnography of the local: Butchers at Black Earth Meats demonstrate stuffing a venison ring baloney for Mark Wagler and students during the Dane County Cultural Tour.

tours with his students. The tours were rooted in Wagler's deep commitment to teaching his students ethnographic skills so that they could thoughtfully explore the world immediately around them and be able to see themselves as cultural beings. Resulting year-long projects included the Dane County Cultural Tour, the Hmong Cultural Tour, and the Park Street Cultural Tour.[3] In 2005 Debbie Kmetz became the WTLC coordinator and proposed the idea for a cultural tour for adults, drawing on her background in tour development as a local history specialist at the State Historical Society of Wisconsin.

Our planning also profited from a neighboring state's successful and popular project, Iowa: Eye to I. Since 1989 Iowa Wesleyan College has invited K–12 Iowa teachers to immerse themselves in an engaging nine-day summer journey through Iowa culture, exploring the state in a multidisciplinary way. We were drawn to the idea of a collective, direct, statewide experience: teachers canoeing together on an Iowa river at dawn, listening to regional music, eating a dinner served by local church women, and, most of all, meeting Iowa residents. Loren Horton, one of the Iowa organizers, answered numerous questions about the tour length, content, and logistics and offered enthusiastic encouragement for a Wisconsin tour.

We received support for the 2006 and 2007 Here at Home tours from the Ira and Ineva Reilly Baldwin Wisconsin Idea Endowment at UW-Madison.[4] The Wisconsin Idea is a century-old tradition that stresses that the boundaries of the university are those of the state. This encompassing view of the university's mission encourages staff and faculty to work beyond their respective campuses. In developing the tour, organizers turned to UW faculty across the state to provide additional perspectives.

As we planned the tour, we focused on exploring environmental and human factors contributing to the development of local culture, identifying expressions and manifestations of that culture, and finding ways we could work with teachers to develop ways of incorporating it into the classroom. Ruth Olson served as staff folklorist, Anne Pryor as curriculum specialist, and Debbie Kmetz as historian and music specialist. Steve Ackerman was resident meteorologist and research scientist. Collectively the tour staff offered scholarly commentary that embraced a diverse range of disciplines, including folklore and folklife, history, climate and weather, art, anthropology, music, and geography.

The tour also benefited from the expertise of guest faculty. UW-Madison professor emeritus David Mickelson offered teachers an introduction to Wisconsin geology, observing that landforms factor into a community's agriculture, occupations, building traditions, and recreation. Mark Louden, of the UW-Madison German department, met the tour in Milwaukee to talk about the events and elements shaping the character of the city's German and Jewish cultures. William Laatsch, of the UW-Green Bay Urban and Regional Studies department, led the tour through the Belgian and Czech heritage areas of Kewaunee and Door counties, where he showed teachers how, as a geographer, he reads the landscape for evidence of persistence and change in cultural traditions. Mark Wagler provided a teacher's perspective

as he led the group on a brief replication of the Park Street Tour he had
conducted with his fourth-grade class.

The Itinerary

The tour route, in combination with the selection of communities, presenters, and activities, was designed to provide opportunities to explore the forces
that shaped local culture and its current expressions and manifestations.
Months in the planning, the final route took teachers through Wisconsin's
diverse geography, beginning in Madison in south-central Wisconsin and
heading first southwest along the broad valley of the Wisconsin River and
then into the surrounding hillsides and narrow valleys of its tributaries. The
route followed the Great River Road along the Mississippi River, which has
served as a highway of cultural exchange for centuries. Winding north into a
rich agricultural area, the tour then followed an older state highway through
early logging settlements, working farms, and recreational areas onto an
Ojibwe reservation and then through dense areas of national forest, much
of it created from failed twentieth-century farms.

The tour carried participants to its farthest point north along the shores
of Lake Superior, the largest body of fresh water in the world, and then south
through more national forests to the reservation of the Lac du Flambeau Band
of Lake Superior Chippewa Indians (Ojibwe). The tour continued southeast to Door and Kewaunee counties along Green Bay and Lake Michigan.
There participants viewed a landscape in transition, where exurban bedroom
communities for residents who work in the nearby city of Green Bay are
replacing small Belgian and Czech rural towns. Then the tour headed south
to Milwaukee, Wisconsin's largest and most densely populated urban area.
There the city route wound through neighborhoods of nineteenth- and
twentieth-century buildings rising in proximity to Milwaukee's three rivers
and the Lake Michigan coastline. On the evening of the final day, the tour
traveled west back to Madison along a late-1950s interstate highway.

The people and activities on the tour were deeply rooted in place.
Wherever possible we chose specific routes to provide visual evidence of
what some presenters might discuss. For instance, the route on the fourth
day of the 2006 tour consisted of a four-hour drive through the "cutover."
Much of the northern third of Wisconsin is land that was earlier Ojibwe
homeland and hunting area. Although the federal government acquired
most of the land through a series of treaties, the Ojibwe successfully retained

Here at Home tour route 2006 & 2007

⭐ Overnight stops

tracts as reservation land. In the decades following the treaties, the land owned by the U.S. government was sold, and the dense forests were logged so dramatically that the region is often called the cutover. Once the treeless land became useless to those interested in lumber, it was sold to incoming settlers, many of whom bought acreage sight unseen from agents who spoke their native language. Settlers found the land highly variable in quality and the task of removing the pervasive stumps arduous.

The day-four ride began in the rich agricultural area around Eau Claire. Kmetz and Olson's commentary on the bus addressed the landscape of successful farms and talked about the immigrant settlers, their land holdings, and barn architecture. As we went farther north, the farms became fewer, and woodland stretches appeared. The bus traveled through the Lac Courte Oreilles Reservation, where—despite Ojibwe resistance—ancestral land had been flooded in the early twentieth century to build a dam to provide electrical power for the Eau Claire area. Continuing north, the bus reached a region where the land was agriculturally marginal and the earlier farm-failure rate substantial. The mature forests there had been planted during the 1930s by young men working in the New Deal's Civilian Conservation Corps (CCC). In this stretch of forest, the bus pulled over while Ackerman explained the dramatic effects of a recent year's straight-line winds.

The ride ended in Drummond, a small town of about two hundred people originally built as a company town by a lumber concern in Eau Claire. Local residents met us at the museum and library, where Drummond native James Unseth reminisced about his childhood and Larry Gagner spoke about his 1930s work in the CCC. Other residents described their museum's exhibit—"Drummond: Life in a Company Town"—and shared photographs documenting the area's massive nineteenth- and twentieth-century logging and subsequent reforesting.

Next, teachers toured the current Drummond sawmill, where they saw the equipment that transformed logs to lumber and talked with the manager about his experience as the third generation in his family to work with wood. Afterward, the bus carried teachers several miles into the Chequamegon Forest, where participants spent the night in cabins on the grounds of one of the area's former CCC camps.

The next day, U.S. Forest Service staff guided the bus north into another part of the Chequamegon Forest: the Moquah Barrens. There—deep in the woods—we met a contract logger who demonstrated contemporary logging with a large, powerful, and expensive piece of equipment that allows one person to choose specific trees and harvest many in a single day. Next, the Forest Service staff accompanied us to the Pilsen Town Hall in the small rural crossroads community of Moquah. Here the teachers met the Moquah Homemakers Club, many of them descendents of early-twentieth-century Slovak and Croatian settlers who had been eager to farm the recently cutover land. The club has been in continuous existence since the 1930s. The homemakers served a traditional Slovak luncheon, including *holubky, halusky, pirohy,* and *kolace* made from family recipes. Later that day, the tour stopped at the Tetzners' family farm, one of the few complete dairy operations in the state, where people can purchase milk and ice cream made on the premises from the milk produced on the farm.

The past in the present: Teachers and faculty learn about logging on a tromp through the woods with U.S. Forest Service staff.

In the course of four hours one day and the equivalent of two hours the next, teachers rode though a landscape where the visual evidence bespoke almost 150 years of change. In little more than a day, they met people who recounted family and community stories about earlier eras, shared their memories and firsthand experiences, and offered distinctly contemporary perspectives in an area where, despite the changes, many occupations, food-ways, artistic traditions, and recreational pursuits are still based in local natural resources.

Multiple Ways to Perceive Local Culture

In many instances, tour staff modeled interviewing with local residents. In other cases, presenters gave short talks. Teachers were encouraged to ask questions, and sometimes there was additional time for small group conversations with the local residents. Useful skills included active listening and polished questioning. Teachers also drew upon their experiences to increase their understanding. Several teachers commented on their families' connections

Photo by Anne Pryor.

Contextual learning: Steve Ackerman uses a Mississippi bluff vista as a teaching tool.

to logging. Others—especially those from rural areas in the state—found resonance with the homemakers or the people on Tetzners' farm.

The tour provided a variety of sensory experiences. Vistas ranged from a high overlook above the Mississippi River Valley, where Ackerman offered meteorological insights, to reading the landscape analytically for evidence of settlement patterns, to perceiving the meaning and deep family connections in the components of the Day of the Dead altars created by Rosa Zamora. Sounds ranged from the subtle, windlike tones of Frank Montano's flute to the collective cheers at the Ashland Protractors baseball game, to memories quietly shared at lunch tables where meals often consisted of local specialties. Kinesthetic experiences included walking the grounds of a Norwegian farmstead, learning to dance the polka from the Happy Hoppers at Slovan

Country Inn, and experiencing the heat of the lumber drying room at the sawmill. There were also aesthetic moments when the beauty of the landscape, architecture, artwork, or music became an intangible component of the local sense of place. Additionally, there were deeply human moments when teachers and local participants connected. Some evoked laughter, others, flashes of recognition or understanding, still others, gratitude.

The teachers spent an intensive eight days with the faculty, the bus driver, and each other on the tour. Although we did not purposefully try to exclude access to media—Internet, television, or radio—there was only limited access. The days began with breakfast by 8:00 a.m. and ended well into the evening. Participants were immersed in local culture. A quality of surprise also characterized the tour. Generally teachers had little idea of what was coming next. For those accustomed to schedules, the lack of a published agenda may have been disconcerting. However, according to a view shared by a teacher, the lack of a printed schedule helped create an atmosphere of participation, rather than anticipation. Whatever the response, as each of the days progressed, immersion became a characteristic of Here at Home.

The layering and juxtaposing of sensory, intellectual, emotional, and aesthetic elements offered a continual array of multifaceted experiences. The tour sought to create circumstances where teachers perceived local culture in new ways. Also important was the creation of community. We made many efforts to extend a sense of welcome and hospitality to the teachers before the tour began. Another pretour goal was providing participants with enough information to make them comfortable embarking on an eight-day trip where each day brought new experiences. It was important to build a sense of trust. All participants received in advance a list of the other teachers on the tour to encourage carpooling and post-tour networking. Additionally, each tour staff member wrote a short autobiographical piece and chose some pretour reading for the teachers, sent to participants in advance. When teachers met at the beginning of the tour, there was a sense of happy excitement.

There was also a sense of shared exploration. Most of the specific places we visited seemed to be new to the teachers. However, as the bus drove through familiar places—and especially home communities—we encouraged the teachers to share their stories. Some were informational, some humorous, and some inspiring. Additionally, each day several teachers introduced themselves, often sharing deeply personal reflections on their teaching, educational background, career choices, and communities. We all experienced exhaustion, frustration, and laughter during our long days. Group difficulties included the sometimes-uneasy combination of heavy and light sleepers in shared cabins. But there were also moments of hilarity, featuring recurring jokes developed over the days or a funny story told around the campfire.

Some of the most powerful community-building experiences involved hospitality. People throughout Wisconsin went out of their way for the teachers. The Ashland Protractors scheduled one of their baseball games so we could attend. They called our group "teachers in the bleachers." A few places waived standing no-tour policies specifically because our group contained K–12 teachers. Receiving so much hospitality was at times very humbling, but its collective nature also drew tour participants together as they frequently remarked on the generosity of people throughout the state. During the tour, the teachers, staff, and bus driver built a community based on shared experiences, long days together, and deeply moving moments of connection with people throughout Wisconsin. As they traveled, they found themselves "here at home."

Learning Outcomes

The evaluations and reactions of many teachers suggested that the tours were life-transforming experiences. They personally had been moved deeply and powerfully by the interactions with the people and places they visited. As one participant wrote in an unsolicited e-mail, "This is the kind of experience that alters a person's entire paradigm of daily life. It would be impossible to grow so much as a person and not expand that understanding into my teaching."

That comment—and others like it—reflects the goals of the Here at Home tours. The first goal—to inspire and enable teachers to return to their communities with increased recognition of the value, accessibility, and richness of their local cultures—complemented the second—to have the teachers apply those newly gained insights to their teaching, treating their home communities as places ready to be explored and experienced in new ways with their students. Through post-tour communications, teachers revealed ways that they translated their tour experiences into classroom curriculum and also gave us insights into our success in meeting our learning goals. In 2007 we organized a two-day reunion and professional-development retreat for teachers from the 2006 tour. Fourteen teachers from around the state

Photo by Anne Pryor.

Hands-on learning: Artist Kim Swedowski teaches Polish egg decorating to tour alumni gathered for a midyear retreat.

attended, evidence of the strong sense of community that the tour had fostered. After a daylong cultural tour of Wausau, the host city, we spent the second day with ten teachers presenting their curricula.

Additionally, in 2008 WTLC recruited teachers from the 2006 and 2007 tours to make presentations at the statewide Wisconsin Education Association Council conference. Twelve volunteered, which created enough panels for a local-culture track throughout the two-day conference. What follows is a sampling of the teachers' self-described efforts, collected at the 2007 retreat, in planning conversations for the 2008 conference, and through interviews and a written report. Their efforts show that the teachers who participated in the tours—both veteran and novice educators from all grade levels, all types of schools, all sections of the state, and many different curricular areas—could relate to the organizing tour principles. Each adapted those core ideas to his or her unique teaching situation. All found pedagogical value in the concept of local culture and then used the philosophy and methods modeled during the tour to meet their particular curricular goals.

Champions of the Local

Several teachers took the tour because they teach fourth grade. The state's fourth-grade social-studies curriculum mandates a focus on Wisconsin, especially on examining change and continuity over time. By taking the tour, these teachers wanted to expand their knowledge of Wisconsin to meet required curriculum standards. While they certainly did gain more information and perspective about the state, they reported less on including specific content than on implementing the larger principle of looking locally for content. One fourth-grade teacher in Lodi, a rural south-central Wisconsin city, applied the technique of ethnographically investigating his home community. He explained that he was devoting the academic year following the tour to exploring local culture:

> What I have accomplished so far is discussing what culture is and how my students see culture. We started out [with] a very vague and broad term. I asked students what they think of when they think of American culture. Then we have been narrowing it down to Wisconsin culture and the many aspects of that. We started talking about agriculture and how that is a huge part to many Wisconsin families. We also incorporated a visit to the local curling club in Lodi to discuss how curling really is a part of Lodi culture.[5] We are currently working on discussing different cultures in our families and hopefully will have a cultural fair at the end of the year.

As Gregory Smith notes, teachers who engage in place-based education ". . . become the creators of curriculum rather than the dispensers of curriculum developed by others. . . . Unlike curricula drawn from elsewhere and transmitted by a school system more concerned about the perpetuation of national rather than local knowledge, these school studies build on the familiar and then extend it. This curricular focus also validates the culture and experience of students' families, acknowledging them as worthy of inquiry" (2002, 588).

Validating the worth of community life and the value of local knowledge has long been a hallmark of folklore and other disciplines that structured the Here at Home tours. This fourth-grade teacher developed a locally shaped curriculum using community resources. Rather than use a curriculum that fed facts to his students, he employed the organizing principle that constructed the tour: experiential inquiry. He looked locally, saw that curling was a community activity that embodied key cultural elements representative of Lodi, and arranged for his students to learn directly from the people who embodied the knowledge specific to that place.

Post-tour conversations with the teachers indicated that before they created local-culture curricula, they reflected on their tour experiences from several perspectives, including personal and pedagogical. Craig Roland describes this reflective process: "Teachers unfold, examine, and reshape their own educational beliefs and assumptions so that they are able to integrate new conceptions of teaching, learning, and subject matter within their own emerging knowledge structures" (1995, 123). The curriculum development of another fourth-grade teacher who participated in the tours is an example of such reflection. She took the tour to strengthen her knowledge of the state but had a revelation on the first day that made acquiring facts a secondary goal for the subsequent days. She explained that while we were on Park Street—being guided through a miniversion of the Park Street Cultural Tour—she suddenly understood something: "Wow, I've lived in Wisconsin all my life, and I've never realized what a rich state it is. I've been so focused on travel around the country and to different places around the world that I missed out on Wisconsin's culture." This teacher said that insight affected her deeply on a personal level, and curricular change flowed from it.

After transferring to teach fifth grade in Junction City, a rural village of four hundred in her central Wisconsin school district, this teacher considered and tried different ways to address local culture, such as having her students develop a tour, adding more discussions of different cultures, and not focusing solely on international cultures to the exclusion of American culture. However, she found herself unsatisfied: "It felt shoved in here and there," she explained. "We would only get to it when there was available time, and there was never enough." In the following academic year, she sought to remedy this by making local culture the structuring theme for the year: "I don't think it's as meaningful to the kids unless you really focus on it. I got that idea from Mark Wagler and the Park Street Cultural Tour."

Photo by Debbie Kmetz.

Deep listening: Teachers learn about Slovak immigrant culture through meaningful interactions with the Moquah Homemakers Club.

She wrote an enrichment grant to her district and received funds for a yearlong multicultural peace project. The plan includes having the students read books about children from a variety of family lifestyles and other cultures, followed by writing about cultural traditions in their families and milestones in their lives. "One of my goals is to have kids appreciate their own culture," she emphasizes. Sharing will occur not only among students in her classroom but with pen pals in another part of the state (Milwaukee) and another country. Students will take photos of their lives outside the classroom and compile their writings and photos and those of their pen pals into a book. They will visit their Wisconsin pen pals and share their books with them. Their culminating activity will be a classroom museum presentation for the rest of the Junction City school with all the students creating a display highlighting the milestones and traditions of their lives and those of their pen pals, looking at the similarities and differences, and celebrating both.

This teacher's version of local-culture studies purposefully incorporates an emphasis on reading and writing because of other curricular goals. Like so many K–12 teachers, she feels pressure to address required curricula and high-stakes achievement tests while making learning meaningful to her students by integrating content with their lives. Her project plan illustrates four points that allow a teacher to develop and implement substantial local-culture pedagogy: integration with multiple curricular areas, continued focus on state tests, positive administrative support, and funds for travel or new materials.

We found that several teachers' jobs had changed since their participation on the tour but that, even with new school or grade assignments, they continued to incorporate local culture. One teacher, a high-school counselor in Appleton when he took the tour in 2007, retired soon afterward. He subsequently began to teach a graduate course for community and school counselors seeking a master's degree. He used his tour experiences in the course:

> I created a special Here at Home photo story that I shared with my class. It made a deep impression. As a result, several students are using this model to research and create their own projects surrounding their own local culture. It has been very exciting to see the first results. One of the graduate students did a presentation on his Czech roots and background while detailing his great-grandfather's settling in Wisconsin. Another woman spoke about her immigration from Laos and the transition for her parents and herself. She expressed many details about the Hmong culture of Green Bay and the many challenges occurring with keeping their own cultural traditions versus assimilating into a "white privileged" culture. I could share many more examples about my class.

The school counselor's experience on the 2007 tour—exploring the Czech settlement area of northeastern Wisconsin and meeting several Hmong refugees who are wrestling with resettlement issues—helped create a platform for his students' explorations of these same issues. His statement illustrates the ripple effect we hoped for, in this case occurring with students much older than we had anticipated.

If the counselor found the tour valuable for his adult graduate students, another teacher found similar value for her kindergarteners. This cross-age applicability brings to mind Jerome Bruner's assertion: "We begin with the hypothesis that any subject can be taught effectively in some intellectually honest form to any child at any stage of development" (1960, 33). The kindergarten teacher had always focused on cultural studies with her young students in Lena, a small village near Wisconsin's border with Michigan's Upper Peninsula. She had a successful yearlong curriculum—"Around the World in 180 Days"—that had her students taking pretend journeys to multiple foreign countries. After participating in the 2006 tour, she found herself reflecting on her curriculum: "I definitely looked at it differently after the tour." Then she added, "I look at everything differently." She decided to insert local connections: "What I took away from my experience on the bus tour, which I thought was fantastic, was trying to tie in with the local people and get local people to come into the classroom with information about their ancestors."

This relatively small change to the existing curriculum added local relevancy to an already-participatory unit. This teacher has moved to teaching first grade now and plans to devote the fourth quarter of her new social-studies curriculum to studying local culture. She summed up a simple, but key, asset that will work in her favor in that endeavor: "Everything for us is walkable in Lena. There are lots and lots of opportunities."

Creative Applications

Art was another curriculum area for creative application of principles from the tour as demonstrated by an elementary art teacher in Wisconsin Dells, a city in south-central Wisconsin in the traditional homeland of the Ho-Chunk Nation. Along with a large Native population among her K–5 students, this teacher also has many students from international families who came to work in the city's bustling tourist industry. A new teacher, she rewrote her school's elementary art curriculum to infuse it with a cultural focus. During the tour, she was especially impressed by Ellis Nelson, an artist whose studio (a former garage now spilling over with sculptures) she had passed many times as a child but had never visited. His unique reuse of materials to create inventive objects inspired her to do a recycled-arts project with her students. Rag rugs for sale at the Slovan County Inn gave her the specific idea. "It's like making a giant potholder," she told us enthusiastically at the retreat as she displayed eye-catching rugs made on homemade weaving frames. The students wove tube strips from old T-shirts gathered from

Photo by Anne Pryor.

Applying tour insights: Teacher Kate Clausius Thompson
explains her students' local-culture project.

students and staff, tag sales, and leftover inventory from tourist venues. The
project proved wildly popular among the students, their families, school
staff, and community members who now request rugs.

In another part of the state, a third- through sixth-grade art teacher
connected a unit on local culture with a fourth-grade teacher's existing cul-
tural-history project. Both teach in the Luxemburg-Casco school district
northeast of Green Bay and went on the 2006 Here at Home tour. (We
were especially pleased to have multiple teachers from a school or district on
the tour because they could then understand, reinforce, and support each

other's curricular innovations.) In an extensive unit on cultural heritage, social-studies students researched facts about the countries of their ancestors. They also worked closely with their families to research the rich stories and treasured family heirlooms that enliven their cultural backgrounds. They created paper quilt blocks that depict what their families think are the most important things for others to know about them.

The art teacher built on the social-studies curriculum by taking advantage of the research the students had done on their heritage. She also used the idea of students making lists of cultural observations as a prewriting exercise that she had learned on the first day of the Here at Home tour from Mark Wagler. She described the process as she applied it: "Every day that they came in, we did lists on different topics, and many of them had to do with their own families." This preparatory work paid off later. She explained, "Every single one of the kids had no trouble starting on a story about something they absolutely loved about their family." She used those stories in a unit on Hmong story cloths in which the students looked at examples of those hand-stitched fabric and embroidery representations of traditional tales or contemporary war experiences:

> We talked about why they were made and the stories that they told. From there we went on to a paper version of the Hmong story cloth, and I said, "I want you to think of a family story. Possibly it's related to your history or your relatives because you've done all this research." But then I said, "Twenty, thirty, forty, fifty years from now, your stories now are going to also become family heritage." So I gave them the choice of doing an historical story or something that was more contemporary.

At the 2007 retreat, she showed us examples of her students' cut-paper images and read the accompanying written work. The following example incorporates the sophisticated technique common on Hmong story cloths of showing several different events all in one image: "In my picture is my grandpa coming over from Belgium to America. Back in Belgium his brother is waving good-bye to him. In America I am waiting for my grandpa to arrive. It is a windy day, and there is a chance of some rain in America." Another is an example of an important contemporary story from a child's life: "This is a picture of when my parents got married. I was about four years old. It's special because it's when I had two parents and not just one." The compelling images and moving stories show the power of everyday life and the ordinary worlds that students inhabit. They reveal students profoundly appreciating and possessing their own lives and cultures, meeting a goal of local-culture pedagogy.

The projects and curriculum adaptations discussed so far demonstrate ways that teachers independently applied local-culture principles. Another teacher worked closely with WTLC staff to develop her post-tour project. Following a panel discussion at St. Bede's Monastery with leaders from three local religious communities during the 2006 tour, a Madison middle-school teacher partnered with Debbie Kmetz to modify an existing curriculum on ancient civilizations and world religions. Support from the Wisconsin Humanities Council (WHC) allowed the teacher to expand that curriculum to make it more contextual and therefore successful. She makes the case for the value of learning through community-based explorations:

> In order to really understand a religion, I needed to incorporate the culture behind the religion as well. If students could see and learn about the culture, they would then see and understand how the religion grew out of that culture.
>
> As I began to look for speakers from each religion/belief, it was very important that my students actually go to their places of worship and not just have speakers come to our school. . . . [In the past] often students lost interest because the speaker could not make the religion come alive only through words. Also many of these speakers thought they could just talk and students would understand. This was not the case. In fact, sitting and just listening leads to behavior issues. I wanted to avoid these problems by putting the students directly into the worshipping environment.
>
> Actually going to the place of worship, the speaker has so much more at hand to explain and use to teach about the religion. The speaker can then also incorporate how their religion functions in the local community. Students would then see world religions live and at work right in their own backyards and not halfway across the world. Building these connections helps with understanding one another.

The result was an innovative curriculum that studied Christianity, Islam, Judaism, Hinduism, Buddhism, and Hmong animism with successful multidisciplinary visits to local religious sites to meet with host practitioners. The class also investigated ancient local Native beliefs by visiting effigy mounds in the Madison area with a former Wisconsin state archeologist. The teacher worked with a colleague at her school so that two classes took part, and—as a condition of the WHC support—she is sharing information with other teachers who wish to study places of worship in their area.

Meeting Our Goals

The Here at Home multidisciplinary philosophy is grounded in an ecology of place, where the local environment is critical to the learning experience. Focus on the local demonstrates that communities can be a context for learning. The methods employed by the faculty model ways that natural, cultural, and historical local environments can be integrated into a holistic learning experience. Were the tours successful in meeting their goals? We think they were, based on the variety of statements we collected from the teachers in recorded small-group or individual interviews and whole-group reflection periods during the tour; through anonymous evaluative surveys completed on the final day of the tour and unsolicited letters and e-mails after the tour; and by the unabated enthusiasm with which teachers have maintained continued contact with WTLC and adopted local-culture teaching practices.

One teacher's comment—"I always thought exploring other places was more interesting. . . . There is so much richness in this state, so much I didn't know. Our students don't need to travel six hundred miles to see culture"—responds to our first goal. We wanted teachers to recognize the value and accessibility of their local cultures. Many evaluative comments related directly to that, as in this succinct example: "This trip has helped me to look at my community in a different way."

We sought to make Here at Home a launching point for including local culture in curricula so that teachers would explore their communities in new ways with their students. These sample comments illustrate the successful attainment of this goal many times over, as does this one:

> We can incorporate this into our teaching, not just by telling people
> what we did but having the students go out in our own community.
> There's so much culture right within our own communities that
> I don't think we realize or the students even realize. I think that's one
> big thing I've gotten out of this: use what we have right in our back-
> yard. It doesn't have to be a historic museum or anything; it just has to
> be people who live there.

Creating a Learning Community

In reflecting on the tours, the organizers and faculty have pondered why the project was successful in achieving its goals. We considered many factors, including the immersive quality of the days, the variety of multifaceted experiences, the intellectual quality of the content, the ethnographic modeling of the faculty, the rich theme of place, the holistic multidisciplinary presentations, the power of aesthetic moments, the deep human connections among teachers and with hosts, and scrupulous planning. One factor in particular aligns our experience with current educational research: the development of a learning community.

The sometimes-arduous shared experiences of an eight-day trip of about a thousand miles built camaraderie. This camaraderie quickly grew into a learning community in which participants collectively worked toward achieving common goals and objectives they had brought with them (the most basic of which was to learn more about Wisconsin) and those established by the tour faculty. The tour engendered feelings of belonging to this new and dynamic group, feelings that can be so strong that members report changes in identity as a result.

Learning communities bring people together for shared learning, discovery, and generating knowledge. Learning communities thrive when all participants take responsibility for achieving these goals. Drawing from educational research on learning communities (Brower and Dettinger 1998; Hesse and Mason 2005), we find that the Here at Home cultural tours contained four core factors that define an effective learning community.

Shared Discovery and Learning

Collaborative activities in which participants share responsibility for learning and research that take place are important to the development of a community. Here at Home facilitated structured experiences that enabled participants to learn from and with one another. The teachers took responsibility for achieving goals by being active learners: they took notes and photos, practiced active respectful listening during interviews, and fully engaged in all activities. They shared their discoveries through conversations and structured reflections during the tour and adapted curricula after it.

The Here at Home cultural tours thrived because the expertise of the leaders at structuring authentic and powerful learning opportunities met the

Shared learning: The Here at Home tours foster the development of learning communities.

needs of the teachers to expand their knowledge and improve their teaching. Participants valued their interactions with local community members, as well as with their fellow travelers. This shared time was valuable to them and the learning community itself.

Connections to Other Learning and Life Experiences

Learning communities flourish when implicit and explicit connections are made to experiences and activities beyond the immediate program its members are participating in at any given moment. The tour enabled teachers to consider new ways to see their communities and use local culture in their teaching. Participants could situate their learning in a larger context, solidifying their place in the broader community and decreasing any feeling of isolation. They felt a sense of connection and have built on that by staying in contact through an e-mail list and attending WTLC-sponsored and other local-culture events.

Functional Connections among Learners

Learning communities thrive when the interactions among learners are meaningful, when they are functional and necessary to accomplish the work. Here at Home valued the unique contribution of all participants and recognized that intellectual growth stems from relationships among all group members. The organizers encouraged sharing personal stories and experiences on the bus, during meals, and in the evening. Participants turned to each other to explore ideas and get feedback on issues of teaching and place-based experiential learning.

Inclusive Environment

Learning communities succeed when the diverse backgrounds and experiences of participants are welcomed in such a way that they help inform the group's collective learning. The tour brought together teachers of varied backgrounds and skills to inspire alternative ways of thinking about their teaching. The tours were structured so that teachers had easy and diverse access to fellow members, faculty, and guests, not only during the presentation but in informal situations as well. The teachers appreciated this communication.

The Here at Home cultural tours have been the heart of WTLC's professional-development offerings. But WTLC extends beyond the tours with its material introduction of the many perspectives of local cultural study. WTLC is itself a rich, developing resource as these creative teachers spawn their own projects and inspire their students to view themselves within their home places. As organizers of the cultural tours, one of our greatest delights occurred when the teachers from the 2006 Here at Home tour gathered at the 2007 spring retreat, where they realized that they, in fact, *are* teachers of local culture and equally with us have the responsibility to share their cultural work with other teachers in the state. They continue to offer each other support, network, and share ideas. WTLC has become a statewide learning community of local-culture education enthusiasts thanks to the fires sparked through the Here at Home cultural tours.[6]

Notes

1. Other partners for the WTLC Here at Home cultural tours have included the Wisconsin Humanities Council and the Chippewa Valley Museum.
2. More information is available online at http://csumc.wisc.edu/wtlc

3.   See the Web sites for the Dane County Cultural Tour: http://csumc.wisc.edu/cmct/ DaneCountyTour, the Park Street Cultural Tour: http://csumc.wisc.edu/cmct/ ParkStreetCT, and the Hmong Cultural Tour: http://csumc.wisc.edu/cmct/HmongTour

4.   Additional funding for the 2006 and 2007 tours came from the National Endowment for the Arts, the Wisconsin Arts Board, and the University of Wisconsin.

5.   More information on Lodi culture is available online at http://www.lodi.k12.wi.us/ schools/es/Krueger/lodi%20culture.htm

6.   The author responsibilities in this chapter are as follows: Steven A. Ackerman, introduction and "Creating a Learning Community"; Ruth Olson, "More Than Folklore" and "Contextualized Knowledge"; Debbie Kmetz, "Our First Here at Home Tour," "The Itinerary," and "Multiple Ways to Perceive Local Culture"; and Anne Pryor, "Learning Outcomes," "Champions of the Local," "Creative Applications," and "Meeting Our Goals."

4

Art at the Threshold
Folk Artists in an Urban Classroom

Amanda Dargan

SITTING ON THE FLOOR BESIDE POTS OF RICE flour and brightly colored powders, Madhulika Khandelwal takes a pinch and slowly releases it between her fingers, drawing a fine curved line. Starting with a simple flower shape, she builds outwardly in concentric circles of ornamentation until the flower blossoms into an intricate design of stems, leaves, and petals. This traditional art, called *rangoli* in regions of India, is practiced solely by women. Khandelwal learned to draw rangoli from the women in her family. She describes how many women—both in India and the United States—draw rangoli at the entry to their homes, sweeping the designs away each morning and then creating them anew.

Often drawn at the boundary of sacred and secular space, rangoli designs mark both physical and ritual thresholds—at the main entry to the home or temple, in front of a home altar, and at a wedding, birthday, or *namkaran*, the Hindu naming ceremony held soon after a child is born. Festivals, such as Diwali, call for more elaborate and colorful designs. During these festivals, families go from house to house to view the designs. Khandelwal recalls that in the evening, the rice-flour designs shimmered in the moonlight on the stones of her family's courtyard.

On this day, however, Khandelwal draws rangoli on the floor of a fourth-grade classroom at Public School 11 in Woodside, Queens, New York City. She has been invited to demonstrate her art by George Zavala, a visual artist

Amanda Dargan is the education director of City Lore, a nonprofit organization located in New York City and dedicated to fostering the city's living cultural heritage.

Madhulika Khandelwal demonstrates the Indian art of *rangoli*.

who will be working with these students in an artist-in-residence program over the next fourteen weeks. A student born in Bangladesh and another from Pakistan raise their hands and describe similar traditions in their countries. Khandelwal responds that this art form is found throughout southern Asia, where it is known by different names. She writes some of the names on the board: *alpana* in Bengal, *kolam* in parts of southern India, *mandana* in Rajasthan, *aripana* in Bihar, *muggu* in Andhra Pradesh, and *chowk* in Delhi. Like many folk-art traditions, the designs, materials, and techniques differ from region to region, but their purpose is similar: to adorn, protect, and welcome guests and deities to a place.

Embedded in daily life, folk arts and the artists who create them can be a rich resource for teaching and learning in school settings. The experience of working with artists like Madhulika Khandelhal helps students make connections between what they learn in school and at home, between the arts and traditions of their families and communities and those of other communities and cultures. Traditional arts like rangoli offer ways to look at practices that are both universal and particular to a cultural group. Even those students unfamiliar with the south Asian art of rangoli can connect to the universal practice of decorating and protecting the entrance to the home, as well as marking rites of passage, such as birthdays, baby-naming ceremonies, and weddings. Christmas wreaths, Jewish mezuzahs, Chinese red-paper envelopes, evil-eye charms, horseshoes, garlic braids placed on doorways during Greek Easter, even doormats are among the customs throughout the world to protect the home or observe a religious holiday or belief. Working together to investigate these threshold arts and customs, students begin to make personal connections and notice cross-cultural similarities and differences, both important for navigating successfully in an increasingly diverse society.

This chapter draws on my work as a folklorist directing K–12 arts-education programs at City Lore and other nonprofit organizations over the past thirty years and the evolution of my thinking about what folk arts and the field of folklore can contribute to teaching and learning in school and community settings. It describes different models that folklorists have used to bring folk artists into classrooms as guests or teaching artists and highlights the models and practices that inform my current work. These include 1) professional-development tools and strategies to prepare folk artists for school visits; 2) folk-arts residencies that explore not only the art skills and cultural context, values, roles, and meaning of these arts for their practitioners but also their traditional pedagogical practices; and 3) collaborative residencies cotaught by artists from different folk and fine-arts disciplines and cultural backgrounds. Finally, it seeks to make a case for developing models and strategies that permit more expansive roles for folk arts and folklore study in K–12 education.

Folk Artists in Schools (FAIS) Models

I met Madhulika Khandelwal in 1982 when I initiated a Folk Arts in Schools (FAIS) program for the Queens Council on the Arts, adapting a successful model used by other folklorists around the country. Funded by the National Endowment for the Arts (NEA) Folk and Traditional Arts Program, beginning in 1976—often with matching support from state and local arts councils—FAIS programs, modeled in part on artists-in-schools (AIS) programs, proliferated across the country in states such as New Jersey, Florida, Kentucky, Michigan, Ohio, Nebraska, and New York.

In these programs, a folklorist conducted fieldwork in a community or region to identify and prepare folk artists to conduct workshops in local schools. The folklorist often worked closely with classroom teachers to plan and prepare students for the artist's visit. The folklorist then facilitated the workshop, in which artists demonstrated their art, followed by a participatory activity with students. A lovely example of this model appears in the video documentary *Folk Artists in the Schools,* directed by Nancy Groce when she was the folklorist for the Council on the Arts and Humanities for Staten Island from 1984 to 1986 (Groce 1985). Groce brought a wide range of artists and local residents to a Staten Island elementary school: a ferryboat captain, Norwegian *rosemaler,* Ukrainian *pysanky* maker, Haitian dancer, Italian marionetter, Chinese calligrapher, Irish musician, Philippine cook, and pigeon flier. Groce writes that her goal was "to demonstrate that 'art' existed within the student's own community and was not confined to annual field trips to Manhattan" (1985, 3).

A central goal of FAIS programs like the Staten Island and Queens projects was to give students and teachers an appreciation for the rich folk-arts traditions in their local communities and—through experiences with a wide variety of artists and art forms—an understanding of the nature of folk arts and their role and meaning to particular culture bearers and communities. The folklorist Mary Hufford, who directed an FAIS program at a school in Camden, New Jersey, notes a distinction between these programs and other AIS programs: "Whereas AIS (Artists in Schools) deals with the products of individual creativity, FAIS emphasizes the position of the artist and his creation within a larger social matrix. It aims to show students that art does not begin and end with the creation of beautiful objects but that its beauty encapsulates the values of the community in which it thrives and is inextricable from the lives of its creators" (1979, 5).

Creating New Program Models

A modification of FAIS, the Folk Arts in Education (FAIE) model required direct participation by a folklorist in every classroom workshop to facilitate students' interaction with the artists, many of whom had little or no experience in school settings. Essentially a folklorist residency with multiple guest folk artists, this program model is very time intensive, and we could manage programs in only one or two schools at a time. In addition, this model emphasized the role of the folklorist, rather than empowering folk and community-based artists to teach the residencies themselves.

Thus, we moved toward an artist-in-residence program model that arts-education providers and their school partners throughout the country still use widely (Remer 2003). It requires working with folk artists with experience or interest in teaching in long-term residencies of ten to twenty contact sessions with students. These longer residencies permit a sustained, in-depth experience for students, teachers, and artists with time to develop inquiry-based investigations and community field trips, attention to process as well as product, and culminating projects that are more ambitious than the smaller art-making activities possible in one or two visits by artists. This model also allows education staff and folklorists to assume different roles and responsibilities in the residency programs, such as identifying and preparing artists to teach in classrooms, locating guest artists and community experts for classroom visits, developing resource materials and community field trips, and documenting and evaluating the program's impact on teaching and learning in our partner schools.

We also expanded our roster to include community artists who work in both fine and popular art forms, such as murals, sculpture, dance, theater, popular dance, hip-hop, and spoken-word poetry. Some of these artists specialize in bringing children and local community residents together to share stories and personal experiences as inspiration for creating collaborative art projects (Davis and Ferdman 1993). Others engage students in researching family and community history and culture. In these residencies, students draw on their traditions as a resource for making art. They work with songwriters like Leo Schaff to write songs based on interviews with community residents (Schaff 2009) and theater artists like José Garcia and George Zavala to write and perform plays inspired by the stories told by local seniors or the experiences of their peer group. These residencies teach important lessons about traditional arts: they serve both as an expression of a community's shared aesthetic and cultural values and a resource for creating original work that expresses a personal vision or the collective ideas of a group of artists.

Artist Collaborations

In addition, we continued to recognize the value of bringing in guest folk artists, who have rich traditions, expertise, and personal experiences to share with students. Although these artists may teach young people in their families or communities, they may not have time or interest in teaching in long-term residencies. We decided to create models that integrate guest folk artists and other community experts into the longer artistic residencies. In these programs, students create original artwork inspired by the guest artist's visit and their research into both local and world cultures and historical events. Guest artists and community experts offer many opportunities for student learning in artist-residency programs: 1) they introduce students to a wider range of art forms, cultural backgrounds, and areas of expertise or personal experience; 2) they allow teaching artists to make connections between the residency theme or art form and a particular folk-arts tradition; and 3) they share firsthand experiences from the cultural and historical context of the art forms or events students are studying.

Third-grade students in one residency, for example, explored telling stories through different art forms. The residency integrated the arts with the social-studies curriculum focus on communities around the world and the English language-arts unit on traditional narratives. In the fall, half the classes worked with theater artist Lu Yu and half with Chinese dance artist Margaret Yuen to retell stories from the beloved Chinese novel, *Journey to the West,* written by Wu Cheng-en during the Ming Dynasty (c. 1500–82). The novel features the Chinese monkey king and his adventures accompanying the monk Xuanzang, an historical figure, on his pilgrimage to India to bring back Buddhist scriptures. Students explored how the stories are told through theater, including Chinese opera, and dance, but they also brought in examples from home of these popular stories depicted in television shows and comic books. In the spring, we divided the classes into three groups who worked with Lu Yu, Indian Bharatanatyam dancer Malini Srinivasan, or visual artist Jenna Bonistalli to explore stories and characters from the *Ramayana,* the ancient epic known throughout South and Southeast Asia that is also depicted in many traditional and popular art forms, such as dance, drama, puppetry, comic books, and movies.

Bonistalli's students retold the stories through narrative paintings inspired by the *patachitra* scroll-painting tradition from West Bengal. She invited Srinivasan to visit her class for a lesson on gesture in painting and dance. Srinivasan led students through the movements and gestures associated with the characters in the stories they were studying. These students also visited the home of rangoli artist Samantha Mukhavilli and the nearby Hindu Temple Society of North America, where they saw statues of the characters depicted in the stories and learned that the entire *Ramayana* had been recited in the temple the week prior to their visit. This yearlong residency program

Photo by Jenna Bonistalli, courtesy of City Lore.

A third-grader paints an image inspired by stories from the *Ramayana* and scroll painting from West Bengal.

provided rich experiences and varied entry points for students to make cross-cultural and cross-disciplinary connections and develop a deeper understanding of the elements of stories and the qualities of powerful storytelling.

We also invite guests who have firsthand experience of the topics students are studying. For a residency where students created and performed a play based on their research of the Japanese American experience, we invited Madeline Sugimoto, who described her personal experiences and shared images of her father's paintings that depicted life in an internment camp that housed Japanese American citizens during World War II. Guests like Sugimoto provide compelling evidence of the impact of historical events on individual lives and communities. They are also powerful catalysts for student creativity and art making.

Photo by Amanda Dargan, courtesy of City Lore.

Samantha Mukhavilli draws rangoli designs in front of her home in Flushing, Queens, for students from Public School 11.

This brings us back to the fourth-grade classroom where Madhulika Khandelwal guides students in an activity inspired by her rangoli. She gives students a chance to try drawing a line by releasing rice flour between their fingers. This is a challenging task, and these young students are amazed that Khandelwal can draw such beautiful designs using this technique. Rather than plan an activity that may be an exercise in frustration, Zavala and Khandelwal focus instead on building a design by elaborating on a central image, using oil pastels rather than rice flour. Most of the children quickly grasp the idea and create brightly colored rangoli designs.

Before the class ends, Zavala asks students if they have questions for Khandelwal. One student wants to know how she keeps the powdered designs from blowing away or getting "messed up" when people walk over them to enter the house. Khandelwal explains that for the women who draw rangoli, it is the act of creating the designs—not their permanence—that matters. Zavala observes that this is an ephemeral art, meant to last only a short time. He writes the word "ephemeral" on the board and asks students to think of other examples of ephemeral art. One child says "sand castles," but no other examples are offered, so Zavala asks students to talk with their families and think of more before he returns the following week. He reminds them that they will explore their own threshold traditions during the residency and create artwork inspired by their discoveries.

In the weeks that follow, Zavala and his students explore threshold traditions—both material and ritual—and discuss what they reveal about the cultures and beliefs of the people who practice them. Students talk with family members and look for threshold amulets and ornaments in neighborhood stores and homes, including their own. Zavala has them gather images, symbols, colors, textures, and memories of threshold customs to use in their artwork. He introduces them to the art of assemblage and shows them the work of fine artists who work in this form, such as Joseph Cornell, a Queens artist whose boxes incorporate found objects, and Betye Saar, an artist who uses family memorabilia and photographs in her assemblage art. On the final day of the residency, each student and the classroom teacher share their assemblage boxes with the class and respond to questions about their artistic choices, materials, and ideas.

Residencies like this have several goals. One is to support a social-studies unit—in this case, the fourth-grade focus on immigrant communities in New York—and through guest visits and family research, generate discussion around the ways that immigrant communities both maintain and adapt their traditions to their new homes in the city. Another is to compare the ways that folk and fine artists incorporate their cultures and surroundings in their art. A third is to give students—many of them first- and second-generation immigrants—a lens for connecting their practices to those of their classmates and guest artists. And fourth is to provide an artistic form—in this case, assemblage—that allows students to develop skills and techniques associated with this form and express their understanding and ideas around a common theme: physical and ritual thresholds.

These folk-artist visits give students a deeper understanding of traditional arts but also serve as a springboard for them to draw on their cultural traditions as inspiration for creating original work. Many of our teaching artists practice both traditional and personal art inspired by their cultural heritage and identity. George Zavala is formally trained in theater and visual arts. His personal art explores issues of identity and his relationship to his Puerto Rican and American heritage. Madhulika Khandelwal is an associate professor in urban studies at Queens College and has written about Indian communities in New York, inspired, in part, by her own immigrant experiences (Khandelwal 2002). Continuing the traditional arts she learned from her mother connects her to the rich cultural milieu of her childhood in India and the Indian community in New York City.

Opportunities to work with artists from a wide range of backgrounds, training, and expertise can help dispel common perceptions that folk artists, who often learn their art informally, are not as skilled as artists with formal education or that their art requires less rigorous training When students interview guest folk artists, they discover that many began learning their craft when they were very young from family members or mentors who set rigorous standards. They hear stories of quilters whose mothers made them pull out their stitches until they sewed them evenly spaced, or dancers who secretly practiced steps before daring to perform for others.

We work with folk artists like NEA National Heritage Fellow Juan Gutiérrez, a Puerto Rican *bomba* and *plena* musician, who learned this traditional music informally from older musicians but has a degree in music and worked as a Broadway composer for many years before founding a performing group and nonprofit organization, Los Pleneros de la 21. And we work with artists like Leo Schaff, who teaches songwriting to students but does not read music—his formal education is in theater. These artists exemplify the variety of ways that artists learn and use their artistry in their professional or everyday lives and help dispel the notion that only those with a formal arts education can be professional artists.

Preparing Folk Artists to Teach in Schools

All the teaching artists City Lore employs to work in schools are practicing artists, but they also consider teaching an essential component of their professional lives. Many instruct children in their own community-based settings but are also committed to teaching students of diverse backgrounds in public schools. Their challenge—and ours as folklorists who prepare them to work in public education—is to design program models and teaching practices that provide them with the tools that, in turn, encourage students to develop skills and understandings that they can use in their lives. We have designed professional-development programs that address the unique challenges and gifts that traditional artists bring to their work in K–12 education.

One challenge for folk artists working in schools is deciding what to teach students from diverse backgrounds who may never participate in this art form again. Many folk artists feel responsible for presenting and teaching their art form in a way that respects their teachers' and communities' notions

Photo by Amanda Dargan, courtesy of City Lore.

Kwok Kay Choey performs tai chi to a Puerto Rican bomba beat at a teaching-artist institute sponsored by City Lore and Local Learning.

of authenticity. In their communities, they often teach students who plan to continue practicing their art throughout their lives. What can they teach students in such a short time that will encourage a deep understanding of their art form's function and meaning in its cultural context and, at the same time, help these students develop skills and knowledge that they can apply to their lives?

To address this challenge, we ask artists in our professional-development workshops to articulate what they want their students to understand and know how to do by the residency's end. We also spend time discussing the influences on their decision to become artists, who their teachers were and how they were taught, the cultural values their art embodies, and the community contexts in which they learned and continue to perform their art. We ask them to think about what learning and working in this art form have taught them beyond art skills and what they hope that it will teach their students.

We also spend time discussing what they consider to be essential components of their art that they want their students to learn, their "nonnegotiables."

What are they willing to sacrifice, simplify, or adapt? How do they deal with the religious contexts of many art forms, and how do they convey the complexity of the tradition and at the same time make it accessible for even very young students? Malini Srinivasan, an Indian Bharatanatyam dancer, said that she realized very soon that in these settings, she must sacrifice an emphasis on technique. She uses her assembly-hall performance to show students how the dance is performed by artists who have studied it for most of their lives. Her nonnegotiables are that every class must begin and end with a blessing expressing gratitude to Mother Earth, noting that she calls it a "blessing," rather than a "prayer," with these students, but she refers to it as a prayer in her performance. Srinivasan explained her choices:

> One thing I haven't dropped out of my teaching, whether it's long or short, is the prayer to Mother Earth, which became "hello" to Mother Earth and "good-bye" to Mother Earth or the "greeting" to Mother Earth, because one teacher was very specific that the word "prayer" not be used so as not to offend. It's a prayer or greeting in motion directed to Mother Earth. . . . It's an important part of our dance's culture, not just that it's directed to Mother Earth, but just the idea that you ask for blessings, ask for forgiveness, ask that you need the support of the world and the people around you. That is very, very strongly embedded in this tradition. After a dance class you do your prayer for Mother Earth and then you touch the feet of your teacher or you touch the teaching tool, which is a stick. It's not something I ask any of my students to do, simply because I don't feel ready. But I do always, touch the feet of my teacher always, and in that way ask for his blessings, that no matter what our personal differences may be that they do not enter my homage to him. It's a kind of submission, "Okay, I follow you and I take your teaching, in some part of my soul, without question," and then with the other part of my mind I can play around with it and cultivate it, but there's an aspect of it which says, "I submit to my tradition, and I need your blessings to continue." Although I don't say this to my students, I hope something of that gesture conveys this. . . . You don't just start; it's not anywhere, anytime. We make a conscious effort to begin. And we close. . . . The other thing I don't negotiate is bare feet. I really feel that this art form is about contacting the ground with your body. It does not work with shoes. . . . So much of our tradition is that weight and that attachment to earth, that grounded, rhythmic movement. Without it, you don't have the dance. The quality of the movement requires it. It's also attached to this Mother Earth idea. We are planted here.

Similarly, Cote d'Ivoire dancer Yahaya Kamate ends each class with a ritual blessing, which he also has adapted for a secular setting. He explains that "we believe that we get energy from the earth and the sky and from each other, and so we express our gratitude." As he accompanies students on the *djembe* drum, they put their hands over their hearts, raise them up, then reach to the floor and turn around as they say, "Thank you, heart. Thank you, sky. Thank you, heart. Thank you, earth. Thank you, everyone." For Puerto Rican bomba dancer Julia Gutiérrez-Rivera, her "nonnegotiable" is the gesture of respect to the lead drummer before beginning and ending the dance. She shows students the way that female dancers raise the edge of their skirts and bow slightly, but she gives them permission to use their own nonverbal ("dancers communicate with their bodies, not their words"), but respectful, greeting.

These opening and closing rituals are part of the traditional pedagogy of these arts. They encode cultural values as surely as the rhythms of Puerto Rican bomba and the stitched patterns of Ukrainian embroidery. And, although each uses different gestures and words and acknowledges different sources of inspiration—teachers, fellow artists, Mother Earth—they all insist on marking the beginning and end of a class or performance by showing gratitude and respect. We can discuss the religious nature of some of these rituals with students while adapting the rituals for a secular setting by focusing on the cultural values or ideas they convey.

The ethnomusicologist Patricia Shehan Campbell makes a case for designing music instruction that incorporates traditional pedagogical practices, teaching that "strives to reach beyond queries of 'what' and 'why' to questions of 'how.' Those working to evolve this pedagogy have studied music with culture bearers, and have come to know that this music can be best understood through experience with the manner with which it is taught and learned" (2004, 27). Not all traditional pedagogy is appropriate for schools, of course. We would not incorporate the tactic that a local stonemason used with his new apprentices when he was dissatisfied with their work—he smashed it to pieces with a sledge hammer. Nor would we require that students spend their entire residency mastering a basic stitch before moving on to more complex ones, as many embroiderers have told us they were taught. But we do encourage artists to talk with students about the ways they were taught and how this pedagogy shaped their artistry and their teaching practice.

Another challenge is how to align traditional pedagogies both with our core values and practices as an arts-education provider and with state and local arts-education standards. Kwok Kay Choey, a Chinese brush painter, teaches by demonstrating different strokes through symbolic imagery: bamboo shoots, dragons, fish. Students imitate his drawings to practice learning the strokes. As they progress through the residency, students develop a repertoire of imagery and strokes that they can use to compose unique paintings. Sometimes we get criticism from teachers—especially art specialists—about this approach. While it diverges from current pedagogy in arts education, we have observed an artistic freedom and skill that comes after repeated imitation and practice.

As an arts organization, we also believe in devoting time for students to discuss and reflect on what they have learned and the artistic choices that shaped their paintings. We feel that students will understand this art form better if they compare it to other tools and forms of painting. And so we pair Choey with City Lore teaching artist and staff member Jenna Bonistalli, who leads the discussion and reflection sessions with students as well as oversees the observational drawings on field trips to the Chinese Scholar's Garden in Staten Island. Choey, who enjoys this coteaching experience, describes some of these practices as "very Western" and unfamiliar, which we try to highlight in our discussions with students.

At City Lore, we ask each teaching artist to write an artistic statement—framed as a letter to students—that we use as a tool to design their residencies and identify core practices and goals. In his letter, Foley Kolade, a Nigerian musician and fabric artist, shared a story of a woman who influenced his thinking about his art:

> I'm totally dedicated to my work. Being an artist requires being a disciplined person. I take all my work seriously; I respect it all. I learned this from a woman who took care of the river gods, the *osuns*. One day she told a story about the only time she ever got furious with someone. It was the time she saw a man throw his artwork in the garbage because he thought it wasn't good enough. She said, "Never throw your art away! All your work is valuable. It's not perfect; it's not supposed to be. We always have room to grow and our work reminds us of our imperfection and encourages us to grow." I try to have that philosophy about my life and my art.

Working together as a group, we circle words and phrases the artists have written and discuss ways to design instruction that supports their core values as artists and teachers. Nego Gato, a Brazilian capoeira artist, writes in his letter, "Capoeira teaches sensitivity, flexibility, coordination, stamina, and how to read people." In our artist workshops, we may ask, "What do you mean by flexibility? Is it just flexible bodies, or do you also mean flexible minds?" We can stretch and warm up muscles to build flexible bodies, but how do we construct flexible minds? Many traditional arts, including Puerto Rican bomba and plena, require the skill of reading people, so we gather ideas from all the artists in the room.

Another artist wrote that his art form teaches patience. How do we teach patience? One way is to model patience in our own teaching, but we can also design activities that require it and give students opportunities to practice this skill, refrain from rescuing them when they lose patience, and give them tools to help them persist through frustration. And we can tell stories about a time when we lost patience and what it taught us. If we value our "mistakes"— as Kolade does—we can offer activities that build on them, use teachable moments to talk about our mistakes and what we learned from them, or show examples of our art that grew from work we considered imperfect.

Our goal in these workshops is to give artists opportunities to gather their memories and experiences and identify their core values and practices as artists and educators. Then we work with them and their partner teachers to design residencies and instruction that respect their tradition and artistry, support the goals for their students, provide rich learning experiences, and build skills and knowledge that students can use in other areas of their lives.

At a recent artistic workshop, Juan Gutiérrez performed a plena that he often plays with his students. Then Shobana Raghavan Raj, an Indian Carnatic singer, sang the same melody from a folk song she remembered. Gutiérrez accompanied her, and when she finished, he said, "Amazing—my hair is standing on end." Gutiérrez then asked the group if they had drums in their cultures with the root word *boula*, like the Puerto Rican drum *buleador*. "I've heard it means 'to remember,' which makes sense because it remembers the beat." Then Raghavan Raj spoke, "We have a similar word, but it means 'to forget.'" Connections and epiphanies like these that occur when traditional artists are working together inspire and reinvigorate our work.

Designing for Inquiry and Arts Integration

Increasingly both schools and funders require that artistic residencies support learning both in the arts and another subject. Because part of City

Lore's mission is to document, advocate, and educate the public on the cultural heritage of communities in New York City, we design arts residencies that integrate primarily with social-studies and language-arts curricula. Our goal is that students and teachers view the city as a resource for teaching and learning in the arts and social studies. We draw on our experience documenting city neighborhoods and communities to give students and teachers tools and skills to investigate and document community traditions, historical events, and cultural settings. We encourage research as a preparation for making art and drawing on a variety of resources—books and the Internet but also people and places in city neighborhoods and institutions. Students learn to conduct research using tools and primary sources that folklorists, anthropologists, and historians employ: interviews, ethnographic observations, note taking, reading documents and artifacts, mapping, and audio and video recording. They learn to analyze and interpret their research through the questions they ask and the art they create.

Working with the teaching artists and their classroom teachers, we begin most residencies with a big idea or question that guides our design and often leads to more questions that students investigate independently. Sometimes the questions change as we move through the residency. This happened in a residency that focused on the Mexican Revolution. Our initial inquiry question was, "What ideas inspired the Mexican Revolution?," but a few weeks into the program, we realized that we—artists, teachers, students— were more interested in the roles that artists played in spreading these ideas. So we changed our question to, "How do artists bring about social change?" This required altering scenes in the play that we had already developed and researching more stories to include, but the excitement was infectious, and other staff specialists (social studies, art, technology) volunteered to teach lessons that supported our study.

Two traditional Mexican dance and music artists—Alfredo Ortega and his daughter Cecilia—dance/theater artist Lu Yu, and visual artist Diana Evans collaborated on this residency. Students learned about the role of visual artists such as José Posada, whose populist engravings helped spread political ideas to a largely illiterate population and who influenced a generation of mural painters, including Diego Rivera. Students painted a backdrop of Rivera's painting "Dream of a Sunday Afternoon in Alameda Park" and opened and closed the play with pre- and post-revolution tableaux. They performed traditional dances taught by the Ortegas for scenes depicting the *soldadares,* women of the revolution, and Anna Pavlova's visit to Mexico during the revolution, when she performed in a bullring, inspired by a traditional courtship dance. The teachers whose classes participated in the residency reported that students made connections between the ideas and social conditions that shaped the Mexican Revolution and other conflicts in the Americas, the focus of the fifth-grade social-studies curriculum, throughout the year. They also learned that artists play many roles in society beyond creating art that is interesting or aesthetically pleasing: they can be agents for change.

The Role of Folk Arts in Arts Education

If folk arts are to have a central place in K–12 education, they must contribute not only to students' understanding of cultural traditions but also to their ability to think critically, gather and analyze evidence, and express their ideas and interpretations through personal creativity. Folklore and the tools of the folklorist can support learning in a variety of subjects, including the arts. Folk arts are uniquely suited to explore the ways in which traditional art forms reflect the history, culture, geography, and values of different cultures and subcultures.

Folk arts manifest ways the arts enrich our daily lives, even for those not seeking a career in them. Too often the arts are viewed as valuable only to children with talent and a desire to pursue an artistic profession while others are relegated to the role of audience members. Folk artists show students that you do not have to make your living as an artist for creating art to be an integral part of your daily life.

Learning through folk arts values authentic, hands-on learning strongly connected to the real world; draws on students' prior knowledge and experiences in their families and communities; provides opportunities for student inquiry and the acquisition of deep knowledge and sustained research using a variety of resources, including their families and peers; and offers access to community experts and people with firsthand experience of historical events and cultural practices.

The study of folk arts also makes a strong case that arts education should include an understanding of the social, cultural, and historical context of the arts (Chalmers 1996; McFee 1966; Sandell 2009), Eliot Eisner writes,

> Arts education should enable students to understand that there is
> a connection between the content and form that the arts take and
> the culture and time in which the work was created. Why is such an

outcome important? It's important because the quality of experience
the arts make possible is enriched when the arts are experienced within
the context of ideas relevant to them. Understanding this cultural
context is among the most important ways in which such enrichment
can be achieved. (1998, 97-98)

Although understanding the nature of folk arts is not the primary goal of
every City Lore residency and many of the art forms that students study
are not folk arts, these arts and the discipline of folklore inform all our programs, from the tools that students employ to conduct their research to the
questions that guide their inquiry. They draw each residency's attention to
the cultural/historical context of the art form(s) studied and the cross-cultural comparisons and interdisciplinary connections students make. They
are visible in the emphasis on artists telling personal stories about their practice and educational experiences in the arts, both formal and informal. And
they influence our efforts to allow the core values, cultural practices, and traditional pedagogy each artist brings to shape the program design and goals.

Making Connections through Folk Arts

For artists and teachers, artistic residencies rooted in folk and traditional arts
such as rangoli connect to other broad themes or ideas. George Zavala chose
to associate rangoli with thresholds, but he could have developed a residency
that made other connections, such as women's, ephemeral, sacred, Indian,
or Asian arts. Each lens offers promising avenues for student inquiry and
creativity. If teachers are hesitant to take on the study of an unfamiliar culture, the focus on themes and asking questions to guide students' research
and inquiry makes these studies more accessible. Graeme Chalmers writes,
"If the focus is on the why of art, art teachers in multicultural societies need
not worry that they do not know enough about art in a plethora of cultures.
Rather than viewing teachers as transmitters of huge bodies of knowledge,
we should see them as leaders and facilitators who are able to focus on the
process and assist students in their investigation and understanding of the
commonalities in the functions and roles of art across cultures" (1996, 38).

    In some of our partner schools, we connect our residencies across grades
and arts disciplines around a common theme. For the 2007–8 school year—
the year of Madhulika Khandelwal's visit to George Zavala's residency—we
explored a number of possible themes but found it difficult to find a common

Photo by Amanda Dargan, courtesy of City Lore.

A fifth-grade student models a Broadway gypsy robe.

thread to connect the diversity of residency topics and art forms teachers had chosen. The school's art teachers, for example, had developed a yearlong study of environmental art with students. The same year, teachers in another residency program insisted on doing Broadway theater, not an art form we considered aligned with City Lore's mission. At first we resisted, but then we decided to challenge ourselves to integrate the study of traditional arts and culture with this popular art form. Students worked with theater artist Lu Yu to perform scenes from plays that reflected important social issues from different decades. We invited Terry Marone of Actors' Equity to visit each class with an example of a "gypsy robe," a Broadway tradition dating back to the 1950s, in which a robe freighted with good-luck mementos passes from one chorus line to another each time a new show opens. Marone explained the imagery in the patches contributed from different shows and described the rituals and traditions associated with the robe, including the rule that it must go to a musical with a chorus line and be given to the chorus member with the greatest number of Broadway credits. The robe is delivered a half hour before the opening-night curtain, and the new recipient—who is crowned king or queen of the gypsies—puts it on and circles the stage three times while each cast member touches the robe for good luck (Groce, 2000–2001, 14).

Lu Yu, the lead teaching artist for this residency, described rituals and beliefs associated with theater in China, such as lighting incense for the god of theater, Guan Gong, before a show opens. He asked students if they were familiar with the theater expression "break a leg,"—used to ensure that no such misfortune befalls a member of the cast—and he encouraged students to investigate their good-luck traditions.

Other City Lore residencies that year included a quilt residency in which students explored the question, "What is home?" They discussed ideas of home that included their country of origin, the home where they lived with their families or caretakers, and their neighborhood of Woodside, Queens. They visited a local quilt shop, where they saw traditional and contemporary designs and learned a basic stitch. Children created squares depicting their homes and contributed to a central image of their neighborhood. Quilters from the shop they visited stitched the pieces together.

We were well into the school year—mounting student artwork for the spring arts fair—when we began to see a common theme that had eluded us. In different ways, each residency—and the art teachers' study of environmental art—had explored ideas of home—home as the dwelling where you live, as your neighborhood, as this country, and as your family's country of origin; Broadway as the home of American musical theater; and the Earth as home for us all. While stories that students shared and portrayed in their art revealed ways that these homes did not always feel safe or welcoming, they also expressed ideas of what a home should and could be: a place of safety, nurture, and belonging.

During her classroom visit, Madhulika Khandelwal talked about the challenges for Indian women living in New York City who want to continue drawing rangoli daily in front of their homes. Many live in apartments and work outside the home; the time pressures of life in New York can be overwhelming. She acknowledged that few Indian women of her generation continue the tradition in New York. Yet, even when she lived in an apartment, Khandelwal continued to draw small rangoli designs in front of her door, both to adorn her new home and to feel connected to the family she had left behind in India. By sharing her art and experiences as an immigrant, Khandelwal inspired her students to reflect on their experiences and create art that expressed their ideas of home.

It may seem, at first, a simple question—"What is home?" But the rich learning that followed when artists, teachers, and students spent time

Photo by Amanda Dargan, courtesy of City Lore.

Quilt panels created by students at Public School 11 were inspired by the question, "What is home?"

together exploring answers to their questions and drawing on a variety of community resources revealed the complexity of students' ideas of home. Encouraging inquiry through folk arts into the diverse experiences and meanings of home inspired these students—many of whom are first- and second-generation immigrants—to think deeply about their relationship to their many homes and each other.

5

From "Show-Me" Traditions to "The Show-Me Standards"

Teaching Folk Arts in Missouri Classrooms

Lisa L. Higgins and Susan Eleuterio

Dear Mr. Moore, I like the music and the sound, but I think that the dancing is really fun. But I love how you taught the people with the drums. I got the part of the garabato girl and I got to dance with a skeleton dude and these two boys fight over me. This dude named Gabe has to dance with me, but I have never danced with a boy before. So it's kind of awkward, and he is going to be a skeleton, so I love this and the music that you do. How do you do so good on the drums? Where do you live?

—Jordan B.

So wrote a student from Shelbina Elementary School in northeastern Missouri after a weeklong residency taught by Colombian folkloric dancer Carmen Dence and her percussionist Arthur Moore. In Jordan's letter to Moore, she exhibits newfound cultural knowledge, an enthusiasm for learning, and the ability to overcome challenges—all goals for Missouri's Folk Arts School Residency Project. Ultimately, Jordan appears well on her way to achieving performance goals outlined in the state of Missouri's K–12 academic criteria, known as "The Show-Me Standards" (Missouri Department of Elementary and Secondary Education 1996).[1] This chapter

Lisa L. Higgins is the director of the Missouri Folk Arts Program, a program of the Missouri Arts Council and Museum of Art and Archaeology at the University of Missouri in Columbia. Susan Eleuterio is a professional folklorist and educator who is based in the Chicago metropolitan area.

explicates an ongoing, multiyear project that strives to develop successful school residencies through strong collaborations among educators, local arts administrators and traditional artists with the guidance of professionally trained folklorists. The project is designed to engage students and enhance school curricula through hands-on activities grounded in Missouri's rich cultural heritage.

As folklorists we recognize that learning takes place every day in every setting. Perhaps that is why we are often eager to learn and are as full of questions as Jordan. Inevitably, the first question that folklorists ask traditional artists and tradition bearers is this one: "From whom and how did you learn?" The next question follows logically: "Where and when did you learn?" Folklorists can create cultural maps of regions, states, counties, and—as we get more local—school communities with our questions and the responses we garner. Asking from whom and how tells us whether the art form has been passed directly from tradition bearers within a specific community or from a bearer in one community to an apprentice in another. Asking where and when tells us as much about the specific community as about the individual artist. These questions and their responses also provide teachers with tangible cultural resources from their own neighborhoods, counties, regions, and states. Those real—but sometimes invisible—resources are multidisciplinary and relate directly to the goals and standards of contemporary school systems. Since 2004 the Missouri Folk Arts Program (MFAP) has piloted new programs to deliver these cultural resources into Missouri classrooms.

MFAP was established in the mid-1980s at the University of Missouri in partnership with the Missouri Arts Council.[2] Over the years, MFAP folklorists have produced educational projects for schoolchildren, including traveling exhibits and performances. One project developed in 1988 continues today, a partnership with the Missouri State Museum, an entity of the Department of Natural Resources. With "Tuesdays at the Capitol," our two organizations coordinate performances and demonstrations at the capitol building in Jefferson City by master and apprentice artists who participate in MFAP'S Traditional Arts Apprenticeship program (TAAP). Students who tour the capitol—typically fourth- and fifth-graders who are studying Missouri history, government, and culture—are the primary audience for "Tuesdays." Despite the long life of the program, the length of its sessions has steadily diminished as school groups began to arrive at the capitol with full agendas that included meeting legislators, participating in tours of the building and the Supreme Court of Missouri, and viewing exhibits at the Missouri State Museum. With considerations for both the students and the artists, MFAP staff tweaked "Tuesdays" into four-hour demonstrations in the galleries of the museum, housed in the east and west wings off the capitol rotunda. MFAP staff also began to research Folk Arts in Education (FAIE) projects that might better fulfill our mission to "build cross-cultural understanding by documenting, conserving, and presenting our state's living folk arts and folklife in collaboration with Missouri's citizens" (http://maa.missouri.edu/mfap/about.html).

In 2005 MFAP and the Missouri Arts Council submitted a successful National Endowment for the Arts (NEA) grant application to fund a pilot folk-arts residency project. After receiving the grant, MFAP began to explore outreach to schools via in-depth residencies. The project was inspired by the twentieth anniversary of Missouri's TAAP, which pairs master folk artists with apprentices to pass traditions on to the next generation, and the fortieth anniversary of the Missouri Arts Council Arts Education Program. We knew that few of Missouri's exemplary traditional folk artists conducted school programs.

The absence of traditional folk artists on the arts-education roster was not surprising since Missouri's residency program required teaching artists to spend a minimum of twenty hours in the school and conduct pre-residency planning sessions with the teachers. Most traditional folk artists are not full-time artists. They often work forty or more hours a week at regular jobs—sometimes more than one—and cannot meet the minimum residency requirements. Additionally, the most masterful folk artists may not have the educational expertise to develop in-school/after-school residencies nor ancillary materials like study guides, assessment strategies, and standards-aligned student activities. Furthermore, most of these artists are unfamiliar with classroom culture, statewide education standards, and performance goals. Still, folk artists in the schools provide rich content for cross-curricular learning, as well as reinforcing important skills like observing, listening, interviewing, mapping, analyzing, organizing, and communicating. Folk artists are also important reminders to small-town young people that every community has art, even if there is no local fine-arts museum or symphony.

From Whom and How Can We Learn?

For this new project, MFAP staff members identified three master traditional artists with both strong backgrounds in education and ample time to train for and then conduct residencies. Gladys Coggswell was born and raised in New Jersey but relocated to Frankford in northeastern Missouri, near Mark Twain's Hannibal. She is an African American storyteller, counselor, and education specialist who has received the Missouri Arts Council's Individual Artist of the Year Award. In addition to storytelling, she has been an active community scholar, collecting stories about emancipation, integration, and the day-to-day lives of African Americans in Missouri. Fiddler Howard W. Marshall lives in Millersburg, a small rural community in central Missouri. He is a professor emeritus of art history and archaeology at the University of Missouri, an academically trained folklorist with a long history in the public sector, and an accomplished Little Dixie–style fourth-generation fiddler. Since retirement Marshall has immersed himself in all things fiddling, from producing his own collection of Lewis and Clark–era fiddle tunes to reissuing historic Missouri fiddling albums on CD. Finally, dancer Carmen Dence hails from Baranquilla, Colombia, which is home to the internationally recognized *carnivale* that occurs annually just before Lent. She is a highly sought-after Colombian folkloric dancer, choreographer, and costume maker, who leads her own dance troupe, Grupo Atlántico. Dence is also a research scientist in radiology at Washington University in St. Louis. A lifelong learner, she continues to take university courses in both her field and the arts.

In addition to these three artist educators, MFAP staff enlisted the assistance of Susan Eleuterio, a professional folklorist and educator who has designed and implemented FAIE programs for schools and agencies since 1979. She has also served as a consultant and professional-development workshop leader for arts agencies in five states and a regional arts organization. Eleuterio worked closely with Marshall, Coggswell, and Dence during two intensive workshops to develop residency activities and teach them about school culture—an often-overlooked component of successful educational projects. Eleuterio continued to consult with the artists after the workshops and provided feedback on the materials that they developed. She took particular care to show these budding teaching artists ways to connect their materials and activities to Missouri's Department of Elementary and Secondary Education's "Show-Me Standards," which include six content areas (communication arts, fine arts, health/physical education, mathematics, science, and social studies) and four performance goals. Students are expected to "acquire the knowledge and skills" to 1) "gather, analyze, and apply information and ideas"; 2) "communicate effectively within and beyond the classroom"; 3) "recognize and solve problems"; and 4) "make decisions and act as responsible members of society" (Missouri Department of Elementary and Secondary Education 1996). Working hand in hand with MFAP staff, all three artists booked, prepared, and then conducted intensive residencies throughout 2006.

In 2005 MFAP director Lisa Higgins also announced the opportunity to host residencies to a group of local arts administrators at a meeting of the Missouri Association of Community Arts Agencies (MACAA), a statewide organization that serves a network of community arts agencies, most in rural communities. The director and board president of one organization, the Friends of Historic Boonville (FOHB), immediately asked to host a residency. FOHB is in a central Missouri county seat along the Missouri River. Organization leaders specifically asked for Coggswell, wanting to provide African American children in their community with role models and a deeper understanding of the historic contributions of African Americans to the region. As this example illustrates, connecting through MACAA's network has been important to our project since the beginning. Rather than work from the top down for this pilot project—the Department of Elementary and Secondary Education oversees more than five hundred school districts—MFAP staff partnered at the local level with community arts agencies, especially those with established folk-arts programming. MFAP suspected that networking directly through local arts agencies would provide more opportunities than form letters to state-government officials that might or might not trickle down from superintendents to principals and classroom teachers.

The FOHB proved our suspicions were true. The director contacted the perfect middle-school social-studies teacher, who jumped at the opportunity to bring Coggswell for a weeklong storytelling residency, and we ironed out details for a February date to reinforce the African American History Month curriculum. The FOHB director lodged Coggswell in her home for the week, added a culminating event to the residency, and raised additional funds from local businesses—all on her own initiative. During the residency, Coggswell taught students to ask questions, collect stories, and retell them to new audiences. Before the week was over, students began to perform their stories at the elementary school, and they created a story quilt with the assistance of a local quilter. After the residency, students shared their stories on local radio.

This first residency achieved two Show-Me Standards: "to gather, analyze, and apply information and ideas" and "to communicate effectively within and beyond the classroom." Eventually the principal reined in the students to prepare for standardized testing, but the bond between the middle schoolers and Coggswell had been established. She tragically had a stroke just a few weeks later, and the young storytellers made get-well cards, brought in their allowances, and sent flowers to wish her a speedy recovery. Without a doubt, they helped Coggswell in her recovery. The students also achieved another goal—to "act as responsible members of society" (Missouri Department of Elementary and Secondary Education 1996).

Just three months later, Howard Marshall presented a four-day school residency about Missouri fiddling at two elementary schools in northeastern Missouri's Shelby County, a rural community with a population just under seven thousand. Again MFAP staff connected through a community arts agency, and, again, the local arts administrator knew exactly which school and teacher to contact. The music teacher split her time between both schools and was interested in reconnecting her students with the rich music and dance traditions that have a long history in the region. Monday through Thursday, Marshall traveled nine miles between Clarence (population 915) and Shelbina (population 1,943) to introduce fourth- and fifth-graders to the historic and contemporary significance of old-time music and dance. The month prior to the residency, the music teacher prepared the students by teaching relevant songs and basic square-dance steps. When Marshall came into the classroom, he was able to link the residency content across several disciplines: history, geography, and physical education.

Each day Marshall built on the previous day's lessons by adding a new artist. An eighty-year-old acclaimed rhythm guitarist from nearby Knox County accompanied Marshall daily. A square-dance caller from nearby Sturgeon joined them midweek, and the students practiced their new dance steps with live music. On Thursday a Knox County luthier demonstrated fiddle building. Like Coggswell, Marshall ended the residency with a culminating event—something all three teaching artists agreed upon while training with Eleuterio. Shelby County students topped off their residency with "Fiddler's Frolic," a square dance and cakewalk. Two yellow buses delivered children from Shelbina to the Clarence gym. Clarence students arrived by car and truck, driven by their parents and grandparents. Ninety-six dancers—mostly children—created twelve dance squares and filled the gym floor for the first dance. Onstage a large band surrounded Marshall, including his guest-residency artists, a master artist from MFAP's apprenticeship program, six local musicians, and three Shelby County students on fiddle, guitar, and mandolin. The young dancers executed do-si-dos, allemandes, and the complicated grapevine twist. Surprisingly, many stayed on the dance floor to waltz, although it was no surprise that all of them remained there for the cakewalk.

To reinforce curricula and demonstrate proficiency in communication-arts standards, the music teacher asked her students to reflect on Marshall's residency by writing short essays. Some students responded with one-page essays, and others wrote thank-you letters describing their favorite parts of the week. Their enthusiastic comments included these:

> The first day was fun, but my legs kept falling asleep on me from sitting too long. So, please have more dancing. — Joanne

> I wasn't there on Monday so I don't know what went on, but from what I heard, it sounded like a load of fun! It must be awfully hard to learn to play by ear! — Jacie

> I just want you to know that you all have inspired me to want to even call for square dancing, play the fiddle, make the fiddle, or, the one I want to do the most, play the guitar. — Justin

MFAP staff and Eleuterio used these written responses as gauges to assess the residency as students articulated pieces of regional history, favorite tunes, or difficult dance steps like the grapevine twist or allemande left—which one student mistakenly, but amusingly, called the "Alabama left." Later, Marshall also conducted the fifth school residency of the project for a local cooperative of home-schooled children from mid-Missouri during November 2006 in Columbia.

For the fourth residency, MFAP staff arranged with the West Plains Council on the Arts for a residency by Carmen Dence. This was one of the most difficult projects to organize since West Plains is in south-central Missouri just north of the Arkansas border; the MFAP offices are in Columbia, about three hours north; and Dence lives in St. Louis, also about three hours from West Plains. In addition to logistics, we were all curious to see how a residency by Dence—a bilingual, immigrant artist from ethnically and racially diverse St. Louis—would fare in the rural Ozark region of Howell County, where

As an artist in residence in West Plains, Missouri, Carmen Dence introduced south-central Missouri students to Colombian traditional dance and the annual carnival celebrations of her home country.

Photo by Willow Mullins.

more than 95 percent of the population are white and not quite 2 percent are Latino. Dence, however, proved that dance is a universal language as she worked with a percussionist, a dance partner, the school's music teacher, and students in grades five through eight for a week that October.

Anecdotally Dence's residency proved to be another resounding success. The president of the arts council shared three stories: a lone Latino elementary student with spotty attendance was perfect the week of the residency; a mildly autistic student found new ways to engage and participate with peers; and the culminating event drew a standing-room-only audience in the 450-seat theater—despite being scheduled opposite the high-school Homecoming football game. Dence, Marshall, and Coggswell not only introduced students to Missouri traditions but also helped them to achieve Missouri performance goals and knowledge standards in fine arts, communication arts, physical education, math, and social studies. All three teaching artists also helped students meet grade level expectations, like making connections between the arts and other academic disciplines and learning cultural contexts for artistic expressions.

While students learned about Missouri's rich cultural heritage and achieved state standards, folklorists, teachers, and local arts administrators learned that planning and executing residencies require additional resources. In addition to masterful teaching artists and adequate funding, strong residencies demand many, many hours and an eager, energetic team. MFAP staff served as a liaison among the teaching artists, classroom teachers, and arts administrators to determine the budget, make travel arrangements, and set the schedule for preplanning and the residency. Teaching artists worked with classroom teachers to determine the day-to-day schedule and confirm logistics: number of students, hours in the classroom, necessary supplies, and room dimensions. Community arts administrators, MFAP staff, and teaching artists created press releases and organized culminating events. The process also provided MFAP staff, teachers, arts administrators, and teaching artists with the skills necessary to enrich the curriculum and the students, rather than simply entertain them. After completing the first phase of the pilot project, we could establish a model for school residencies that worked well and assess needs for the project's second phase.

Where and When Did We Learn? (A Case Study)

Assessment led our funding proposals for the next three phases of the project. From the beginning, MFAP staff determined that the Folk Arts School Residency project should be guided by more than annual grant cycles. Rather than propose a project that would be completed during the life of a one- or two-year grant, Lisa Higgins likened the project to the "slow food movement," noting that a worthwhile FAIE project should be organic, individually crafted for each occasion, relevant to the "climate" and culture of the locale, and never rushed. Our assessment also revealed a few ingredients that were missing in phase one of the project: a guide for teachers that connects the residencies to state standards and grade-level expectations (GLEs in educational vernacular), a larger menu of teaching artists, and technical assistance for school districts that want to host residencies.

When we questioned the teachers from phase one, all of them indicated that they felt inadequately prepared to host the residencies in regard to content; they wanted to be able to prepare themselves and their students before the artists arrived at the school to plan and execute residencies. Therefore, we requested and received a second two-year NEA grant for MFAP staff and Eleuterio to create a guide for teachers specific to Missouri folk arts, complete with activities, lesson plans, and links to state education standards on every page (Eleuterio et al. 2009). Eleuterio noted that many admirable, carefully crafted, beautifully illustrated, but wordy, curriculum materials have been created in the past only to end up on shelves, forgotten in the flurries of the real-life, day-to-day realities of teachers, staff, administrators, and students. Therefore, the Missouri guide was field tested and revised after input from teachers and teaching artists. The guide will continue to be field tested and revised via ongoing residencies with changes reflected in an ever-evolving online version.[3]

The first field test was conducted in May 2008, when Shelby County music teacher Lola Rist volunteered, based on her readings of drafts of the teachers' guide and the prior residency with Howard Marshall. This time Rist chose Carmen Dence as the artist to connect with her goals for teaching music and dance. Rist always tries to connect with local traditions while also introducing her students and the local community to customs beyond the county line. Additionally, this residency—which included basic introductions to Spanish, kinesthetics, and world geography—helped students meet performance goals like recognizing and solving problems and acting as responsible members of society. Rist also partnered with Shelby County's Title I and fine-arts teachers to connect the residency to communication and fine-arts standards.

Susan Eleuterio traveled to Shelby County to observe, provide technical assistance, and assess the residency. She kept meticulous notes, which generated additional data to evaluate the project. Here are some excerpts from her field notes with input from the teaching artist and the teachers.

❦ ❦ ❦ ❦ ❦ ❦ ❦

Shelbina Elementary School

Shelbina is in a rural area, two and a half hours northwest of St. Louis, where the rolling Mississippi Valley hills just start to become the flattened prairie of the Midwest. Redbud trees were in full rosy bloom and contrasted with the bright green of spring and the weathered exteriors of many buildings. Shelbina Elementary School is a low frame building with a small trailer behind where Title I coordinator Monica Mitchell's office is located. The walls were covered with brightly colored artwork. We were enchanted by a series of drawings focused on dance; the students clearly had thought about how people's bodies move when they are dancing, and a number of the works depicted couples with the woman dipped backwards as in a tango.

I arrived in Shelbina on Wednesday, May 7, to observe the third, fourth, and fifth days of the residency. By this time, Carmen Dence and percussionist Arthur Moore had been in town since Sunday evening and had already spent two full days with the children. Dence kept and shared the extensive notes she kept on the residency; she included artistic and educational concepts, daily logistics, and dance-movement techniques. She wrote, for instance, "The first day, after being introduced by contact teacher Lola Rist, we gave the students an overall description of what the residency would entail: the learning goals and the expectations. We encouraged the students to be an active part of their learning, to develop creativity, and to gain a sense of trust for their residency teachers." With updates on the first two days of the residencies, I was eager to observe the artists, the children, and their teachers in their third day.

Day Three, Shelbina

We met briefly with Monica Mitchell to review the day's schedule, then went to the school cafeteria, which was small but cheerfully decorated with posters and serves as the gym as well. Moore set up chairs with drums, maracas, and *guiros*, a gourd instrument, with scrapers for the kids. The first class, fifth-graders, arrived, and Dence had them begin with a series of warm-up moves. The students had been divided already into two teams: musicians and dancers. Moore took charge of his eleven percussionists as Dence's team practiced a variety of dance roles for the carnival. She used a flip chart to teach them about how the Baranquilla Carnivale was designated by the United Nations as a Repository of Oral Patrimony. She began with the Colombian flag, noting, "This is the flag of my country, Colombia, and it has three colors." She then demonstrated the movements of the *cumbia* and ways to use the flag in dance, moving from high, to medium, to low as it is waved. She told the kids, "You have to keep moving because you're in a carnival." The students were already divided into flag bearers, *puya* dancers, *animalitos* (tigers), a *monocucos* (like a drum major with a stick with ribbons), *garabato* dancers (girls with skirts), and a character representing Death, who uses a white hooked stick to take the dancers off the floor.

Among the roles that students danced in the carnival celebrations that were the culmination of Carmen Dence's residency were animalitos, in this case, tigers.

Photo by Willow Mullins.

Dence sketched a short choreography for each group of dancers, demonstrating the moves and repeating them. Rist helped the students with their moves and wrote down their steps with them. The monocucos and Death have a play fight in which the monocucos dies. Dence told the children, "We all die, so you must live your life and enjoy it; this is a happy dance." Each group learned about five moves and practiced them with Dence and the teachers while Moore and the student musicians provided rhythm. When the fourth-graders came in for their session, Dence welcomed them with "Buenos dias" ("good day" in Spanish). She began with the warm-up then quickly moved into rehearsal of the carnival dances.

Day Three, Clarence

Clarence Accelerated Elementary School is about twelve miles from Shelbina, an older brick building with benches indicating "Girls' Entrance" and "Boys' Entrance," a remnant from the past. The school has a large gym with a stage, which was a great space to set up the musicians. The halls, like those at Shelbina, were decorated with posters and children's art. We met Mary Jo Kattelman, the art teacher at both schools. I asked what prompts she gave the students before they started their drawings of dancers. She explained that they focused on the concepts of drawing lines—lazy horizontal lines and vertical lines like people standing—and they danced in class. As I had guessed, they also talked about the popular television show Dancing with the Stars. Dence explained to Rist and Kattelman that she wanted four students to read parts of a poem from an indigenous tradition, *kasipoluin*, a creation myth about the rainbow. She told the kids they would be doing a dance called *chichamaya*, a key component of Carnival, and she wanted them to wear costumes of white T-shirts and red scarves. Mr. Lyon, the fourth-grade teacher, provided a box of white T-shirts, and Dence provided the scarves, along with several other costumes she keeps for educational programs. Dence then selected some girls to be *damas* and dance the cumbia, another group to be a snake, and a group of boys to wear hats and scarves (representing rooster beaks), serving as *caballeros*.

Next, she showed the boys how to wear and move the hats and their hips. Rist and Kattelman practiced with the girls while Dence taught the boys their steps. Moore practiced soft percussion with his musicians. Fourteen girls wore long skirts; four girls were chosen to carry fishing net, representing fishermen from the ocean; and two others were chosen as flag bearers. Dence explained their role in the village would have been to announce, "There is a cumbia tonight," pointing out the lack of telephones and the Internet to spread the news in earlier times. She directed the boys to come in with their hats held high in front, then to kneel down while the girls came in using their skirts to swirl. Dence showed the girls how to pull up the corners of the skirts and move in and out together. Students were learning a folk dance with distinct gender roles, an echo of the boys' and girls' entrances at their school.

Day Four, Clarence

We began the day at Clarence with Mr. Lyon's fourth-grade and Mrs. Bode's fifth-grade classes. Dence announced, "We will be rehearsing for performance today." After a brief warm-up, Dence taught the chichamaya dance. She chose the tallest four girls to wear long dresses; one girl was to dance solo. Dence created a role for a number of kids as a snake. There were two students who had been absent on Wednesday, so

I asked them to help me run the boom box. As some students rehearsed the etiological poem about the creation of the rainbow, Dence explained that in the myth, a snake gave birth to the rainbow. A student was chosen to enter with colorful streamers representing the rainbow. Then Dence turned to the dancers, teaching another dance with a soloist who enacts a "play fight" with two boys. The entire group then gathered to practice the cumbia.

An exciting aspect of this residency was that the art and music teachers, the Title I coordinator, as well as classroom teachers became dance instructors. While Dence worked with one group, and Moore worked with the musicians, one or more of the teachers led the rest of the kids in practice. Too often in arts residencies, teachers are afraid to teach because they are not "experts" in the art form. Dence's method of teaching made everyone feel comfortable practicing and learning together.

Day Five, the Culminating Events

We began the day at Clarence. A group of senior citizens from a nearby nursing home was brought to the performance, and many family members and the cafeteria workers attended as well. An issue to consider with culminating events is that in many families (whether rural, suburban, or urban) both parents work, and they often find it difficult to attend daytime school events. In my own experience, the most successful events are held in the evening, but this was not possible for this residency. Still, parents, grandparents, students, teachers, cafeteria workers, and guests filled seats on the gym floor and in the balcony. Lisa Higgins introduced the program and artists, explaining also that the project was funded by state and federal tax dollars from the Missouri Arts Council and the National Endowment for the Arts. These kinds of announcements may seem obvious, but encouraging support for the arts is easier when citizens can see concrete examples of public arts funding, especially when their children are directly affected. With introductions complete, the students performed two intricate dances, with a solo by Carmen Dence in between, while teachers assisted students in their costume changes. The students were enthusiastic and remembered their dance moves well. The event was a great success, as evidenced by parents documenting the event, snapping photos and telling us about the excitement their children had expressed during the entire week of the residency.

We then packed up and headed to Shelbina Elementary School, where Monica Mitchell had arranged a lunch buffet in the Title I classroom in our honor. Again we were bombarded with stories about the enthusiasm of students and teachers throughout the week. Immediately afterward, Dence helped the students dress in their costumes and apply makeup where necessary. Three hundred parents, grandparents, younger siblings, and younger schoolchildren came to the culminating event at Shelbina, which was tied in with the Young Writers Conference, an annual event that families often attend. Like the morning program in Clarence, this culminating event was tailored to the students, the school's culture, and the space. At Shelbina the fourth-graders and the fifth-graders enacted a Carnival, complete with colorful flags, rousing music, and entertaining dances. Throughout the week, I had watched several very shy students, and I was impressed to see how well they performed at the final program. Dence has a knack for identifying student leaders, who made the more reluctant students comfortable. The enthusiastic participation of teachers as dancers also added to the children's confidence and overall fun. The animalitos dance and the battle with Death were very popular, eliciting shouts of momentary fear, followed quickly by squeals of delight from the audience.

♔ ♔ ♔ ♔ ♔ ♔ ♔

Why Folk Arts? Theory into Practice

On location in Shelby County, Higgins, Eleuterio, and Dence were recipients of positive feedback from parents, teachers, and administrators. Perhaps the most ringing endorsement for the residency was that the principal of Shelbina Elementary School donned a mask along with the other teachers and participated enthusiastically in the carnivals in her school's cafeteria. Once again Lola Rist used short writing assignments to help students document and apply the information they had acquired during the residency, as did Monica Mitchell. Additionally, some students spontaneously wrote unsolicited letters of praise and thanks for Carmen Dence and Arthur Moore. As with the Howard Marshall's Shelby County school residency in 2006, the students' written comments are good measures of the impact of the residency:

Dear Mrs. Dence and Mr. Moore, we all are so happy to be performing the show tomorrow. Mr. Moore, you are a good drummer. Mrs. Dence, you are a good dancer. Both teach all of us really well that we will be ready for the show. We wouldn't be ready if we didn't have as good as teachers as you people. We love to see you people doing different beats and different dances to go with the beats. We all are just so excited about doing the show. We love working with you. I wish we could do the show more than two times. I just want to say we are so happy to perform tomorrow and that we are going to ROCK the performance.

Your friend, Tayler

Dear Mrs. Dence and Mr. Moore, I am so excited about our dance on Friday. My family is coming to see the dance on Friday. I've been practicing every night when I get home. Well at least try to. So, my grandma and my mom are coming to the dance. I know my part already. I practiced with a skirt on. I am just so excited. So my grandma will take pictures. I'm just excited!

Your friend, Samantha

These two student assessments are typical of those expressed by their peers, using written language and letter writing to express what they have learned. They took initiative and practiced at home, and they were personally invested in doing their best during the performances. Clearly the children had established collegial bonds with the artists, recognized the artistic excellence of Dence and Moore, and sought to show off their newfound skills. Additionally, the students passed their enthusiasm on to family members, enticing them to attend the culminating event.

Much of what works in the residency model developed by the Missouri Folk Arts program echoes the work of educators James Moffett and B.J. Wagner. In their handbook *Student-Centered Language Arts and Reading K–12* (1983), Moffett and Wagner demonstrate the power of publication for students of language arts. In the case of the folk-arts residencies, performance-based production work with students can create authentic reasons for learning. Students know that they will perform (as the language-arts students know they will publish) in front of the entire school and their family members. The impending performance makes the lessons and rehearsals more relevant as students practice with a clear purpose and audience in mind. In fact, students often set their own high standards of excellence, instead of waiting for teachers and other adults to impose them.

In addition to the students' assessment, we also looked to the teachers for written feedback. The biggest challenge facing every classroom teacher is time, and a reality of every school—rich or poor, rural or urban, large or small—is that education is delivered in strictly measured segments: classroom periods are dictated by the bell. Little time is available for planning, execution, and evaluation, and what time remains is dictated by everything from federal mandates to school-improvement plans, individual student needs, the economy, and even the weather. Monica Mitchell is all too familiar with these time constraints and regulations, and she was new to the residency process, unlike Lola Rist. However, Mitchell quickly sensed the music teacher's enthusiasm for the residency, took a risk, and joined the planning process. She remained enthusiastic throughout the residency and provided positive feedback in notes to Susan Eleuterio:

> I feel like we all worked together so well, wanting the experience to benefit the kids. When everyone has the students as the main focus things will come together beautifully, and this residence was proof of that. I don't think it could have gone better. I heard so many positive comments from the kids, teachers, and parents—everyone involved. What a tribute! Many, many parents that I saw during the week said how their children hardly share anything about school, but they couldn't tell them enough about the residency and would show [their parents] some of what they learned that day. Wow!
>
> They couldn't say enough great things about it all! They LOVED [Mrs. Dence and Mr. Moore] and all of the activities of the week. I think the Carnival was the ultimate for them. It all helped them to realize more that there are other cultures out there besides just our little Shelby County here in Missouri. They need that because some of them don't get to travel and experience these differences.

As evidenced by this teacher's assessment, one beauty of a residency is that students begin to know the artists and develop a relationship with them and the content. Not only does Mitchell's evaluation reiterate lessons learned by the children, but she also recognizes the importance of the cultural content so pertinent to a folk-arts residency. Much of traditional folk learning takes place in informal settings—after work, around the dinner table, at family gatherings, or during community events. A residency—especially one sustained with interactions between teaching artists and students—can help recreate that informal learning setting. The residency artist can transmit knowledge and enrich learning in a less academic manner, a manner that is often more familiar to students and—dare we say it—fun.

Although Missouri's folk-arts residency project is new and being implemented slowly, we have learned how valuable the teaching artists, their accompanists and guest artists, and their stores of local knowledge are. We are also learning the challenges of the project:

- Although folk artists make excellent teaching artists, like most artists, they require training in statewide educational standards, tutorials on school culture, and strong support from arts administrators to maximize the impact of their residency.
- Educators are more receptive to new opportunities and resources when respected leaders in the community suggest them; for example, local arts administrators can link teaching artists with local schools more effectively than can rosters and mass mailings.
- Successful planning and execution of a school residency is time and people intensive.
- Schoolteachers also require strong support from arts administrators and funding agencies to host residencies, especially with the ever-growing time constraints imposed by standardized testing, the demands for teacher qualification, and other administrative duties.
- Opportunities for cross-generational and cross-cultural learning come during residencies with sustained contact among teachers, teaching artists, and students.

Missouri's folk-arts school residency model relies heavily on strong partnerships and active collaboration between teachers and school administrators, local arts councils, artists grounded in local knowledge, and folklorists with strong experience in the classroom and community arts.

Folk artists can become effective educators when they become students of school culture: honing skills in timing and information delivery, understanding students' complicated needs, and building appreciation for local knowledge and traditional culture. Additionally, folk artists are strong resources for teaching state standards through knowledge that is familiar, engaging, and accessible to teachers, students, and their families. However, teachers are often unaware that these resources are available. To harvest them, teachers need to expand their networks to include directors and board members of local community arts organizations. Schoolteachers often are eager to connect local knowledge to the curriculum but require concrete resources to expedite planning and funding. Teachers interested in folk arts in education need to learn how to access funding, find ways to make their schedule flexible for a residency, and make connections between their curriculum and the arts. School districts and state departments of education expect teachers to link all classroom content to educational standards, outcomes, basic skills, and critical thinking in key areas of knowledge like reading, writing, math, science, communication arts, and social studies. Arts-administration professionals at local and state agencies are a key link between teachers and the resources needed to enrich classroom learning. Community arts directors in Missouri have cultivated a rich, statewide network through MACAA and can tap into it to connect teachers with teaching artists, arts-education specialists, and folklorists. State arts-council staff members are eager to provide technical assistance as teachers plan school programs and apply for funding.

Our experience is that the results are worth the expense of resources. Through folk-arts residencies, teachers gain much-needed human and curricular resources; students are deeply engaged and learn to connect a sense of place with community knowledge; and folk artists are recognized as expert teachers. When teachers, students, and artists engage in content-rich, well-planned residencies—ones that are strongly linked to established educational standards—the results are not only exciting but also valuable. Through Missouri's newest folk-arts-in-education project, we have been able to show stakeholders ways to achieve their objectives with exciting outcomes based in the "Show-Me" state traditions and clearly linked with Missouri's educational standards.

Notes

1. Colloquially Missouri is known as the "show-me" state. According to the Web site of Missouri's secretary of state, the origin of the nickname is unknown. The most common legend, though, is that Missouri Congressman Duncan Vandiver, who served from 1897 to 1903, proclaimed in an 1899 speech, "I come from a state that raises corn and cotton and cockleburs and Democrats, and frothy eloquence neither convinces nor satisfies me. I am from Missouri. You have got to show me." Available online at http://www.sos.gov/archives/history/slogan.asp (accessed 15 January 2011).

2. With the success of a grassroots group called Missouri Friends of the Folk Arts, a program was created in the mid-1980s under the auspices of the University of Missouri's Cultural Heritage Center. A decade later, the center closed, and the Missouri Folk Arts program (MFAP) was established at the university's Museum of Art and Archaeology. Since its inception, the Missouri Arts Council has provided significant funding for MFAP's projects and operating budget.

3. A PDF copy of the guide is available online at our Web site at http://maa.missouri.edu/mfap

6

Every Student Rich in Culture
Nebraska Folklife Trunks

Gwendolyn K. Meister with Patricia C. Kurtenbach

THIS CHAPTER DESCRIBES THE AUTHORS' WORK COLLABORATING AS folklorist and teacher—along with other teachers and a state historian—to bring Nebraska history to classrooms across the state authentically, yet economically, and, most importantly, use folkloristic material to meet state education standards. Marrying the expertise of folklorists and educators produced the successful design of traveling trunks filled with culturally accurate resources relevant to current teaching demands and allowed students to learn state history firsthand through the experiences of a variety of the state's cultural groups. Social-studies educators today often emphasize point of view and primary source materials as well as artifacts. The involvement of Gwen as a folklorist who has been documenting Nebraska folklife for many years meant that trunks would include real-life primary sources and objects. Students would learn from interviews with tradition bearers from around the state, traditional music, images of authentic cultural expressions, an array of artifacts, and children's books that do not reinforce stereotypes. A veteran classroom teacher, Pat Kurtenbach outlines a variety of practical ways that teachers can easily use these trunks with their students. Teachers' input

Gwendolyn K. Meister is the executive director and folklorist for the Nebraska Folklife Network, a Lincoln-based nonprofit organization that documents, presents, and assists traditional artists and conducts the state folklife program.

Patricia C. Kurtenbach teaches fourth grade at Elliott Elementary School in Lincoln, Nebraska, with the goal of continuing to learn and grow, even after forty years in the classroom.

matched folklife content to essential education standards in social studies and English language arts and current education policy and practices.

Why Cultural Trunks

The Cultural Encounter Kit project began in 2004 when the Nebraska Humanities Council (NHC) and Meister's organization, the Nebraska Folklife Network (NFN), committed to a partnership to produce a series of history and folklife trunks to help address a problem identified by the Nebraska State Historical Society and other state educational organizations. Schoolchildren statewide were receiving very little instruction about Nebraska because few educational materials existed. The last comprehensive textbook about the state had been produced decades before. Most information about Nebraska in general social-studies and American history books was either inaccurate or focused only on the overland trails, homesteads, and Indian tribes of the pioneer era. Indeed, Nebraska was portrayed as a place people traveled through on their way to somewhere else, where nothing important had happened since pioneer days.

Conceptualization of the Nebraska history curriculum was influenced by another NHC program emphasis, New Nebraskans, focusing on newer immigrant groups in the state. NHC Executive Director Jane Hood was intrigued with the potential of profiling both newer and earlier immigrants to Nebraska through their folk arts, customs, and other cultural traditions and began a conversation about collaborating with NFN, resulting in the traveling-trunk concept. Both the NHC and NFN realized that to create trunks that would make sense in existing classroom curricula and practices, they needed to work closely with teachers enthusiastic about using them, and so collaboration with Kurtenbach ensued. She is a fourth-grade teacher with thirty-eight years of experience teaching in the Lincoln Public Schools (LPS), all at Elliott Elementary, a school in a low- to moderate-income, older neighborhood just south and a little east of downtown Lincoln.

The NFN offered staff time, volunteers, and travel costs to conduct fieldwork interviews and undertake research needed to create traveling cultural kits. The NHC agreed to fund the costs of producing the kits, housing the trunks, and checking out and distributing them to schools and other educational organizations across the state. As of 2010 the partnership had produced kits on the cultures of Mexican Americans, Germans from Russia, Vietnamese Americans, Swedish Americans, Iraqi Americans, and Irish Americans in Nebraska with additional kits in planning stages or process of development. Subject to the availability of funding, the partners want to profile the largest and most significant cultural groups in the state, which entails approximately twenty kits.

Outside and Inside the Kits

Cultural Encounter Kits travel in a heavy-duty plastic, wheeled box meant for storing and hauling tools. The toolbox has a pull-out handle on the front, a four-inch-deep plastic tray that nests just inside the top cover, and two seven-inch wheels on the back. The cover can be completely removed by unfastening two metal hasps, which accept various types of locks for security when the kits are shipped. UPS or comparable delivery services can ship them easily and relatively affordably. The kits are compact and mobile so that users can pick them up and transport them in car trunks or backseats.

The content of each kit varies with the cultural group, but in general the teacher's manual consists of six lessons—some divided into two or more parts—and master copies of all student handouts. Kits have a history timeline and a packet of up to fifty images, such as maps, drawings, charts, and many photographs on 8½ by 11 numbered, captioned, and laminated pages. Each kit contains excerpts of audio interviews with Nebraska traditional artists and tradition bearers from the featured cultural group, CDs of traditional music, videos of the culture and history of the featured group, and artifacts such as traditional clothing in various sizes to fit students, cooking utensils, games and toys, holiday decorations, a national flag from the home country (if appropriate), and other culturally relevant objects. Kits also hold one copy each of a number of publications appropriate for fourth- through eighth-grade students. These are bilingual when possible and usually include an ethnic cookbook, a bilingual dictionary, a general history or social-studies book about the cultural group's place of origin, picture books of folktales and other traditional stories, a book of proverbs or traditional poetry, stories of immigration by or about children and teenagers who are members of the cultural group, and books on the holidays, traditional arts or crafts, and other cultural activities and traditions of the group. For example, one kit contains the following:

❦ ❦ ❦ ❦ ❦ ❦ ❦

A Treasured Heritage: Mexican Americans in Nebraska

☐ Teacher's guide (eighty-five pages of lesson plans with background information for the teacher and connections to state educational standards) and student handout masters
☐ Image packet (timelines, maps, charts, forty-five laminated photos)
☐ Artifacts
   • Traditional clothing
      o two girls' embroidered blouses similar to traditional ones in many Mexican regions
      o one red "practice skirt," a double-full long skirt used in many Mexican folk dances
      o one boy's long-sleeved shirt with embroidery detail
      o three rebozos—long fringed scarves or shawls
      o two waist sashes (one red and one striped in colors of the Mexican flag) usually worn with traditional dance costumes by men and boys
      o three bandanas (one each red, yellow, and black) usually worn around men's necks along with western shirts in the northern Mexican states
      o one miniature sombrero
   • Additional artifacts
      o one large Mexican flag
      o one miniature piñata
      o one box of Mexican chocolate used for hot chocolate
      o one *molinillo*—a wooden stirrer for frothing hot chocolate
      o one set of *molcajete* (mortar) and *tejolote* (pestle) of black lava stone
      o one *escobeta*—natural bristle brush for cleaning the *molcajete*
      o one tortilla press
☐ Media
   • Audio
      o CDs of various genres of traditional Mexican music
      o CDs of interviews with Mexican Americans living in

Eighth-graders examine a tortilla press from the Mexican American folklife trunk.

different parts of Nebraska and transcriptions
- Video
    - *Chulas Fronteras* and *Del Mero Corazon* by Les Blanc
    - a video of the Sangre Azteca dancers, a Lincoln Ballet Folklorico group, performing traditional dances from many parts of Mexico at the Nebraska State Fair
- Print
    - Children's books—many bilingual—including fiction and non-fiction titles

❦ ❦ ❦ ❦ ❦ ❦ ❦ ❦

Teacher Involvement

After researching folklife trunks and curricula in other states and local museums, Meister was convinced that teachers should be involved as early as possible in creating the Nebraska cultural kits. The first to come on board was Lois Herbel, an NFN board member who was a retired teacher from Gering, Nebraska, and had done exemplary classroom cultural projects focusing on Mexican Americans and Germans from Russia in her western Nebraska community. She and Meister went to work writing and designing the first two kits. The plan also included NHC-funded stipends to compensate teachers for reviewing draft materials and testing prototypes. Six fourth-grade classroom teachers and two eighth-grade social-studies teachers signed on: four from Lincoln and four from small-town or rural school districts in various parts of the state. Meister corresponded with them for several months and met each in person at least once when delivering kits to the teachers at their schools. Teachers wrote evaluations in the teacher's guides and a report about their experiences with the kits they tested. In addition, Meister visited several classrooms to observe students interacting with the materials and talk with the teachers.

Kurtenbach worked closely with Meister and now makes presentations at teacher in-service training workshops and conferences on integrating the kits with required curriculum. In 2008 Kurtenbach's school, Elliott Elementary, had 38 percent English-language-learner (ELL) students, predominately from Mexico and other Latin American countries but also from Asia and the Middle East. There were 33 percent European American students, and the remaining 29 percent were African American, Native American, and multiracial. The school is more than 80 percent low income and so qualifies for Title I funds. Kurtenbach said, "Our school has grown in ethnic diversity over the years I've taught there, but it has always been an interesting and lively place to teach."

She teaches the LPS educational-equity class for teachers, exploring racism, sexism, ageism, prejudice against people with disabilities, and other equity issues. She has also been involved in the LPS Multicultural Committee, which intends every Lincoln school to model cultural diversity through programs and curricula. She agreed to test the kits because the project strongly connected to fourth-grade curriculum, commenting, "We're very tied into standardized testing right now. That's been everyone's priority and ours especially because we're a low-income school where you might start the year with maybe half the kids in your class up to grade level in reading and math, if you're lucky. That's a real challenge. So we didn't have time for things that weren't tied into the curriculum." She continued,

> I looked at the teacher's guide when we first met, and I saw that you had done all that work of looking at the Nebraska social-studies content standards and matching each lesson to specific standards. I could see how the kit material fit into what I was required to teach. The topics covered in the lessons fit with the U.S. Southwest-region studies that we were doing, as well as Nebraska studies and learning about the

increasing numbers of Mexican Americans coming to live and work in Nebraska. I could see the tie-ins, so it made sense to get the kit and give it a try.

When asked how she figured out how to use the kit in the classroom, Kurtenbach said,

I had to study the teacher's manual a bit. It covers a lot. It's very comprehensive. After all, you designed it so that it can be used by teachers in fourth through eighth grade. Also it's designed so that teachers can pick and choose what parts they use. I looked through it and chose the lessons on Mexican American immigration and cultural integration. Those had the strongest connections to what I was teaching. To set the framework, I also used the first lesson, "What Is Culture?" I wanted to make it really clear to kids—think it through with them—that culture isn't something just "other people" have. Everyone has traditional foods, common sayings and expressions, certain ways they dress, things they believe, ways they perform, and so on. I wanted to help them make those connections so that not only the Hispanic kids but all the kids saw themselves as rich in culture.

I used the bilingual picture book *In My Family/En Mi Familia* (Garza 2000) from the kit because on each page is a different Mexican family custom, like a birthday barbecue or a traditional treatment for an earache. So I read some of these to the class, and then we talked about what their families did in those situations. I asked if there were any home remedies they had, or if there were any birthday traditions.

So, using the framework of culture and folklife as they were defined in the kit, we took pages from the book and brainstormed ways that category fit with their lives. Kids who thought they didn't have any traditions then realized they have lots of them. They said, "Oh yes, we do a certain cake every year for the birthday cake," or "My mom checks my temperature by kissing my forehead."

I talked about my background being a mixture of Swedish and Irish. It's not just about pumping for information and trying to get kids to reveal themselves. You need to share and reveal yourself, too. The whole idea is recognizing that what seems common and ordinary to you is often an important expression or component of your culture. It's realizing those ordinary things *are* your celebrations, your traditions, and your beliefs. Using the kit, I helped my students become more conscious of that.

Asked about parts of the kit that she felt were not appropriate for her class, Kurtenbach replied, "The history part and the acculturation and assimilation part both go into more detail than I would for fourth grade. Also

Photo courtesy of the Nebraska Folklife Network.

An eighth-grade girl models clothing from the Mexican American folklife trunk.

the part on language—learning about culture through language—has more depth than needed in fourth grade but is useful in higher grades."

Kurtenbach found that some of her Mexican American students were familiar with artifacts from the kit such as the *molcajete* (a black lava mortar for grinding chilies and spices), *tejolote* (pestle), tortilla press, and miniature piñata. She chose to display the traditional clothing, rather than let students dress up in it, even though some students had been in dance troupes and had the experience of wearing such things as the double-full practice dance skirt. She later thought that she might do that differently and choose volunteers to try the clothing on to emphasize that the clothing is not a party costume but should be worn or used respectfully.

Teaching in Activity Centers

Kurtenbach shared the titles and covers of all the books from the kit with the whole class and many of the images as well, especially those of Mexican American children or families in Lincoln, Scottsbluff, and other Nebraska communities. She gave an overview of everything in the kit as an introduction to setting up activity centers so that students could experience the components more closely:

When using centers it's very important to make it clear to students that there's a purpose for each that is tied to social-studies objectives. It's not a time to socialize with your friends or catch up on the latest TV show. It's not something you can just spring on kids without planning, setting your goals, and practicing. You need to show students what it looks like to work well at a center without direct teacher supervision. I had the objectives in written form both on a little stand-up chart in each center and on individual handouts for kids. So they knew exactly what to do in each center.

Also when developing centers, I always think about what learning styles and modes provide a balanced experience once a student has rotated through all of them. There is usually a center where kids make something. In this case, they made tissue paper *papel picado* banners to decorate the classroom. There were centers featuring listening, reading, looking at images, taking notes from videos, and handling and describing artifacts in depth. So the centers really tied into reading and writing objectives as well, not just social studies. And that's really important, too. Anytime you can overlap other disciplines and strengthen everything that students are practicing, it's a plus.

For the photo center, I chose photos that were Nebraska related and would mean the most to students, such as three boys on their low-rider bikes, mariachi bands, a young Scottsbluff woman's *quinceañera*, and so on. I asked them to choose one to write about either in a descriptive paragraph or a shorter description and tell the ways that the subject of the photo contributes to Mexican American culture. As a last step, I asked all the students to list similarities between the photo and their own cultural experiences. In the case of the boys on low-rider bicycles, for example, students might have modified their bikes in some way or made a homemade skateboard. They might have worked with a parent on some other project in the same way that the boys in the picture worked on the bikes with their fathers.

My approach was to do the centers forty-five minutes a day for five days so that by the end of a week, everyone got through all of them. Students were explaining what they were thinking and telling how they made their choices. The lessons also lend themselves to being taught in the traditional format, where you introduce them, do a guided activity with the class, and then have the students do an independent activity. You could also have students work individually. They could each make their own family trunk. Alternatively, you could do a class or a school trunk. If kids did their own, they could just make a shoebox trunk, for example.

Assessment was part of the reason I decided to tie the kit closely to the study of the Southwest region and Nebraska history. Both units have

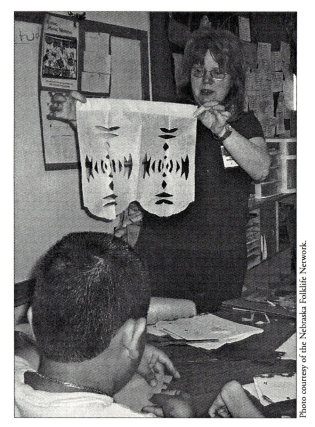

Pat Kurtenbach uses samples from the Mexican American trunk to teach *papel picado*.

curriculum-related tests (CRTs) that teachers are required to administer. So those are what I used for assessment. Otherwise I would have been taking time away from what kids were actually going to be tested on.

Making Kits Teacher Accessible

It is evident that Kurtenbach, as an experienced teacher, had a number of advantages in using the cultural kit effectively in her classroom. It takes a certain amount of extra effort for all teachers just to reserve the resource and fit it into an already-tight schedule, but using the kits makes certain intellectual demands for which Kurtenbach was already quite prepared. Some of the more challenging were the following:

1. Choosing the parts that most closely fit with the curriculum units she was teaching;
2. Introducing students to the activity-center experience and modeling ways to work appropriately in them;
3. Setting goals for the total learning experience that she wanted students to have and thinking through the activities, directions, and products that would create that experience;
4. Structuring experiences in the activity centers to use different modes of learning and incorporate various reading, writing, drawing, and thinking skills; and
5. Creating and maintaining an atmosphere of respect for the culture being studied.

In addition, Kurtenbach needed to know or learn some practical things beforehand to use the kits effectively. These ranged from writing effective instructions for the self-guiding activity centers to anticipating the ways that students were likely to behave in various situations and helping them focus on the tasks at hand. She suggested a number of ways to help less-experienced teachers gain the knowledge and practical skills they need to use the kits. These tips also can enhance use of other folklife resources.

1. Give teachers the opportunity to examine the resources first-hand when possible.
2. Provide written suggestions (and training, when possible) that give teachers the opportunity to think and plan beforehand about ways that they can incorporate the resource into their curricula.
3. Provide as complete a depiction of the kit as possible in print, photos, and online promotional materials.
4. Make sure that teachers know it is important to familiarize students with the activity-center experience and provide clear directions and expectations.
5. Give teachers information on respectful ways for students to interact with materials such as traditional art objects, clothing, flags, and other cultural symbols.

Conclusion

The Cultural Encounter Kits have proven very popular with educators as well as students. NHC checks them out for three weeks on a first-come, first-served basis to librarians, museum educators, classroom teachers, and other Nebraska educators. Tying lessons to the state standards in English language arts as well as social studies was essential to success, as was creating flexible lesson plans that guide educators in using some or all of the items and activities in each kit. Involvement of folklorists has meant that the information, images, and artifacts are authentic to the cultural groups represented. The partnership of NHC and NFN is certainly key, and both organizations anticipate continuing to develop these kits, connecting young people with ancestors and neighbors old and new.

7

Folkvine.org
Exploring Arts-Based Research and Habits of Mind

Kristin G. Congdon with Karen Branen

FOLLOW A VIRTUAL BACK ROAD TO A VISITOR's center to learn about Florida folk artists. Folkvine.org marries folklore, folk art, arts education, and technology through rich, accessible, and compelling media. Over a period of four years—with the support of seven grants—faculty and students from the University of Central Florida (UCF) worked with artists and their communities to create individual postcard Web sites of ten different artists (or groups of artists), four tour guides, several podcasts, and two curricula. Although the product is primarily a Web site (http://www.folkvine.org), the project also included public events and scholarly publications and presentations. This chapter 1) briefly describes the Web site and the team's arts-based research approach, 2) explores the practice of using Folkvine.org in an elementary classroom based on three of the Harvard University Project Zero's eight Studio Habits of Mind, and 3) describes ways—based on working with this rich and varied Web site—folk art and folklore can enrich teachers' and students' learning experiences.

The Project

In the early stages of the project, our goal seemed simple: to document folk artists creatively on the Web. We were interested in the way that learning

---

Kristin G. Congdon is a professor emerita of philosophy and humanities and former director of the Cultural Heritage Alliance at the University of Central Florida.
Karen Branen is an elementary art teacher in Seminole County, Florida, and an adjunct faculty member at Rollins College.

Front porch of the visitor's center, the information focus of Folkvine.org.

was becoming more Web based, and we wanted to explore ways that a Web site could be developed from a folkloric perspective. We wondered how ethnographic research could be presented in an interactive manner, and we wanted to investigate ways that an artistic presentation of folklore material could compel a participant to learn.

Craig Saper, a UCF English professor, and coauthor Kristin Congdon wrote a grant to the Florida Humanities Council to explore how they might translate works of art and ethnographic processes to a Web environment. Because neither of them knew much about the technical aspects of the project, their first team members were doctoral students in the UCF Texts and Technology Program. However, it wasn't until Chantale Fontaine, an undergraduate art student who shyly asked if she could help, joined the team that they had the dynamic technological and artistic vision they desperately needed. Faculty and students from various disciplines joined the group from 2003 to 2007, the four years of active work on the Web site. All but one of the selected artists had been highlighted in Congdon's coauthored book, *Just above the Water: Florida Folk Art,* which was just being finished when the project started. The many years spent working on this book proved to be invaluable because Congdon had established relationships and trust with all the artists she had interviewed. Team members collectively selected the artists who would be documented. Choices were made based on an attraction to the work, interest in the artist's creative motivations, and ease in gaining access to the artist and his or her community. Considerations of diversifying the Web site according to race, ethnicity, gender, and economic class were also part of the selection process.

The artists—in the order they were documented—are 1) Ruby Williams, an African American farmer and produce-stand owner whose paintings grew out of the signage she made to sell her fruits and vegetables; 2) Ginger LaVoie, a Hawaiian quilt maker who is culturally, but not biologically, Polynesian, having lived and studied with an elderly quilter for twenty years; 3) Diamond Jim Parker (now deceased), a retired clown and circus historian who created miniature model circuses; 4) the Scott family, including Wayne and Marty and their son Allen, who make clown shoes and props; 5) Kurt Zimmerman, a retired engineer from Florida's Space Coast, who paints parallel universes as a way to reconcile the trauma he experienced during World War II; 6) Lilly Carrasquillo, who designs and constructs Puerto Rican *vejigante* masks; 7) Taft Richardson, who works to heal his African American neighborhood and the children who live there by making sculpture from the bones of roadkill; 8) Nicario Jimenéz, a Peruvian *retablo* maker whose subject matter reflects both his Andean heritage and his new life in the United States; 9) Eileen Brautman, a *katuba* maker (Jewish wedding contracts); and 10) a bobbin lace-making group in central Florida. The Web sites on Lilly Carrasquillo and Nicario Jimenéz are in both Spanish and English. Artists' Web sites are displayed as interactive postcards that sit on a rack on the counter of a Florida visitor's center. You get to the visitor's center by virtually driving down a road, stopping at the building, and opening the porch door. The idea is that you can get to know a lot about Florida by learning about our Folkvine artists.

We quickly realized that the artists and artist groups were so different that we needed humanities concepts to weave them together as a collective that had similar experiences related to their artistic lives. Three "tour guides" were created that addressed issues that became titles for the booklets: "Recreative Identity," "Social Economy," and "Placemaking Imagination." These guides unite the artists in universal processes, thereby communicating to the Web participant that the Folkvine artists are connected in ways that reflect their creative processes and human needs. In designing these tour guides, we recognized that—in the case of each of our artists—creating art was clearly and carefully linked to a process of shaping identity, building a life based on social capital, and imaginatively making a place to live

Photo courtesy of the Folkvine team.

Postcard of Taft Richardson, who creates sculptures from roadkill.

and work. For instance, in the "Placemaking Imagination" guide, artists are linked to their landscape as readers learn how interaction between artists and the environment changes both. The ways that inspiration, reflection, and identity can come from understanding one's place in the world become clear. Lisa Roney and Chantale Fontaine later made a fourth tour guide on the process of making Folkvine so that Web participants can gain some insight into the ways that creative and technical Web-design decisions were made.

Documentaries, as we all know, are never just about the subjects of projects. They are also about the researchers and producers.[1] As we progressed, we understood that we—as team members (apart from the artists/subjects)—also had a presence in the site. To acknowledge this important fact, we created bobble heads to represent some of the team members and placed them on a shelf in the visitor's center. We speak—not on the artists' sites—but through the virtual tour guides. On the bottom shelf of the counter is a radio, where we experimented with podcasts. Follow the arrow in the visitor's center to the game room to find two curricula. One is a board game for elementary students; the other is a zine (a small magazine) for high-school students. Both connect to Florida's "Sunshine State Standards."

Photo courtesy of the Folkvine team.

The counter in the visitor's center with its colorful displays.

Arts-Based Research

Increasingly we are realizing that how we see has become as important as what we see (Mondloch 2007). When using an arts-based research methodology, researchers become as engaged with the questions that are raised about the way that something is constructed as what is constructed.[2] Arts-based research in educational practices has its roots in a number of dissertations written at Stanford University under the direction of Eliot Eisner. This new methodology is called *educational criticism.* According to Melisa Cahnmann-Taylor, "Eisner's student, Tom Barone, took educational criticism and developed it into a new arts-based methodology, *narrative storytelling*" (2008, 5–6). While educational criticism comes from the position of a connoisseur, narrative storytelling allows and encourages the researcher to participate in creating the story. As postmodernism gained favor with those doing qualitative research, arts-based research became even broader and riskier as it incorporated artistic processes. Today there are a wide variety of ways that this method of doing research is incorporated into educational practices (Cahnmann-Taylor 2008, 6).

In the case of Folkvine, we not only constructed a narrative among our artists and ourselves, but we also allowed the artwork to pose questions for us as researchers. As the project progressed, we raised questions about the artists' aesthetics and how to present them, the ways that the tour guides should function and why we needed them, and how we constructed learning by creating the Web site as we did, complete with nonconventional navigation routes. We also asked how Folkvine.org changed or extended the process of navigation. Continuously we wondered what exactly it was that we were creating. Was it a Web site about our artists/subjects? Was it a work of art motivated by our artists/subjects? What, exactly, were we teaching others with this Web site? And what was our ethical responsibility in creating Folkvine.org (Congdon 2006)?[3]

We recognized, as Jacques Derrida has argued, that as translators of artists/subjects' lives and work, we are privy to more meaning than we can communicate effectively on the Web (Di Stefano 2002). We sort through numerous still pictures and video and audio clips and select the story we want to tell. Our selection perhaps says more about our needs and desires for the lessons we wish to present than about our artists/subjects. Although we try to represent what the artist would want us to say about him or her, if we are truthful, we choose those things that interest us most. These may be snippets of knowledge or information that fit current theories. Or they may be ideas that our disciplines have told us are important to address. These ideas may or may not be of primary interest to the artists. An arts-based research approach tries to make these processes visible. It is important to make this point clear to elementary students as they engage in the game that we designed for them. We want them to know that when you design a Web site, plan an event, or do ethnographic research, you make choices. Consequently, there are many ways to construct knowledge in the arts.

Elementary Curriculum and Habits of Mind

A Florida Department of State, Division of Cultural Affairs, folk-arts grant funded the elementary curriculum. Karen Branen,[4] an art teacher from Sterling Park Elementary School in Casselberry, Florida, led the pilot testing on this educational component of the Web site. Sterling Park is in a suburb north of Orlando, and the students who attend it come from varying ethnic groups and all economic brackets. Branen worked with six classes of fourth-grade students, including children who were in special-education and English as a second language classes. Students in her classes are ethnically diverse, coming from South and Central America and the Middle East, as well as Europe. Including art from different cultures has always been central to her teaching approach. Despite the challenges posed by students who speak various languages, Sterling Park consistently is recognized as an excellent school. For many years, it has received an A in Florida's grading system for schools. At the time of this writing, the game remains in the school art room on the computer as a DVD so that students can play it when they have finished their assigned projects.

We selected three artists for the elementary board game: Ruby Williams, Kurt Zimmerman, and Lilly Carrasquillo. We chose these artists because we felt they would appeal to young children, they were less controversial in content than some of the other artists (for example, they didn't deal with violence), and they represented diversity in creative expression and approaches to art making. Branen's students engaged in the Web site in three main ways: 1) helping design the site, 2) making masks based on the work of Lilly Carrasquillo, and 3) evaluating the site to recommend changes.

Nathan Draluck, a UCF philosophy graduate student who was studying for a degree in liberal studies, was the primary Web designer for the site.[5] Draluck had experience working with folk artists at the House of Blues in Orlando[6] and had taken classes that included folklore study. Working with the other members of the Folkvine education team,[7] Draluck suggested that we have students at Sterling Park draw certain components of the Web site so that they had ownership in the process. This approach would also make it "feel" like a game for children. They made animals, fruits, and vegetables for Ruby Williams's site; UFOs, spaceships, and planets for Kurt Zimmerman's site; and suns, animals, reptiles, and birds for Lilly Carrasquillo's site. The drawings delighted the team members and quickly became part of the game.

As the game was being developed, Branen introduced her fourth-grade students to Lilly Carrasquillo's artwork. They enjoyed knowing that she was Puerto Rican and immediately identified her with their Puerto Rican classmates. The Puerto Rican students were thrilled to have an artist represented who was like them. Like Carrasquillo, the students used papier-mâché and their imaginations, taking ideas from many cultures and places to make a character or a statement. By the time the game was ready for the students to pilot, they already had a great deal of knowledge about this one artist and her traditions.

The third way the students participated was by playing the game and giving the team feedback on what worked and what didn't. They immediately saw that their drawings had been incorporated, and this pleased

Photo courtesy of the Folkvine team.

Board with avatar for Kurt Zimmerman's game, one of several possibilities for playing Folkvine's innovative, interactive game.

them very much. Branen reports that they knew exactly who had done what drawing, and this became an important participatory aspect of the game.

Similarly to an old-fashioned board game, players first get to create their avatar—or player—in our game. The students quickly communicated concerns with this aspect. Although the avatar was designed in a cartoon manner, they felt there were not enough diverse options to represent them all as individuals. In response Draluck expanded the ways that the avatar could be created. It can now have hats, horns, antennae, or polka dots. Skin color can be green or purple, as well as light brown. Many options are included for the body and legs. With the expanded possibilities, this first step became a favorite part of the game for the students.

Students also responded that they liked the humor in many of the questions. They often discussed their ideas and answers with other classmates, laughing at the options presented for selecting answers. For example, one of the possible answers to the question of what to do if your PA system breaks just before the event is to ask all the speakers to yell. Another poses a scenario in which a friend wonders whether she should attend Lilly Carrasquillo's event because she doesn't speak Spanish, and a possible answer is to tell her to learn Spanish quickly. Informal discussion often ensued, and Branen carried on conversations with the class on topics of interest. It also became clear that the content was a mix of easy-to-answer and challenging questions for fourth-graders. Many students played the game on one artist more than once, trying to beat their previous score.

The game is set up to incorporate the player as part of the Folkvine team. The player's job is to learn about the artist he or she selected and plan a public event for that artist, much as we did when we developed the Web sites. Consequently—when playing the game—students need to think about audiences, community resources, refreshments, and program activities. In many ways, they have to think and act like a public-sector folklorist.

The game is designed with a curvy road, and you move on it the way you would on Monopoly or Candyland board games. You pick a card that corresponds to the space that your avatar occupies. There are three kinds of cards. The question mark indicates task questions related to information about the artists. The horseshoe cards are about planning the event, and the cards with two lines that come together at a right angle are the detour cards. These cards pose more conceptual questions about the artists. Detour cards are worth 250 points while the other two are worth 50 points each. If you don't answer a detour question correctly, you must deviate from the main road, and the game takes you longer to complete. If, at any time, a player needs to research a question about an artist, his or her Web site is easily accessed from the game board. There are more questions than can be answered by anyone playing the game, so a student can play the game for any one artist more than once. Questions are generated randomly. Stars that light up on the lower right-hand side of the computer screen record points. At the end of the game, the players are told how well they did as an event planner. Narrative answers can be discussed in classrooms with teachers if the game is played as a group activity.

To help us evaluate the content of the game, we looked to Harvard Project Zero's Studio Habits of Mind. Carefully analyzing the research, Lois Hetland, Ellen Winner, Shirley Veenema, and Kimberly Sheridan (2007) argue that many claims about the value of arts education have not been substantially proven.[8] Instead of false claims, they promote eight Studio Habits of Mind.[9] These characteristics, they believe, are central to studio work in the visual arts. They are also primarily taught through a general arts-education curriculum that encompasses more than just making art. Focusing on these Studio Habits of Mind is important for many reasons. They teach students to be flexible, turn things upside down and shift directions, and imagine unique and innovative ways to solve problems. By building these habits, students can see relationships between things as they gain an ability to explore the power of the imagination. John Dewey built his ideas about education on grounding ideas in experience, and he recognized that these kinds of skills were necessary for a successful democracy to function.

In the Folkvine elementary board game, we concentrated on three of these habits: observe, reflect, and stretch and explore. These three were selected to provide a focus for evaluation. They seemed to fit best with Folkvine because they appeared to mimic what so many of the Folkvine artists do in their creative lives. We evaluated these characteristics based on observations made by Branen and written comments from students.

Habit of Mind I: Observe

Many of the students looked at the Web site on their home computers before playing the game. When the Folkvine artists were introduced in class, these students recognized their work and could talk about it. From looking at Lilly Carrasquillo's work, they understood where she got her inspiration and could then apply that idea to their own creative process of making masks. When asked to make drawings for the board game, they readily understood why certain subjects were associated with selected artists. For example, it made sense that a board for Kurt Zimmerman would feature UFOs and spaceships, since he painted parallel universes and worked at the Space Coast. Students discussed how artists were able to take ideas from their everyday lives and experiences and make them relevant in their artwork. They also recognized that art could be made from many kinds of materials, not just those they had thought about as traditional "art materials."

Habit of Mind II: Reflect

The students had many kinds of reflections on the project. They talked about how and why masks sometimes hang on walls instead of being worn, and what the differences are in making masks for different occasions and functions. They talked about the kinds of masks they made and what they communicated, much as Carrasquillo does on the Web site. Students explored ways to elicit emotional responses to their work such as making a mask funny or scary. They incorporated textures and patterns that were identified in the Folkvine artists' work into their personal artwork as they explored ideas about communicating personality and identity. To answer the questions in the board game, they had to reflect on information they

Photo courtesy of the Folkvine team.

Puerto Rican mask maker Lilly Carrasquillo working in her studio.

had learned about the artist to make the best decisions possible as an event planner.

Habit of Mind III: Stretch and Explore

Branen observes that her students today are very savvy about technology. This is true even for low-income students. They all know how to use computers, many have iPods and cell phones, and they all play video games. They also play educational games in school, especially for reading and math. So playing a video game in art class made sense to them. Stretching and exploring therefore did not take place in using the computer; rather, they were experienced in the content of the game. There were, however, many ways that students engaged in this third habit of mind. For example, while they didn't always use the same art materials in their masks that Carrasquillo does, they recognized that materials can come from almost everywhere and experimenting with them is a common practice of an artist. Working with Carrasquillo's masks made them think about previous lessons they had in art class about African masks and those that First Nations people made and used in rituals. They connected the functions to many other cultures, including their own.

In playing the game, they repeatedly had an opportunity to see the way something in an artist's life or background could make a difference in that person's work. For example, they understood that Kurt Zimmerman's birth in Germany made it difficult for him to fight against his homeland when he was a young man. They were then asked to think about the place where they had been born to see what significance this might have in their lives and artwork. Time and again, the board game asked them to notice how something influences an artist and that a similar situation might impact them as artists and human beings.

It seems clear that students involved in the Folkvine elementary game build skills in at least three of the eight habits of mind. The game uses technology, which is familiar and compelling to young children, and it is engaging enough that students learn by observing and reflecting on what they see and learn. They also stretch and explore ideas and concepts largely because the narrative section of the game asks students to apply a question or idea to their experience. This Folkvine game is but one example of the ways folklore is a valuable component of an arts-education curriculum.

Folklore and Education

There are many ways to approach folk art in arts-education settings beyond simply having students replicate a folk-art tradition, which can be problematic (Congdon 1987; Delacruz 1999). And there are many lessons that can be learned from the Folkvine.org site besides those we've described. Among them are these: 1) both tradition and innovation are important to our lives and creative work; 2) community context is a significant factor in understanding artwork; 3) shaping our identities depends on looking at multiple lives; and 4) creativity and acceptance of diversity prepare students to participate in the new market economy of the creative class. These are lessons that cross educational disciplines and have relevance to teachers in social studies and language arts, among other disciplines.

Tradition and Innovation

Modern art has created such a strong focus on innovation that tradition is often devalued. While we need to acknowledge and raise the value of tradition in our lives, we also need to see folk art as full of innovation. It is difficult to function effectively without both the stability provided by tradition and change initiated by innovation. According to David Lowenthal,

We cannot function without familiar environments and links with a recognizable past, but we are paralyzed unless we transform or replace inherited relics; even our biological legacy undergoes continual revision. Yet to cope amidst change we also need considerable continuity with the past. The cultural legacy, too, is conservative *and* innovative: survival requires an inheritable culture, but it must be malleable as well as stable. (1985, 69)

It is clear that Folkvine artists have demonstrated ways that they both adhere to cultural traditions and invent new ways to engage with them. This decisive place where tradition and innovation merge is a position where students should become comfortable. This is the space where opportunities for critical thinking reside. Ruby Williams needed to make a living on her ancestors' farm after moving back home from many years in New Jersey. While adhering to her family's traditional farming practices, she expanded the function of her produce signs to make them folk art that she could sell along with her fruits and vegetables. Nicario Jimenéz took the traditional *retablo* practices from his Andean ancestors and began telling nontraditional stories with them. These stories related to his new home in the United States. They incorporated the history lessons he had learned about civil rights and the experience of visiting New York City (Congdon and Bucuvalas 2006).

Lucy Lippard argues that rootedness doesn't necessarily only come from time spent in a certain place. She claims that "psychological ties can be as strong as historical ones and they can be formed by 'rootless' individuals" (1997, 42). It all depends on how strong one's longing for roots is. Ruby Williams became a folk artist because she is innovative enough to extend her family's farming traditions to painting signage. In doing so, she paints folk wisdom she learned from her community, like "it hurts to hate," or she makes up new sayings that reflect on her own personal experience, like "timing me is wrong." Through her innovation, she grounds herself more deeply in her identity.

The same is true for Nicario Jimenéz as he uses the traditional *retablo* art form of his father and grandfather and applies it to the experiences of his new home in Florida. His tradition helps him better connect his new life to his heritage. When you think of innovation and tradition in this manner, they are no longer simply linear aspects of a creative process. Instead, they fully entwine. They also constitute valuable approaches and practices of problem solving and inventiveness for students.

Community Context

All the Folkvine artists appear on the Web site in their community contexts, whether they are occupational, regional, religious, ethnic, or some other form of cultural association. It is impossible to evaluate the artwork without some understanding of context. Often the community or communities where the artist primarily creates have their own evaluative criteria. It is important that audiences understand the function of the particular art within that context (Congdon 2004; Brenson 1995).

Some Folkvine artists, such as Ruby Williams and Taft Richardson, reveal an interconnectedness to other than humans. Increasingly our relationship to plants, animals, and the natural and built environment is becoming crucial to our survival and that of the Earth. Michael Brenson explains that it "is this fact of interdependency or interconnectedness, of shared circumstances or interests which constitutes the unity of community and which enables solidarity—the acknowledgement and valuing of relatedness in the midst of differences within a community" (1995, 21). Ruby Williams could not adequately be studied as an artist without understanding her connection to her family's land and the joy that she gets from growing and eating fruits and vegetables. Taft Richardson, who makes sculptures from the bones of dead animals, creates his art as a way of enacting resurrection, not only of the animals but also his neighborhood, which has fallen victim to crime and poverty. Caring for bones, synthesizing the material, for Richardson, replicates the resurrection of Christ. As he teaches neighborhood children art, he incorporates the lessons he has learned in his church community and shows his students ways to renew themselves as productive, healthy individuals.

Shaping Identities

Regardless of age, we are all always shaping our identities. Mary Catherine Bateson, whose parents were the famed anthropologists Margaret Mead and Gregory Bateson, recognizes that we "need to look at multiple lives to test and shape our own" (1990, 16). Through the eyes of a group of Florida folk artists, Folkvine offers students diverse views of the world and many ways of interacting with it. The goal is to acknowledge the creative choices we have in forming our identities. While each Folkvine artist is rooted in one or more traditions, each individual explores his or her place within that space by adhering to its cultural values, changing or adapting them, or rejecting them. Lippard understands that being a part of a community doesn't mean that you accept all aspects of that group; rather, it "means knowing how to work within differences as they change and evolve" (1997, 24).

Kurt Zimmerman, for example, was deeply troubled by his involvement in World War II, despite his wanting to stop the Nazis. This example demonstrates to students that someone can have mixed emotions about doing what he or she believes is right. By painting pictures of roadkill, Zimmerman liberates animals that have been smashed by an object they didn't see coming. Using this as a metaphor for people who were bombed, he paints the animal spirit as an energized soul, living in a parallel universe. This creative process—imaginary or real—recasts Zimmerman's identity as a liberator, instead of someone who bombs villages and destroys lives. In this way, he heals himself as he softly and wisely communicates messages of caring to his art audiences. He models for us a way of constructing identity based on creative action.

Art educator Dipti Desai (2005) asks that we move beyond simplistic and troubling notions of identity as we learn new ways to contextualize artwork. She recognizes that identity is complex, and simply noting, for example, someone's ethnicity or home-place can easily lead to grave misunderstandings. Just because Ruby Williams is African American or a farmer, or Lilly Carrasquillo is Puerto Rican, for example, doesn't automatically indicate how someone lives or what he or she believes. Multiple approaches to understanding an artist's identity must be incorporated into curriculum practices.

Creative Class

Richard Florida (2002) claims that in the future, individuals who are creative and comfortable with diversity will spur economic growth through innovation. He further states that a community must have technology, talent, and tolerance to attract creative people. Folkvine.org tries to address each of these qualifications in an embedded manner. Using the Web as a teaching tool encourages students to explore its potential uses for creativity, play, and information. By interacting with Folkvine's artists' sites, they can explore multiple ways to identify and develop creativity and talent. And because each artist creates with different materials (paper, bones, threads, wood, and paint, for example) and gets inspiration from varying sources (such as UFOs, roadkill, religion, and animals), students who study these artists can learn about many ways to find meaning in life. There is no one set way to think about one's place in the world.

Students in Karen Branen's class learned numerous things from Folkvine. They now know that artists create in many ways using a multitude of materials. They understand that the Folkvine Web site is an extension of the artists' work and can in fact be seen as artwork in itself. They are especially pleased that their artwork, inspired by the Folkvine artists, is part of the Web site. And they have begun to understand that art is a process more than a fixed thing and it is connected to other parts of one's life experience. Perhaps the most striking thing Branen's students learned is that great art doesn't have to be in a museum to be valuable.

Folklorists and educators (especially arts educators) have a great deal in common (Bowman 2006). Individuals in both disciplines are interested in exploring creativity, educational practices, ways people problem solve, and how individuals and groups make sense of their worlds. Folkvine.org is one example of a project that brings folkloric and educational content together to explore questions and practices of mutual concern. Students of all ages can benefit by learning more about ways that traditional cultures use creative practices to establish a place for themselves in our amazing world.

Notes

1. In Ruth Behar's book, *Translated Woman* (2003), the author reports on many years of fieldwork studying the lives of women in one small rural Mexican village. Her main subject is Esperanza, a woman whom villagers claim is a witch. Behar makes herself visible throughout the story as she raises questions about her right to tell someone else's life history. As with arts-based research, the questions that are raised can become more important than the answers.

2. Much has been written recently about arts-based research. *Studies in Art Education* did a special-topics issue on arts-based research in arts education in 2006, 48 (1). In 2008 an anthology titled *Arts-Based Research in Education* appeared, edited by Melisa Cahnmann-Taylor and Richard Siegesmund. This text examines the ways that arts-based research is being used in the broader realm of education. Since it is a relatively new form of research, tensions have been expressed about how much credibility it should receive.

3. For a broader discussion about the ways that Folkvine.org relates to these questions, see Saper (2008). For an article that addresses the ethnographic decisions made in creating the site, see Underberg and Congdon (2007). And for an article that addresses ideas about teaching about religion in educational settings, see Congdon and Underberg (2006).

4. Karen Branen is an award-winning art teacher who has been active in the National Art Education Association for decades. She has been very helpful in testing new ideas in art education over the years. Her school has been ranked A ever since testing based on the educational mandate of No Child Left Behind began.

5.   Shortly after he completed the elementary game for Folkvine.org, Nathan Draluck transferred to the University of South Florida to work on his PhD in philosophy.

6.   I recognize that many readers may have trouble with my designating works at the House of Blues as folk art because there is ongoing debate over the definition by those who study and collect it. I use the designation here to point out that Draluck's approach to our work was contextual and folkloric.

7.   The Folkvine education team members were Karen Branen, Kristin Congdon, Nathan Draluck, and Natalie Underberg. Lynn Tomlinson and Chantale Fontaine also consulted on the project.

8.   These claims include arguments that studying art will increase reading skills or is correlated to better grades in academic disciplines. For more information on this topic, see the chapter titled, "Making the Case for the Arts: Why Arts Education Is Not a Luxury," in Hetland, Winner, Veenema, and Sheridan (2007).

9.   The eight Studio Habits of Mind are develop craft, engage and persist, envision, express, observe, reflect, stretch and explore, and understand the art world.

8

"When Lunch Was Just Lunch and Not So Complicated"

(Re)Presenting Student Culture through an Alternative Tale

Lisa Rathje

THE STUDENTS HAVE NAMED THE ASSEMBLAGE "PARENTLESS GENERATION."[1] It is striking, filling the room with images that seem to evoke childhood—a teddy bear, Mickey Mouse, basketball—and chillingly contrast with graffiti texts—"free dem South Side Savages," "R.I.P. Quarter," "Lost-Neverfound." Standing nine feet tall and twelve feet wide, and composed of multiple stand-alone pieces, the structure demands attention and evokes contemplation. Kayla,[2] a student whose story is included in the visual art, wrote part of the accompanying interpretive text:

> Parentless Generation is the theme of my art. You see the people being burned by the fire. You see crack, weed, guns, cars, rims—these are the things that corrupt the minds of today's youth.
>
> Every kid wants to have money, but instead of getting a job, they start selling drugs. They get caught up in it; cuz there wasn't anybody there to tell them that there is a different way of life.
>
> All that God has done is burned by the fire, so we turn to the streets cuz the streets show us love, the streets become our family, the crack heads are our aunts and uncles, they show us love. If you're not getting

Lisa Rathje is an independent folklorist whose areas of interest include folklife, cultural heritage, and ethnographic research methods, as well as applying cultural knowledge in social-justice efforts.

what you want, the streets got whatever you want or need.

The kids are being burned by the fire. Getting sucked up by the streets. Kids are killing each other. There are a lot of young people who are in eternal life because of something stupid.

Nowadays, you can get killed for no reason. There are too many young people locked up or dead for no reason. I say it's the '70s generation's fault. This is what is going on in the streets of Harrisburg. I know. I grew up in the streets of Harrisburg.

This work is the centerpiece at an end-of-the-year open house hosted by students in a small program of the alternative-education high school in Harrisburg, Pennsylvania. It acts as a showcase for the program The Art of Many Voices, an ethnographically based arts-residency and mentoring program designed by folklorists at the Institute for Cultural Partnerships (ICP), community artists, and teachers to work with at-risk teens to increase their academic achievement.[3] Offered in both classroom and after-school settings, the program afforded high-school students the opportunity to earn humanities, English, or social-studies credits as they worked with folklorists, folk and traditional artists, and other community members over the course of the school year. The goals that informed the development of the curriculum for The Art of Many Voices include these:

- Students will learn ethnographic skills, including how to develop an interview protocol and the practical and ethical considerations of observation and interviewing;
- Students will bring their own research to bear in a variety of project-based activities;
- Students will recognize the characteristics and use of personal narrative stories, oral histories, and other spoken-word traditions;
- Students will experience and practice art with recognized master artists;[4]
- Students will value academic achievement because education standards are embedded in the creative process of Many Voices; and
- Students will gain a better understanding of themselves, their community, and social processes, especially as expressed through the arts.

The Art of Many Voices seeks to provide students with the ethnographic tools to document their community and not only collect their own stories but also contextualize them in a more deliberate community project. Early in the process, we realized that success necessitated a student-centered program of high quality and demanded that we use our ethnographic skills to their fullest to understand better the school culture and those who were actors in it. We later found the following branding very useful in helping teachers, administrators, and others understand our complex program more quickly: we DARE students to engage with this program and use their stories to create new visions for the future:[5]

    Discover: use the ethnographic process to observe and document community;

    Analyze: reflect on information gathered, explore the important stories and issues;

    Represent: express student research findings through art;

    Engage: provide a forum for discussions with the public and create visions for the future.

Many Voices modifies the artist-in-residency model to address education standards by engaging students first through an ethnographic project to document creative art on the street, as well as community stories, followed by intense work in visual arts and the spoken word to express the stories the students have identified and collected. The documentation includes working with digital videos, audio recordings, and photography.

The assemblage was one component of the second year's culminating project in June 2008. A few parents attended the open house. Student invitations attracted a local television station and Harrisburg newspaper, and the district superintendent and the director of alternative education also came. In his remarks, Superintendent Kohn looked at the students and said, "I want to let you know that what I see here has really touched me." He said that he felt very proud of the students for the work that they had done to get to this point. Many staff and faculty members from the local community college joined us, including Kim Bannister, the coordinator of its art gallery, who had worked with our students during a field trip to see an exhibition in her gallery. She pulled me aside after the program and expressed her amazement at the discernable difference between the students she had first met in March and the same people at this June open house. In March she had seen students who could not be engaged, did not know how to have a conversation with an adult, and were generally hostile. In their art and presentations in June, she saw a level of engagement that she could have never imagined.

Part of what stunned Bannister was an unscripted moment when Kayla spoke about the project to those gathered:

> I mean, I learned a lot [other students nod their heads; some say, "I did, too"], just from this right here, and working with the teachers and working and being up at William Penn. . . . I am so proud of this. I am so proud to be with you all and to be able to say that I did this, that I've got something that I can show and put on display. Like— when this goes on display—I'm everywhere this goes because we don't get opportunities to do this because we are in alternative ed. Because they look at us—well, they label us—as behavior and education students. I mean they label us; they put a stereotype on us. So, like, if we brought this up to [the district high school] or someplace like that [another student says, "(The principal) would be mad"]. . . . Yeah, [she] would be mad, you know what I mean?, because this is basically everybody who she kicked out, you know? I mean, [she] never really gave me a chance. . . . She told me that I wasn't going to finish school. . . . She told me that I was dysfunctional and all this other stuff. But to see this [pointing to the mural; other students nod their head in agreement—they have essentially elected this student as their spokesperson], I know what I am capable of. I'm just proud, and I represent alternative ed, and I don't think nothing's wrong with it. I really don't.[6]

All the other students clapped. When they realized that everyone there was also applauding them and their work, they all broke out in wide smiles and congratulated each other. This powerful articulation from one of their peers demonstrated the transformative power that comes from using ethnographic tools in the classroom to elaborate a critical consciousness— VOICE—among disengaged and oppressed student populations.

As I consider the spaces where many folklorists find themselves working most often, it is our attention to the nexus of narrative and custom that proves significant. Social psychologist Michelle Fine and her cowriters argue for creating a "space of intentional interruption" in the classroom (2000, 171). The concept is familiar to those who understand the power of storytelling to make a space to create alternative stories that contest, disrupt, or mask master narratives that have heretofore seemed impervious. While many students in any school have a number of narratives about them from a neighborhood, a generation, and an ethnicity, there are also narratives—or cultural constructs—in the school system that reinforce and prescribe attitude, behaviors, and learning aptitudes.

In data from 2001, 97 percent of the students in this alternative school fell below the poverty line, and only 24 percent graduated. By 2006 the school had a much higher graduation rate, yet students tested 75 and 98 percent below basic scores (reading and math, respectively) on the Pennsylvania System of School Assessment tests.[7] Before our team implemented the 2006–7 folklore and arts-residency program with outside funding, the school had dropped all arts curricula.[8] Resources are scarce for many activities, especially those seen as "extracurricular."

Bruce Wilson and Dickson Corbett note the growing achievement gap associated with poverty (2001). Yet, drawing upon Christopher Jencks and Meredith Phillips's research into black and white test-score gaps (1998), Wilson and Corbett bluntly argue that "the performance gap can be reduced by paying much closer attention to the nature of students' classroom experiences. Dwelling on matters of heredity and background . . . is unproductive and, in fact, simply wrong" (2001, 63). Taking this argument to a logical end indicates that poverty is not exclusively and directly causing the achievement gap. Rather, various cultural constructs that surround students from poverty contribute to the gap. Katherine Magnuson and Greg Duncan reviewed research on achievement gaps and noted that some "obvious explanations" should be ruled out to explain their growth. Drawing upon research from multiple studies they noted that "less than a third of the growth in the gaps is due to differences in school or class quality" (2006). They offer an alternative hypothesis, articulating two possibilities: "teachers' differential treatment of and expectations for black and white students as well as the emergence of stereotype threat" (2006). In other words, it is not necessarily a question of the school's physical or curricular features, but rather how cultural narratives and subsequent constructs affect students' and teachers' classroom experience and expectations of one another.

Folklore and folklorists bring something unique to the classroom, and this chapter describes the ways that the tools of folklore can participate in the difficult task of empowering and enabling students to engage with the narratives that inform the social constructs of their identities. Grounded in a model that resembles good fieldwork, the implementation of The Art of Many Voices in an alternative school setting meant that folklorists worked to understand youth culture critically within the school structure and enable students to tell their stories in their voices. The case study highlighted in this chapter uses the concepts and ethics of folklore to reveal the youth as a kind of folk group, capable of creating authentic expressive culture. I propose that the ethnographic sensibilities developed through a study of folklore support an alternative vision of the educator working with urban youth, namely, a teacher whose curriculum supports youth finding their voices on their terms and in ways that may disrupt, critique, and expose popular narratives about urban youth.

The Teacher-Hero and the Exception/al Student: Representing Roles and Identity

A whole genre of films with stories of teachers and their students "based upon" or "inspired by" "true events" exists, and many have predictable scripts. As a subset of popular culture, these films perpetuate images that appear to represent urban youth and their relationship to teachers. As a folklorist working in an educational setting, I have grave concerns about the implications of these images—especially the role of the urban teacher as a missionary who rescues children from themselves. These films are often very formulaic and therefore provide interesting insight into images that exist in popular culture about schools and students in urban areas. Looking at how teacher/student films were described by those who posted on the Internet Movie Database message boards provides one quick method of characterizing these narratives: "'teacher turns rotten kids into good kids' genre," "movies about kids in highschool [*sic*] getting along despite their race under the guidance of an amazing teacher"; "'really bad students become angels because of one caring teacher' theme"; "'teacher comes in and changes everything' type of movies"; "the 'intelligent white teacher goes to a school with black people and Hispanics who listen to hip-hop and are involved in crime and eventually manages to educate them even though they diss him at first' genre"; "'stranger-comes-into-lives-of-troubled-inner-city-youths-and-changes-them-for-the-better' variety"; and so on.[9] In other words, there are enough references to these themes in popular culture and media that it takes little prompting for someone to grasp immediately what typical characters, the type of school, and the expected plot development are like (see also Bauer 1998; Farber, Provenzo, and Holm 1994).

As I read these descriptions, made specifically in reference to *Take the Lead* (2006) and *Freedom Writers* (2007), interesting assumptions emerge and provide points for discussion about the way cinematic representation relates to urban educational systems today and public perception of them. The image of the teacher as stranger (outsider) means that he or she is usually white and always intelligent, caring, amazing, and visionary (can effect change/transformation). The teacher is portrayed as having agency and being above or outside prevailing systems (therefore sometimes also characterized as a hero activist, renegade, or maverick). The students, on the other hand, are depicted as local, usually rotten or bad, members of an ethnicity other than white, criminal, troubled, and unable to shape their futures positively. Although created by Hollywood, the characters and story represent a reality with which the audience is asked to engage. Building upon arguments first articulated by Cameron McCarthy, James Trier notes that "television and popular film fulfill 'a certain bardic function' in society, singing back to white America lullabies that maintain the suburban myth of security and economic plenitude, while simultaneously creating 'the most poignantly sordid fantasies of inner-city degeneracy and moral decrepitude'" (2001, 129–30). Because film suspends the usual tensions between fiction and reality, audience members assume comfortably that their screened experience is real and their ideas about these schools, neighborhoods, and youth are validated. I use the term "validated" deliberately, for this insistence on truth on the part of the cinematic text reinforces the "truth" of master narratives, or dominant-cultural "texts", about urban youth[10] (Bauer 1998; Bettis 1996; Britzman 1992; Cook-Sather 2006; Robertson 1997; Trier 2001; Weis and Fine 2000).

As legitimization strategies for preserving the status quo with regard to power relations and difference in general (racial, economic, etc.), master narratives have been given more visibility (and, by extension, weakened) by postmodern and feminist thought; yet—as sociocultural forms of interpretation—they continue to inform invisibly (even sometimes more overtly) much of the public's perceptions of people and places (Bhabba [1989] 2001; Butler 1990; hooks [1990] 2001; Lanser 1993; Lawless 2001; Lorde 1981; Mascia-Lees, Sharpe, and Cohen 1989; Trinh 1989). When we return to our list of adjectives describing the two character types of teacher and student in these films, some of the master narratives that surround the profession of teaching (especially in urban or alternative schools) become clear, as well as the ways that these narratives construct identities for students who come from the city or are in alternative education. This chapter probes this narrative of students and teachers to extrapolate ways that it interfaces with pedagogy and educational programs. These master narratives written larger through cinema texts suggested theoretical and practical concerns that influenced the type of folklife-in-education program that we designed in The Art of Many Voices.

How does the hero activist motif affect the self-representation of those working in the alternative school setting? What pedagogical choices must be made to account for and work with the cultural expectations that inform the urban school environment? This teacher/student cultural script has become so well known that it is an expectation to be reinforced, rather than questioned. Managing these expectations—of *representations*—informs my argument that teaching pedagogies and public programming are inherently representational. Many folklorists working in education understand this dilemma of being perceived as hero activists, and they offer interesting answers to resolve the practical curricular questions. Providing expertise on specific cultures and communities, bringing teaching artists and tradition bearers into a classroom, or proposing projects that ask students to use ethnographic methods to document their communities all engage different levels of representational praxis. At the same time, the ethnographic sensibility that a folklorist brings to a project can engender new perspectives on the research already conducted on outcomes from arts-in-education programs.

A look at the culture of the classroom and the ways that cultural assumptions inform teacher behavior points to another hypothesis that may be drawn from the research of Wilson and Corbett: namely, the narratives that exist about "these students" affect the ways teachers teach and students learn. Magnuson and Duncan outline evidence for this claim, citing multiple studies that conclude that teachers' "lower expectations for black students are likely to account for a portion of the gap" and "children's awareness of cultural stereotypes increases during middle childhood, and . . . this elevated awareness was linked to the underperformance of minority children on challenging tests" (2006). Magnuson and Duncan call this awareness "stereotype threat," noting that anxiety results from a student's fear of confirming cultural stereotypes (2006).

I think this also affirms the ways that representations can dangerously shape and mediate pedagogy. Too often the vocabulary of organizations that fund many of these projects perpetuates this problematic perspective through its emphasis on working with "at-risk" or "poverty" populations. This, then, implicitly requires those seeking grant funds to use the same vocabulary. The narrative about "these students" is already predicted and constructed by race, class, and geography, and only an "outsider" may attempt to "save" these kids by his or her intervention. This presents difficult questions. How can schools who most want or need targeted assistance seek funding without becoming a part of the re/production of this particular narrative—a narrative that by its nature renders the voices of the students passive and disempowered?

Additionally, the challenge for teachers is to understand that their actions are not confined to the glorified teacher-hero role in the movies and other representations manufactured and recycled in popular culture. The film narrative models act as a warning for teachers: if they use approaches that resist dominant narratives, they may be banished from the larger academic community, jeopardizing their ability to work collaboratively. However, it is necessarily within the culture of the school that reform must occur, rather than in the classroom—most secondary teachers have a group of students for one hour or less a day. As Charles Payne notes in his text *So Much Reform, So Little Change*, "The essential problem in our schools isn't children learning; it is adult learning" (2008, 42). He points out the irony that reform efforts that fail to see the school as a complex entity ignore research that has surfaced repeatedly since early reformation efforts in the 1960s and '70s:

> In 1971, Seymour Sarason cautioned that we should expect little or nothing from school reform efforts because reformers so consistently failed to understand schools as organizations with their own cultures and their own power arrangements. In a recent retrospective, he notes that for fifteen years, he kept a file of letters from people who had mounted failed reform efforts. One of the strongest themes in those letters was that reformers "had vastly underestimated the force of existing power relationships and had vastly overestimated the willingness of school personnel to confront the implications of those relationships." (2008, 44)

Rather than expect the solo hero-teacher to change the world of students, the perspective needs to broaden and ask how a culture for learning can be created across disciplines, woven through multiple classroom settings, and implemented at many levels across administration and school bureaucracies.

Inside The Art of Many Voices

The work of the Voices projects engages multiple re/presentational practices: from securing funding to having students gather and present stories from their communities, to presenting the students and their final projects to the public. At their core, the Voices projects focused on narrative and developing a critical consciousness among the student participants. In the course of evaluating our programs, we have come to recognize what Deborah Britzman, a leader in educational leadership and policy development, calls a "pedagogical dilemma":

> These students seem to be caught between the only versions of identity offered by dominant forms of culture: One is either educated or not educated. This selective criterion requires both a dismissal of the self and a dismissal of cultural politics. . . . *The pedagogical dilemma is how to create opportunities for students to make sense of the detours of representing oneself in contexts already overburdened with representations one may not choose but, nonetheless, must confront and transform.* (1992, 254; italics added)

This chapter opened with the argument that images and narratives about urban youth devised by the national consciousness contribute to the representation of their cultural identities. The remainder of the chapter considers how attention to the local—through ethnographic processes—can alter those representations among students. Britzman reaffirms the argument that dominant images of urban youth create narrow spaces to construct identity and restrict students' power to act. In what ways can a folklife-in-education program modify this cynical position? Educational philosopher Maxine Greene—reflecting on Paulo Freire's writing—notes that there exist "surprising ways in which the 'culture of silence' can be broken when people begin analyzing the realities nearest at hand and move from there to national realties. Involved, trying to say everything that is on their minds, they find that their critical discourse on their own world is itself a way of remaking that world" (2000, 297). I often use this approach when speaking with educational specialists, teachers, and administrators to craft the argument that ethnographic and place-based learning methods contribute in significant ways to creating the larger educational experience they desire in their classrooms.

Maxine Greene also argues, however, that engaging with cultural representations implies the luxury of thinking beyond yourself and immediate survival. As she notes, marginalized people have "little use" for metaphors that in the end only "enable people at the center to imagine what it is to be outside, enable the strong to imagine the weak" (2000, 295). Research has shown that those who are oppressed are intimately aware of the oppressor's culture because it determines their ability to successfully live in—and offer any resistance to—the larger world (Anzaldúa 1987; Bakhtin [1965] 1984; hooks [1990] 2001, 1992; Lorde 1981; Trinh 1989). This, in itself, is an act of survival. What kind of experience and knowledge do youth who live in oppressive social conditions have to help them understand how much their culture (over)determines their cultural identities? In other words, can these youth gain some perspective on their culture and, through this, a better understanding of how larger social ideas form their cultural norms and identities? Asking young people to produce their stories has already been done and often ends in supporting preconceived negative images in the minds of a teacher or public that yearns to learn more about a culture they do not understand.[11] I don't believe that it is only cynicism that prompted this kind of response from one young student when she was asked to describe some characteristics of her neighborhood in one of our first sessions in the winter of 2008: she said with a smirk, "What do you want to know about: the drugs, the pimps, how dirty it is? I can tell you all about it. I used to sell crack because it was the only good money on our block 'til I saw a fourteen-year-old girl using, and then I said to myself, 'That's just wrong. That's just really wrong.'" How can producing stories work as empowerment, rather than mere voyeurism?

The students we worked with are not unaware of ways their stories can be co-opted; they are wary of curious outsiders who measure difference through such stories. For example, as we began The Art of Many Voices in the winter of 2008, some of our first activities were scheduled *walkabouts,* guided walks through a community with the students to introduce them to cultural survey work and documentation. We bring cameras, video recorders, and notepads. We encourage students to talk to people and shop owners who are willing to share some of their knowledge of the place. On the first day of our walkabouts, students voiced serious concerns, namely, that they could not be seen going into their communities with a white person and a camera because that would mark them as snitches or worse. They claimed that they could be seriously hurt in retaliation. We sat down in their lounge and talked about the implications of their reaction. They admitted that this fear affected other aspects of their lives—their inability to feel as if they could make a positive difference in their community without being hurt, and their belief that their community was the way it was and they couldn't change it. One student asked in the course of the discussion, "Why don't we go walk around in your neighborhood? I would rather see what is going on there than in my dirty ol' hood."

Educational researchers Lois Weis and Michelle Fine note in their edited collection *Construction Sites* that urban students need and construct spaces "in which they engage in a kind of critical consciousness, challenging hegemonic beliefs about them, their perceived inadequacies, pathologies, and 'lacks' and restoring a sense of possibility for themselves and their peers, with and beyond narrow spaces of identity sustenance" (2000, 3). They also note that "there are no victims here [in these essays looking at student spaces], but there are lots of cultural critics" (2). Based upon extensive fieldwork, the essays in this book provide alternative narratives and highlight approaches that complicate those in the teacher/student movie.

After the Harrisburg students refused to go on walkabouts in their community, we reassessed and decided that the best way to move forward was to walk through a different section of town so that they could begin to learn about the process. We hoped that they could then apply some of these tools to their communities without engaging in a group activity or being accompanied by a teacher or white person (both folklorists are white). The day we spent with them in this neutral part of town (a local market) was a great success, and the students showed a larger level of engagement with the material and process than they had in any previous activity. After seeing the teacher model the interview process once, the students quickly got very involved in the activity. They were polite, asked both the market vendors and consumers thoughtful follow-up questions, and took thorough notes about the day's interviews and photos.

The Role of Audience, the Importance of Critical Consciousness

One of the most important components of The Art of Many Voices is conceptual—creating an "audience," a public to hear the students' voices. Weis and Fine claim that many students like those with whom I worked are aware of the narratives perpetuated, especially by the media, and they provide one starting point to discuss developing a critical consciousness. Similarly critic bell hooks notes that "in relation to the post-modernist deconstruction of 'master' narratives, the yearning that wells in the hearts and minds of those whom such narratives have silenced is the longing for critical voice" ([1990] 2001, 2481). To move beyond Maxine Greene's critique of the ways stories of the marginalized are used in social contexts, I suggest that establishing an audience for student work is essential. Here folklore's focus on emergent culture through narrative and performance enhances the ability of the folklorist in the school to create opportunities for significant engagement with powerful cultural constructs by the students. If there is a heart or core to my argument in this chapter about representation and folklife-in-education programming, it is that an awareness of audience needs to define and drive much of the work. That is not to say that the final product should be valued over the process that students and teachers undergo in the program. However, the idea of an audience informs much of the work because it is inextricably bound up with shaping and enacting cultural identity.

Representation through this program can be defined in two interrelated, but distinct, ways: students finding their own voice and vision, and students using these tools to communicate their concerns, hopes, and fears about their neighborhoods and school to the larger community. Because The Art of Many Voices paid particular attention to the folklore and art forms that are culturally significant to the students and their communities, I believe that these students were able to create a vision of themselves as capable advocates for change and empowerment within their school and community, as well as learn to appreciate diversity expressed through arts and traditions. My realization that my research in folklife and education needed to be part of a larger project investigating re/presentational strategies in folklore resulted from my first year in the school, when it became clear that it was only when the students became aware that they were going to present their project to an actual audience that they began to accept the program. The cynicism that students initially expressed about sharing the stories and traditions of their neighborhoods with people who lived on different blocks began to evaporate when they started to believe that others would listen and care about what they produced and said.

A powerful example of this surfaced about three-fourths of the way through the first year as we worked on the final script. When we had begun our work in the school that fall, two sisters of Puerto Rican heritage responded very little in class. One teacher complained that all Maria and Rayne said in her math class was that they could not participate because they could not write English well enough. It became clear that they were using their lack of language skills as an easy crutch to avoid dealing with the classroom and academic environment. We continued to work with them over the year—inviting them to participate and having all-Spanish dinners when they could teach us their language. On the first day of the spoken-word residency, they sat with their heads down and did not plan to get involved. When poets Iya Isoke and Jason Moffitt came around to help individual students, Iya told Maria and Rayne to go ahead and write in Spanish; she did not care as long as they wrote. So they began to write about love and boyfriends, their brother in jail, and their love of Puerto Rico. As the year continued, Iya asked them to start thinking about a piece that they could share in the final performance. Having recently seen a *Def Poetry Jam* video in the class, they decided that they wanted to do a poetry duet like the poetry duo Yellow Rage from Philadelphia. We encouraged them to work on it and decided to invite Yellow Rage to come lead a workshop for us.

We partnered with Nathaniel Gadsden of the Writers Wordshop at the Imani African Christian Church to host the event, giving the students another opportunity to see what resources exist in their own community for positive self-expression.[12] Also we wanted to invite the Writers Wordshop poets so that they could act as models for how to behave at a poetry workshop and expand the audience for the students. The performance was dynamic, and clearly the students were interested in what they saw. Next, we asked the students to get up and share their pieces. Four students ended up sharing, including the sisters. When the two got in front of the small audience, they began to giggle, and Maria said, "I don't think that I can do this." They both started to back out, saying that they could not remember the words. We convinced them that we were all rooting for them and they just needed to do their best. Quietly—but with increasing energy—the girls performed their poem "Ricans Don't Play":

Maria: *Estos cabrones gringos no saben que nosotros Puertoriqueno no jugamos.*
       Y'all wanna know what I just said, then maybe u should take some RICAN CLASSES. Then u know what I just said. Always trying to tell us what to do or what to say. We r fucking tired of the same shit,

Both: "NO SPEAKING SPANISH PLEASE."

Rayne: You know after a while that shit gets annoying, [louder] always criticizing the way we dress, the way we walk and the way we speak. Just in case u forget Ricans counts as 2, while u count as one. Well, the reason I say that is because we have 2 languages, so what I'm trying to say is

Both: "We are way smarter then u.". . . (*Watzup,* 2007)

Yellow Rage complimented Maria and Rayne and encouraged them to continue their work. Then a member of the Writers Wordshop came forward and introduced himself to the girls. He told them that he was Latino and what their poem said was true and important; other people needed to hear their perspective. As I drove them home that night, Maria said, "Our show is going to be really good because it is real. The issues and the stories are real." Maria hadn't known that there was another Latino in the audience; his comments made her realize how other people heard her and her sister. I think that it was the first time that she connected the power of words to an audience that would take something meaningful away from the performance. She told me, "I think that our words can really make a difference . . . that we can start to change how people see us and how they think. This show is going to be really cool."

This comment heralded a change in attitude that affected the remainder of the work these girls did as part of the production. A project artist, Janet Bixler, noted in her evaluation of *Watzup* that "when [Maria and Rayne] interacted with the audience and performed 'Ricans Don't Play' with such intense power, volume, and ownership, I was floored. They stopped being hesitant students unaware of their strength to two young women that realize their ability to command an audience to listen to their opinions and feelings" (personal communication with the author, May 2007). They were the only two performers in the final production who did NOT require a microphone. Significantly, when one student did not show up to the final rehearsal, Maria stepped forward and offered to read her part, even memorizing it in case she had to perform it the next day. Given that she used language as an excuse not to participate in the class at the beginning of the year, her subsequent command of language as a tool of ownership and performance is one powerful example of what folklorists—using their knowledge of narrative and ethnographic process—can accomplish in schools.[13]

The student production presented to the public in May 2007 offers opportunities to understand the power of art in a school setting. Through rap and spoken word, visuals that included life-sized self-portraits and scenes set in the high-school lunchroom, along with other theatrical pieces, students tried to tell the story of who they are, how they got here, and where they are going. The opening spoken-word piece set the scene at the high-school lunchroom, where Sarah remembered the stares she had gotten from the other girls in her class when her pregnancy began to show—she longed for the days "when lunch was just lunch and not so complicated." In class and afterschool sessions with artists, students wrote the script—scenes that depicted their coming-of-age stories and traditions (or lack thereof). The students named the show *Watzup. Life Unpredictable.* As Janet Bixler wrote in her program notes, "Watzup. No, it isn't a question. It is a statement of TRUTH." Culminating in a hip-hop theatre production for the larger community, the student project provided an opportunity for education and dialogue to begin to mitigate the documented fear and distrust these students linked to class, race, and social conditions.[14]

Developing this program, and learning some of these lessons, provides a context for my critical discussion of issues raised by this type of work, including a critique of how the school itself acts as a culture that reinforces behaviors, thinking patterns, and certain assumptions of the students (see Ritchhart et al. 2006; Kodish and Wei 2002; Winner and Hetland 2000; Moonsammy 1991). The work for a folklorist in this setting is immense and fitting. Armed with our toolbox that includes attention to the local and belief in the power of culture to shape narratives of places and people, we find great need for our services. Yet I also readily acknowledge our shortcomings: most of us are not trained teachers, nor do many of us (and I emphatically include myself) wish to be in a classroom on a daily basis. More than twenty years ago at the 1988 American Folklore Society annual meeting, a panel considered how folk arts in education could best adapt to the needs and trends of educational systems.[15] There was an emphasis on trying to ride the wave of multiculturalism and all its promise (Nusz 1991, 7). Now I would argue there is a leeriness of the easy banality of "multicultural work"; No Child Left Behind has wreaked havoc on the arts and humanities in many school curricula—although *diversity* still has some cachet, and there are a few special programs that go with various ghettoized months in the school calendar. We should shift this paradigm and consider what WE think is important about being a folklorist in the school. Is it about bringing education about diversity to the work, or is it about strengthening the culture and identity of the students who attend that school? What if we do not see ourselves as experts who only bring access to cultural objects or ethnic arts to the educational drawing board, but instead supply tools for fieldwork, cultural surveys, and personal-experience documentation? How can our methods—rather than reinventing scholastic models—provide alternatives that work congenially with or parallel to current classroom methods?

One significant issue about understanding the power of words and the types of representation to which the students were reacting emerged as we attempted to finalize the *Watzup* script. Throughout the year, we encouraged the students simply to express themselves. We did not censor. We invited conversations about the most effective ways to convey messages to a specific audience, recognizing that tone and register must adjust for different circumstances and scenarios. What we found most helpful in starting these conversations was work at a radio station operated by a local liberal-arts college. While we did not want to censor the students in the school, the radio station had a whole new set of rules dictated by the FCC. The broadcast signal did not extend past the campus, but the Harrisburg students immediately understood that they were on the radio and a number of people—maybe a lot of them—were going to hear what they had to say. They planned their discussions. They created conversations without swear words. They gained confidence by working with young college students on the project and learning to operate the microphones and other basic equipment.

As we moved closer to putting together a script for the final public performance, we asked the students to consider what they wanted to say to that live audience and craft a production that would tell a public that consisted of family, community members, and strangers more about who they were and who they wanted to become. This was much more difficult than the radio shows because it was asking them to imagine a live audience (many students had never attended a play or live show) and plan for something that was still two months away—a task that seemed impossible to many students who were more comfortable with projects where they could immediately see results. Then, on 4 April 2007, as planning continued, Don Imus, a syndicated talk-show host, caught the nation's attention with his comments, using racially charged jibes, about the Rutgers University women's basketball team. A national debate swelled among talk-show commentators and news anchors, and at the local level, people wondered about the intersections of race and language: whether it was ever okay to use any terms—derogatively or not—associated with ethnicities. The Art of Many Voices staff called a meeting and invited any students who were interested to participate. We needed to discuss the language that the students were writing into the play—especially the use of the word "nigga."

As we began the meeting, we described the debates we had been hearing and said that we were not sure if we could move forward with a script that had the n-word throughout. In a private conversation earlier, a teacher working with the team had said that we needed to censor this word. I asked the students how they felt about this suggestion, and they got angry when they heard the proposal. They said that we "couldn't just come in here and change the rules. You said that these are our words and that you wouldn't censor." I responded that this was true and asked them what solution they would like to propose. Tyra responded that she did not even use that word anymore after hearing a poem by one of our artists, Iya Isoke, but that she wanted to leave it in her poem because that was how she had written it, and it reflected who she was at that time.[16]

Tyra's statement is rich in many ways. Most significantly, it reveals her understanding that she was changing as a result of this process. She wanted to have a tangible reminder of the person she had been when we started so that she would not forget. As she continued to change and assess her priorities, she did not want to dismiss lightly products that she had already created. Her friend Jameshya then came up with a plan. She said that we needed to stage a debate within the performance explaining the progression that we were talking about right now. We accepted that solution. Was it risky? Yes. But it was important to have the students feel that we would listen to their ideas and that we personally believed their thoughts were brilliant, though still perhaps controversial for a high-school play.

Jameshya and Tyra worked together on the following script:

> S: "Why can't you be more respectful and not use that negative word?"
> T: "'Cause he's a nigga."
> S: "But our great-grandparents fought . . ."
> T: "They fought to end the use of the word 'nigger,' not 'nigga'—it's different."
> S: "What's the difference?"
> T: "One you use with friends. . . . If you aren't my friend, you can't call me nigga."
> S: "Can I ask you a question? Are you a racist?"
> Pause. Both are quiet.

Iya Isoke reads her poem, "Change Your Vernacular."

> T: (to audience): What people don't know is that when you use a word like that, you are empowering it. My own thinking has changed since I heard this poem by Iya. I realized that I need to get that word out of my vocabulary. My piece that we did earlier reflects a very real time in my life, but when I heard Iya's words, I changed my own thoughts on the subject. (*Watzup* 2007)

Response to the show was overwhelmingly positive. Roughly 55 percent of the audience members at the final production were family members of the students. This success in getting family to the performance is a testament to the importance that the students began to attach to their own work, as well as the effort that program staff had made to be sure parents knew about the upcoming event and why it was important for their students. In the talk-back session following the presentation, many parents were moved to tears—expressing their pride, love, and surprise for the work that the students had put into the production. As Moffit wrote in his final evaluation, "I think for the parents, family, and friends that attended the final production, they have a new sense of the person they came to see" (personal communication with the author, May 2007). This ratifies the voices that the students found and brought to the public and their families in the performance.[17] Community members were also profoundly affected. As one woman (a prominent state employee who works with the Pennsylvania Human Relations Commission) observed, what these students did was courageous, important, and worthwhile and should be commended.

For the students to hear this was yet another important step in the process that this program is all about. What is truly powerful about this work is that students have been equipped with the necessary tools to move forward. As Moffit wrote for the *Watzup* program essay, "We wanted to create a space that these young people could grow in, mentally, emotionally and spiritually. We wanted them to develop skills that they can take far beyond what you will see today."

Next Steps: Finding Voice for the Future

Ultimately, I find that the student voices documented, expressed, and represented through this project reflect stories of lunch and love, maturity and growing up too fast, and community found and lost. The process of developing and articulating these stories reflects thoughtful curricula, dedicated collaboration, and flexibility. I end with the assertion that we need continued research that presents both quantitative and qualitative assessments of folk-arts-in-education initiatives, especially relative to alternative education.

There are several important criteria to consider when reviewing program effectiveness, including evidence of meeting the established objectives,

Students with artist Nataki Bhatti in front of their mural assemblage, "Parentless Generation."

sustained effect, and replicability across multiple sites. Folklorists need to document and qualify—if not quantify—evidence that they are using these criteria. In 2007 a discussion on Publore (a national Listserv for folklorists) resulted from a folklorist's question asking for quantitative or qualitative evidence of the development of student skills through interviewing in the classroom. A number of useful e-mails came in response; none of them could offer quantitative proof, but many compiled anecdotal evidence to underscore the positive results of interviewing. Mark Wagler noted that

> over [20] years I have seen outstanding student learning in two main curricular areas. First, students have developed deep skills in observing culture and seeing patterns, and gone beyond surfaces to profoundly change the ways they think about themselves and others. . . . Second, I have witnessed significant changes in language development when interviewing and other oral language skills are consciously taught and used. (e-mail, 25 January 2007)

Wagler concluded that ". . . I strongly doubt that the most important changes of teaching with interviewing can be observed quantitatively. When instruction is constructivist and project-based, many components combine to support student learning. When these components are isolated for quantitative study, as Wordsworth wrote, 'we murder to dissect'" (e-mail, 25 January 2007).

Ellen Winner and Lois Hetland offer another cautionary note regarding the use of conventional assessment with these projects. They observe that non-arts outcomes should never be used to justify arts-based projects (2000). Too often program directors and teachers are quick to show that a program has contributed to rising test scores or academic achievement to the detriment of the foundation of that very program. What is needed instead is greater attention to ethnography that can assert that—by participating in these types of projects—students are not only gaining valuable knowledge about themselves and their communities but also becoming empowered to engage with the narratives of and about themselves and their folk group and making positive changes in other aspects of their lives and education. Arguing for theory-driven studies of art programs, Winner and Hetland write that "researchers need to carry out ethnographic studies of exemplary schools that grant the arts a serious role in the curriculum. What kinds of innovations have been made in these schools to foster excellence?" (2000).

As we move forward with folklife-in-education programming, we continue to build evidence of ways the program not only interacts with the culture of the school and student but also allows a space where students can engage with their own identity, as well as other factors that influence the learning process. Although the folklife-in-education program described in this chapter may not be a traditional one that intends to expand awareness of and appreciation for the traditions that richly express cultural identity and community, it is uniquely guided by the discipline and methods of folklore. By increasing awareness of the multiple acts of representation that are already inherently in the educational process and continuing to advocate for ethnography as a pedagogically sound educational practice, folklorists have much to offer in the classroom.

Program administrators, myself included, often doubted the process and learned how difficult it is to describe the growth of critical consciousness among the student populations with whom we worked. The open house portrayed at the beginning of this chapter is only one vivid example that illuminates student benefits from engaging with our ethnographic process. Our process insists on being about more than a conventional school mural, or a piece of personal art that can be taken home, or standard writing and poetry. At every stage, students had to think about multiple steps and create different drafts to get to an end. The process meant that the students had to engage with thematic content and understand other parts of their lives or education in a new context using ethnography. It meant they had to commit to additional time—sometimes coming in after school or on a Friday—because they realized that they could be a part of something bigger than their individual selves.

The pride I saw in the students at the open house was not only about their individual contributions. It was also about completing a project bigger than themselves and recognizing the way their individual piece complemented the larger mural. I was especially proud that the students considered why they wanted certain pieces to be together because they would fit and add meaning to the whole and that they thought the mural had a theme they could articulate. All this demonstrates a level of teamwork and collaboration that did not exist when we began the project and the students' only interest in their peers' work was labeling it. As a student named Marcene commented, "This looks better than anything we could have done alone!" For a moment, her realization of the power of community superseded privileging the individual and the drive for personal survival.

Notes

1.   Some ideas and research reported here were developed with support from the Institute for Cultural Partnerships, the Harrisburg School District, and the Harrisburg Institute of Messiah College. The positions taken here are, of course, not necessarily those of the organizations.

2.   All student names have been changed throughout this chapter.

3.   During the 2006–8 school years, The Art of Many Voices was supported by monies regranted through the Harrisburg Institute of Messiah College from the United States Department of Justice to the Institute for Cultural Partnerships. It has subsequently been supported by a number of public and private sources, including the National Endowment for the Arts and the Harrisburg School District. Points of view or opinions expressed in the course of the project do not necessarily represent the official position or policies of our funders, including Messiah College or the U.S. Department of Justice. All evaluation efforts noted in this chapter occurred during the granting period.

4.   In our educational programs, we define *master artists* as those who are considered exceptional within their cultural communities. Some have been recognized through an award from the Pennsylvania Folk and Traditional Arts apprenticeship or fellowship program. Others are artists in the community who use their medium for social justice or advocacy, often by participating in a tradition or adapting traditional motifs. In this sense, the ICP program differs from traditional folklife-in-education programs, for while we do bring traditional artists into the classroom and our curriculum, we also use other teaching artists who complement the ethnographic process that we ask students to learn and use.

5. My discussion further bears this out, but one lesson we learned for those considering implementing a similar program was the importance of branding and marketing this program to students, teachers, and administrators. Without a recognizable identity, it was harder to make the program visible in the overstimulated school marketplace and culture.

6. Transcribed from video that I shot at the open house on 9 June 2008.

7. Data collected from http://www.edportal.ed.state.pa.us (accessed February 2007).

8. Our core team who designed and implemented the curriculum for the 2006–7 project included me as principal investigator, folklorist Amy Skillman, teacher Louise Morgan, and artists Janet Bixler, Iya Isoke, Jason Moffitt, Nataki Bhatti, Nancy Mendes, and Raphael Xavier.

9. All the following comments were accessed on 19 January 2008 at the Internet Movie Database message board for *Take the Lead* (http://www.imdb.com/title/tt0463998/board/threads) and *Freedom Writers* (http://www.imdb.com/title/tt0446046/board/threads).

10. Of course "urban youth" has itself become a loaded term that acts as a signifier beyond its dictionary definition. It has come to mean minority and poor youth, as well as those who are largely disaffected from dominant social systems, including especially education.

11. These images shape the master narratives already discussed: stories of violence, drugs, broken homes, and the occasional exception of a person who can rise above his or her environment.

12. In fact, arguably another advantage of bringing folklorists into the classroom is their holistic understanding of the community. Rather than seeing The School as a separate entity, they understand the importance of connections with other community organizations and resources that can reinforce the work in the classroom.

13. Another example regarding cultivating the students' awareness of audience and their role as enactors comes from a report that I wrote to the Harrisburg Institute in May 2007:

    April has been a very busy and productive month as we have worked to craft and develop the production for May 19th. Of note are the two mini-performances where the students could share their work. The first was April 3rd at the HACC campus. Performing for the drama club in the Rose Lehrman black box theatre, [Tyra, Joseph, and Samone] had an opportunity to feel the pressure and work through the nerves to follow through and give a performance of the piece "Soul Gone Home." It should be noted that Joseph had chosen to not go to school this day. We called and told him that we were picking him up, and that he needed to perform with the others and not let them down. Samone was so nervous that she kept walking around and saying that she didn't think that she was going to be able to do it. However, all three did perform and all three got more in to the piece as they went on—getting more comfortable with the performative aspect of the theatre. They all listened to the feedback following their performance and all three as they walked out of the theatre were calmer and there was a perceptible difference in their attitudes. We saw this as being a tremendous opportunity where they began to see how they needed to be accountable to each other, as well as where they began to sense how the *process* that they have been engaging with was getting them to these moments where real professional and social development could occur.

    What is especially noteworthy is the difference that we noticed in these three in the next week immediately following this performance. The next day was the filming with a crew from CASA [a local art magnet school for high schoolers]. Again there was nervousness, but also a confidence inspired from their work the day before. They were able to joke around, but also get serious to make the art happen. After the filming we told them that they were free to stay or go—that the *Many Voices* staff were going to be staying around and having a meeting about the show and that we would love their input if they wanted to contribute. All three stayed and contributed in really meaningful ways to the very complex conversation about the direction of the show. We see this as an indication that they are beginning to take more ownership in the program. Their comments also indicated a better understanding of how planning is an integral part of making any larger project successful, a goal of our work.

14. See http://www.phrc.state.pa.us for statistics on the elevated numbers of hate crimes in the central Pennsylvania region.

15. The folklorists on this panel were Peggy Bulger, Gregory Hansen, Nancy Nusz, and Janis Rosenberg. A special issue of *Southern Folklore*—48 (1)—was published in 1991, featuring papers from that panel and other solicited essays on folklife in education, edited by Nancy J. Nusz.

16. Here is an excerpt from Tyra's poem:

> I have been here since 10:30–45 am today
> I have been getting into trouble
> I am really kind of hurt cuz I wasn't doin nuttin'
> I got yelled at by 3 teachers
> The whole time they are yellin'
> I'm thinkin' of ways to get back at him
> I'm thinkin' I'm going fuck dis nigga up
> Dumb ass . . . (*Watzup* 2007)

17. As teaching artist Iya Isoke wrote for the *Watzup* program essay,

> These students appearing in this program are no strangers to labels they have born the brunt of being slapped ferociously with them; wearing them like second skin. When Jason Moffitt and I walked into our first Spoken Word Session we felt a willingness to go the distance. Once we lifted the traditional classroom veil and allowed the students to freely speak life to their own lives . . . they became open and eager to express. During my time with these students, humbly guiding them in ways to effectively express their feelings I was find bouquets of roses growing from the concrete (Tupac [Shakur, 2000]). After this performance I'm sure there will be some who will still slap labels on these brilliantly progressive, striving, courageous students and we will continue to equip them to handle it. For now, this is their time to slap back.

9

Turning the University Inside Out: The Padua Alliance for Education and Empowerment

Lynne Hamer

Fɪʀsᴛ, sᴛᴀʀᴛ ᴡʜᴇʀᴇ ᴛʜᴇ ɪɴᴅɪᴠɪᴅᴜᴀʟ ɪs ᴛʜᴇ ᴇxᴘᴇʀᴛ and work out from there. Second, it is not right to ask an expert fiddler to play in a tent for free; she or he ought to be paid to play in a concert hall. These two instructions from my advisor Henry Glassie at the Indiana University Folklore Institute perpetually influence my thinking as an associate professor of education in postindustrial northwestern Ohio. Together they persuade me that our work as folklorists has its most profound potential in our ability to advocate for the value of the knowledge and expertise held by people who have been systematically shut out of access to full education and employment through institutional racism based in cultural bias.

Foregrounding the relationship between individual prejudice, cultural bias, and institutional discrimination provides a framework (Martin 1991) for thinking about folklore and education that I did not have prior to beginning my work in education. Here are two facts that I as a white, female teacher have become familiar with—and motivated by—through fieldwork and teaching here in Toledo. First, socioeconomic apartheid, described by Melvin Oliver and Thomas Shapiro as "sedimentation of inequality" (2006,

Lynne Hamer is an associate professor in the Department of Educational Foundations and Leadership at the University of Toledo and teaches most of her graduate and undergraduate courses as collaborations through the Padua Alliance for Education and Empowerment.

236), or the ways institutionalized policies and practices preventing blacks from buildingwealth generations ago continue to affect current generations, as seen in the startling recent research documenting that black women on average each have only five dollars in wealth (Insight Center for Community and Economic Development 2010). Second, the school-to-prison pipeline, a national trend toward criminalizing—rather than educating—youth through zero-tolerance policies, exacerbated by the pressures of high-stakes testing. The American Civil Liberties Union (2011), Children's Defense Fund (2007), and others have documented the phenomenon: African American students are much more likely than white ones to be suspended, expelled, or arrested for the same kind of (oftenminor)misconduct at school, leading to African American youth accounting for 45 percent of juvenile arrests but only 16 percent of the nation's overall juvenile population.

Although my current work is with a predominantly African American neighborhood in Toledo—and thus it constitutes the demographic focus in these examples—the framework in folklore and education is not limited to a particular group. What matters is that our disciplinary focus and research methods prepare us to work with historically marginalized students and their families. We are positioned 1) to recognize and affirm the value of their knowledge and skills by starting where they are experts, and 2) to advocate for the value of cultural knowledge, here not on the concert stage, but rather in the schoolhouse. This can happen at any level of education but my work is at the university.

Democratic Spaces

In spring 2007 a counselor and a former student in my graduate course Qualitative Research I introduced me to Sister Virginia Welsh ("Sister Ginny"), the founding director of the Padua Center, a community center in the central city in Toledo that opened in 2006, funded by the Toledo Catholic diocese. UT students and I had recently been invited to a participatory action research (PAR) conference hosted by Bowling Green State University at the Sofia Quintero Art & Cultural Center in south Toledo. Upon learning that PAR is based on researchers and the community being studied working together as a team toward common goals, the counseling student asserted that not only should we participate in the conference, but we should reconceptualize the course as PAR conducted at and with the Padua Center.

Graduate students and community members participate in a focus group about neighborhood assets and needs in the dining room of the Padua Center, June 2007.

In opening the center in one of the economically poorest neighborhoods in Toledo, Sister Ginny had insisted that it be dedicated to "education and empowerment." When we approached her, she quickly embraced collaboration with my department and to host the course Qualitative Research I: Introduction and Methods at the center in the summer of 2007. We named our project the Padua Alliance for Education and Empowerment, and with the graduate research course as our main vehicle, we were off and running—culminating our research-team work by making a presentation at the PAR conference that had originally prompted it (Hamer et al. 2007).

Progressive educational philosopher John Dewey identified two key components of democratic education: first, "not only more numerous and more varied points of shared common interest, but greater reliance upon the recognition of mutual interests as a factor in social control," and, second, "not only freer interaction between social groups (once isolated so far as intention could keep up a separation) but change in social habit—its continuous readjustment through meeting the new situations produced by varied intercourse" (1916, 100). Through the Padua Alliance for Education and Empowerment, we discovered how to actualize Dewey's ideas about democratic education by holding university classes in community locations with only brief forays into the university. The move made pedagogical sense. Our graduate students, mostly preservice and in-service teachers and school administrators, had spent between fourteen and thirty years in classrooms—and because of the continuing and increasing de facto segregation in our nation's schools (Orfield and Yun 1999), they had interacted almost exclusively with peers who had very similar socioeconomic, ethnic, and educational backgrounds. What could they learn by having another class in a university setting, interacting again with people very much like themselves? What could I learn by teaching it?

Moving the class location to the Padua Center and working with its members began a four-year, ongoing project creating democratic spaces for education and exchange between faculty and graduate students who work primarily in dominant-culture institutions (teaching, educational administration, counseling and school psychology, health education, social work, criminal justice, and other fields) and neighborhood residents who work primarily outside the dominant culture in their own neighborhoods, after-school programs, places of worship, and businesses—the people whom Barbara Kirshenblatt-Gimblett distinctively labeled "indigenous teachers" (1983, 10). What immediately became apparent is how far apart these two groups were: graduate students and faculty who had lived in Toledo for years, perhaps all their lives, had never been in this neighborhood. Community residents saw the university as entirely extraneous to their existence, even though it was only a few blocks away. PAR is key to making connections between the two and the Padua Alliance approach. Researchers, service providers, parents, and community members form action teams to identify needs, facilitate communication with institutions, and work with those institutions to take action.

This chapter relates the development of the Padua Alliance over the past four years, beginning with the graduate research course that has involved more than a hundred professionals in what is essentially folkloristic qualitative research in the neighborhood near their university, and ending with the most recent development—an undergraduate cohort that is taking a community-based approach to bringing neighborhood residents into the university. Most of the Alliance's work has taken place through the graduate class; this is the secret to the way we have been able to work with no funding, as well as how many graduate students have become familiar with folkloristic approaches without ever having considered signing up for a folk-lore class. The first section of the chapter describes the neighborhood, using historical data collected by the PAR team, as well as two pieces by community residents who continue to be key collaborators. The second section tells about the pedagogical approach and progression of the graduate course. The third section describes our current efforts to turn the university inside out through the Pickett Parent-Community Cohort, a pilot project offering undergraduate classes based in PAR at the local public elementary school.

The Neighborhood

In traveling to the Padua Center, we leave the UT main campus to go to the neighborhood that in the early 20th century was established by Polish immigrants and called "Kuschwantz" ("cow's tail") by German immigrants who lived adjacent to them. Today it is popularly called "the Junction" (after one of its main streets) by the African American community which lives there.[1]

On our way, we pass the original university site, a farm deeded by Jessup Scott to the city of Toledo in 1872. Once the university's two-year college location—intended to increase accessibility to underserved populations—it is now the Scott Park Campus of Energy and Innovation, sporting several wind turbines and a field of solar collectors. Looking east from Scott Park—down Nebraska Avenue and literally "across the tracks"—we see the tallest steeple in the city of Toledo, the old St. Anthony of Padua's Catholic Church. Built in 1882 and serving six thousand mostly Polish parishioners in its heyday, St. Anthony's was one of three Roman Catholic churches in this immigrant neighborhood at the end of the streetcar line.

In the late 1940s, African Americans—part of the Great Migration to the industrial glass and automotive center that was Toledo—were attracted to this neighborhood, which oral history tells us was rich with apricot and cherry trees, thriving vegetable and flower gardens, corner groceries, and affordable houses. By the 1950s and through the '60s, the neighborhood was racially and socioeconomically integrated, consisting mainly of Polish American and African American families, with neat houses and gardens and factory work within walking distance. Polish butcher shops and other businesses thrived along Nebraska Avenue, and six blocks north, Dorr Street was the heart of the African American business district.

In a paper presented at the annual meeting of the American Educational Studies Association in 2009, neighborhood resident Brenda Witcher called for "the possibility of this neighborhood to be like it was years ago, back in 1965" and recalled:

> It was real nice. The people over here kept their lawns up, they kept their houses up; things were nice. They had a "Little Downtown" up on Dorr Street. That's what we always called it. They had the drug stores, the grocery stores, the shops—hat shops, clothing shops, even a seamstress. They had a little of everything.
>
> Then urban renewal came in. The City started buying up all these houses and businesses because, they said, they wanted to make apartments. They tore down the whole neighborhood starting from Dorr, clear down to where it ends. They tore all that down and put in apartments. Then the people along here, in this neighborhood, south of Dorr—they saw all the Blacks were moving in, moving south from Dorr. So they moved out to the suburbs. People wanted to move to where they were more comfortable.
>
> I always would come over here and said, "I'm going to move over here someday," and I did, in 1965. I didn't know it was going to get like this—that people would be moving out. The place I really wanted to be at was somewhere in a nice neighborhood, close to the events I wanted to go to—and the grocery store and that. (Witcher, Mirzoyants, and Hamer 2009)

As Witcher recounts, after World War II, the neighborhood started changing: the old Polish families were lured by federal-housing programs to leave their homes—by now in need of major renovations—and move to the suburbs. For a brief time—during which she bought her home—this allowed the neighborhood to become integrated, and it was a nice place to live because homes were owner occupied, and work and shopping were within walking distance.

This changed suddenly and unexpectedly. Properties became rental. Mobility went up, and upkeep went down. The neighborhood that had recently been integrated became segregated, with some African Americans buying homes, but many renting in this area that was open to them in a city where redlining was the norm. The Civil Rights Act of 1964 did little to change the discrimination against African Americans in housing and—especially for men—getting jobs. The stresses of discrimination and its now-scientifically documented resulting physical pathologies of heart disease, depression, and alcoholism challenged families, but they persisted: as interviewees have noted, in multiple variations, you knew who your neighbor was, and you watched out for them.

In the 1970s, half-hearted attempts at school integration resulted in the neighborhood's public school, Pickett Elementary, being converted from K–8 to K–5, with sixth-to-eighth-grade students bused to Byrnedale Junior High School before returning to segregated central-city high schools. Gregory D. Johnson, who grew up in the neighborhood, described "getting integrated" in an essay published in the local community-college literary magazine:

> I can remember when they told us we were going to be shipped out to Byrnedale. . . . I cannot remember the teachers being happy about the situation. Some of the teachers were offered jobs out there . . . but there were only four or five of them, and they were saddened. And I think that sadness carried over to us students, when we got out to where we were going. . . . I don't know if *fear* would be the best word to use, but there was the unknown; going out to an all-white school, our first thought was, "What's the deal here?" For us, going out to an all-white school, and standards and customs and ways of doing things that we didn't know anything about, *fear* probably describes it best. . . .
>
> One thing I never understood was *why* they shipped some of us out to Byrnedale, and some to McTigue. The only thing that I can see is this: Pickett was a great school, with great teachers. We had a great program—it was probably one of the best schools in the city at the time. There were only a few failing students. Most kids I can remember were A and B students. But after we got to the new schools, to the junior high, we were held to different standards. I'm not talking about academic standards: those were the same. I'm talking about standards for being *included.* (Johnson 2009, 81)

Johnson identifies the breakdown of the school system as central to disrupting progress by African Americans toward realizing the promise of the civil-rights movement. He recalls, "A lot of kids who got shipped out to Byrnedale had to repeat their eighth-grade years" (2009, 84). Such disruptions have contributed to the neighborhood—and national—crisis of the school-to-prison pipeline, whereby zero-tolerance school-discipline policies transfer students out of school and into the juvenile-justice—and later adult justice—systems (Children's Defense Fund 2007). This is the ultimate exclusion.

After the destabilization of the educational system, other community members pick up the story. They unanimously cite the 1980s introduction of crack cocaine with its promise of quick wealth as central to the neighborhood's demise. Witcher's paper continues:

> That's where drugs and prostitution come in, because kids see momma
> is struggling, and dad—most of them don't have dads. They say,
> "I want to get out and make a living," but to do that it's got to be
> illegal. Everything starts at home. You see your parents struggling,
> and you see you never have things that you want—or just the basic
> things in life. You just exist. They say, "I don't want this kind of life,
> where you have to wait for this, wait for that, so I'm going to get out
> there and make it happen." That's their idea, because this generation is
> not like, "Let's go to school, let's get the grades," because they haven't
> had anything, and they want it right now. They want fast money.
> (Witcher, Mirzoyants, and Hamer 2009)

The oral and written histories collected from educators, police officers, business owners, religious leaders, and community members over the course of the Padua Alliance project concur in documenting a cycle that has become common in Toledo, as well as in urban communities throughout the nation. Underfunded, segregated, culturally unresponsive schools resort to severe discipline policies; students drop out and become unprepared young adults; and adults make a living however they can, cut off from dominant-culture options. The phenomenon known as shrinking cities (Jacobs 1992) identifies problems recognizable on a daily basis in neighborhoods such as this: lack of industry to maintain jobs; reduction of tax base due to the shortage of jobs and relocation of industry; and a series of funding choices at the local, state, and federal levels that maintain inequitable, property-tax-based school funding formulas and prioritize money to incarcerate over money to educate, in effect failing to uphold the constitutional guarantee of equal treatment under the law. Witcher's words bring this history to the present:

> Since then [1965], there has been very little help, although the City
> and agencies could help in many ways if they had the will and would
> work with us. We could start by scratch to get the neighborhood houses
> fixed up, instead of building these cracker-jack houses. They could help
> people who want to stay in their house, to keep their place up. . . .
>   Having the neighborhood like it was in the Sixties again is my main
> goal. Kroger's [Grocery], they even had a little hotel down there. Then
> they had a movie theater. Everything you needed to go to was down
> there. (Witcher, Mirzoyants, and Hamer 2009)

It is this goal that motivates community members to give their time, energy, and knowledge to the project and brings graduate students to collaborate with them.

An Ongoing, Integrated Curriculum

In Qualitative Research I, we use PAR pedagogy to develop a social-reconstructionist approach to formal graduate education.[2] Alice McIntyre (2000) provides an excellent explanation of the PAR process, fundamentally characterized by researchers and subjects working together as a research team to identify problems, formulate questions, collect and analyze data, and take action. PAR in this context is akin to service learning, which requires students to use community service to understand content studied formally in coursework more fully while they are using that coursework to provide better service (Center for Community Engagement 2006). My students and I provide the service of research to organizations and thus help them with both their assessment and their visibility while the students learn deeply about the way research really works by experiencing in a real project the issues of entry, rapport building, ethics, and representation, not to mention exercising the tools of participant-observation field notes, interview transcription, and document collection and analysis.

Social reconstructionism provides the underlying philosophy for both pedagogies. Social reconstructionists posit that the purpose of education is "solving critical problems to promote equality, justice, and democracy in the social environment"; the curriculum should be "community and larger social problems that are amenable to social and political action"; the teacher's role is to "raise students' consciousness about social problems and provide the tools for social critique and social action"; and the students' roles should be "active engagement in understanding social problems and taking action to solve them" (Oakes and Lipton 2003, 107).

Three elements, I believe, are key to the success of Qualitative Research I both as a course and as exposure to community folklore as part of social action. First, it is a core research course regularly included on plans of study for master's and PhD students who would not normally sign up for a folklore course. Second, throughout the course, I emphasize to students that they are learning the same research basics that they would in a regular on-campus course. Third, I continually remind participants that they are part of a larger, ongoing effort and therefore should not become frustrated when they question whether their semester's work will really have impact. It is important to view PAR from a long-term perspective because the rapport needed for collaboration between community and university takes time, and the knowledge on both sides to determine and take effective action likewise develops slowly. When we started the courses, I did not plan for them to have anything to do with folklore; however, I have come to recognize that any time a teacher puts mainstream, dominant-culture students in ongoing communication with people whose lives and expertise exist outside dominant-culture institutions and gives those students the tools and framework to appreciate the experiences and expertise of all people, that is a folkloristic approach.

PAR is too complex to be initiated and completed in one semester's coursework; for it actually to have effect, it must be viewed as an ongoing team effort. The following four semester snapshots demonstrate this process, with the first two semesters concentrating on the research part of PAR and the last two moving into action.

Assets and Needs, Summer 2007

TM (graduate student): So, what else do you think that I need to know about your community, your neighborhood, the strengths, the concerns, the areas of change that need to take place?
PJ (community member): You need to know that the area is very delicate. The trust is very low. They've got faith. They've got belief—they want to believe with everything in their heart—they want to believe. We have mostly old senior citizens that's done lived here forever. They done built homes, sent kids to school, and went to the service. They just want the family back. And the weakness is that they don't know what to do because they are too old to do it. . . . That's all they want. They want the trust, they want to trust again. (Interview PA 2007.TM.01, 6 June 2007)

Our first project was to conduct a qualitative assets and needs survey of neighborhood residents because Sister Ginny saw this as the first priority in creating a foundation for the new community center. Two community-center members, both longtime residents of the neighborhood, led us on a tour during which students practiced participant observation and taking field notes. They documented the neighborhood through descriptive notes and began to analyze the assets and needs through analytic ones (Sanjek 1990). Students' descriptive field notes were sprinkled with folklore about the way to cook pokeweed so that it would be nutritious rather than poisonous, where you could find the only pecan tree growing in Toledo, and the hospitality of front-porch culture. Their personal notes contributed to their understanding how easy it was to step across boundaries that had seemed uncrossable—if given the context, a friendly guide, and a shared purpose. As our community partners identified residents whom they thought we should interview and escorted class members to make introductions and facilitate fieldwork, the folkloristic content of our project became even more apparent. We interviewed a cane maker, a barber, owners of three small businesses (one of which carried white clay brought from the South, a medicinal product used by pregnant women), the leader of a youth drum corps, an itinerant gym-shoe salesman, a minister, and several longtime residents. When students and community members went together to the local history archive of the Toledo-Lucas County Public Library, they shared amazement at the dearth of printed information about the neighborhood—even in its Polish days—as well as the similarity between residents' demands from the city in the 1980s and the needs we were hearing about in interviews.

As community and student team members worked together to analyze data, they discovered key assets among neighborhood residents who recognize the need for change and are willing to take part in it, possess skills that can create change, have a strong sense of community, and possess widespread faith and hope for the future. Resident-identified needs included safety, education, revitalized housing and businesses, empowerment, and community involvement. Based on these documented needs, the Padua Alliance forged working relationships with the city of Toledo, Toledo Public Schools (TPS), Toledo Block Watch, and other community organizations within the neighborhood.

Oral History, Summer 2008

MS (community member): I moved here in 1964. . . . They had the civil rights—the NAACP, the Black Panther Party, the Nation of Islam, and a few like that, and then more. . . . I studied with the Nation of Islam. First of all—with them—was to do something for yourself. That is the reason why that wherever I go, whatever I do, instead of waiting on other people for doing something for me, I do it myself. So that is what inspired me [to open this store]. . . . Inner cities have a need for small business and also have a need for a lot of opportunity. . . . Perhaps by my going into a business industry here, it might inspire others to come here and do likewise. . . . And that is the reason why we're here today. (Interview PA 2008.BK.01, 3 June 2008)

One of the assets discovered in 2007 had been a rich sense of history, and one of the needs was to make that history accessible and educate residents and nonresidents alike about its value. Thus in the summer of 2008, the course project was an oral history of the neighborhood. Jean Anyon has written about school reform based on community development: "We can learn from stories of the past how people developed social movements, and what encouraged actors to get involved. History also reveals relationships between public policy, equity, and contention" (2005, 128). We can see this process in the storeowner's words. To look at his unprepossessing store—one of only two stores in the neighborhood not selling tobacco and alcohol—you would have no idea of its relationship to the Civil Rights Movement and Black Muslim tenets of self-sufficiency—both of which contain rich lessons for those involved today in trying to rejuvenate the community. As team members collected and analyzed data, we realized that social movements are based in the care and commitment of people—especially shop owners, religious leaders, and even bar proprietors—who tend to the social and physical well-being of their customers, congregations, and patrons and, through that attention, build the basis of a community that is empowered and can support its welfare.

Perhaps most significantly, interviews with former and current Polish American and African American residents about the neighborhood's history revealed these groups' similar experiences and common interests, even though both local and national media portray them as separate and distrustful of each other. The group community members and students worked together to identify themes that cut across interviews from both Polish Americans and African Americans: roots and history, values and social life, family and generational relationships, churches and mosques, government institutions, local businesses, conflict and struggle, strengths and weaknesses, and hopes and goals. Relating to local businesses, for instance, a student interviewed a political leader with Polish roots who recalled, "Our father's family operated a store around Buckingham and Hoag, one of their first stores. So they were always feeding people. . . . Their oldest son then [had] a store on Junction, and he was very famous during the Depression for . . . letting people buy on credit so they could get food even though they couldn't pay. And they always paid. They ultimately always paid even if it was pennies" (Interview PA 2008.SP.01, 29 May 2008). Compare this account of the Polish neighborhood store, circa 1910 to 1940, with the words of a current shop proprietor and Padua Alliance participant, Erma Blakely: "Neighbors are willing to help each other. Some small businesses

Erma Blakely, proprietor of the $1.50 Plus Food Mart at 1312 Nebraska Avenue in
Toledo is an avid supporter of Padua Alliance projects.

are able to allow the members of the community to pay as they have the
money. There is an honor system and a sense of trustworthiness" (Interview
PA 2008.CK.01, 5 June 2008).

Students and community members enjoyed the interview process and
the stories, which students presented to everyone they had interviewed in a
celebration at the Padua Center at the end of the term, as well as at a national
conference. During the presentation, students and community members
pondered, "What do we do with the stories?" The answers have guided our
work in the following semesters. First, the stories helped develop a shared
sense of history and identity and thus could be a basis for establishing common causes—as will be clear next in the account of fall 2008. Second, the
stories give us an alternative, local history that should be learned in school
as a complement and sometimes corrective to official, textbook information. Finally, the stories can become a model for necessary social action
in the present, as they did by connecting the work from the summer session
to the fall that year.

The first two semesters—with the assets and needs survey, followed by
oral-history collection—were primarily research with little action beyond

individuals coming together to establish common interests. In the third semester, we were ready to move into action.

Light the Night, Fall 2008

AS (community member): I am watching this neighborhood go from a number of businesses on each corner to deteriorating to just a few businesses on each corner. . . . On Blum, where it's so dark and there is no lighting, and . . . there are huge trees and vegetation, . . . they'll park and you'll hear arguments, . . . shouting in the streets, having confrontations. . . . Lighting is directly connected because lighting gets the city involved in the community and because the neighborhood doesn't feel as if the city cares. (Interview PA 2008.ND.1, 14 October 2008)

MS (community member): I guess my personal opinion is that I feel like it is more the system's fault, not so much the neighborhood members' fault. . . . We need help; it seems like that should . . . be a basic right that this neighborhood deserves. (Interview PA 2008.BK.1, 14 October 2008)

In the fall of 2008, our project entered the action phase of PAR. In August 2008, I met with the Padua Alliance board, two members of which had been interviewed for the oral-history project. Since the assets and needs survey in 2007, the board members had been working on several needs, including addressing the safety issue by improving street lighting. In actuality they had made much progress. They had identified and made contacts in relevant city departments and also found federal grants to underwrite pedestrian lighting. However, visible progress was another matter. We decided that the graduate course for the fall semester would prioritize making visible, immediate progress on improving lighting and reach out to the neighborhood elementary school for help because lights for children as they walked to and from school in the dark winter months was a major issue. As one parent explained,

My main concern—with especially the light project—is the kids and the kids' safety. You walk up, you see kids, especially young girls, going back and forth to school, and the bus stops and waiting for the bus and everything, and there is no light. And our time has changed where, you know, the world has become so corrupt . . . and violent and everything, and then [you] send your kids out there to go to school. (Interview PA 2008.JP.01, 11 November 2008)

The organization and requirements for the fall 2008 class were consistent with past courses. This semester, however, we met every other week in the Pickett Academy cafeteria to encourage involvement of the parent-teacher organization and because we believed that residents—many of whom had attended the school as children—would be more likely to attend a meeting there than at the newer, diocese-sponsored Padua Center. We were correct. Thirty community members participated with the Light the Night project. Early in the process, community members wanted to name our group, so we became the Inner City Development Coalition (ICDC). Brenda Witcher's daughter, Danielle, was elected president. Through Danielle's leadership, members from a neighborhood church founded by her grandmother became involved in data collection as well.

Two high points marked the semester's work. The first occurred when a city of Toledo Department of Public Utilities representative attended a Light the Night meeting in November. The ICDC gave him documentation of dim, dirty, burned-out, and missing streetlights that community members and student researchers had collected by traversing the neighborhood together. Following the meeting, a community resident led the city employee on an unplanned tour of the darkest streets of the neighborhood. In response the employee not only contacted Toledo Edison about replacing bulbs, but he also returned to the neighborhood in the following weeks to measure the distance between existing poles (by policy there should never be more than a 150-foot gap between adjacent light poles). ICDC members dubbed him "one of us," and he offered ongoing advice to the ICDC and its later incarnation, Brighten Up. The second high point was a public educational event held on the darkest night of the year (the winter solstice) to which residents, city and state elected representatives, and UT and public-school officials were invited. The mayor of Toledo gave a rousing endorsement of the project, and UT faculty and administrators who attended have remained excellent resources and collaborators in ongoing work.

An understanding shift about the relationship between the UT group and the community members solidified as well. In the previous semester during the oral-history research, UT participants had found that the Kuschwantz/Junction neighborhood was not a foreign country to them and began to share their insider knowledge on neighborhood tours. I had interviewed my next-door neighbor, who had grown up in the area and still owned rental property there, while a student had interviewed her secretary, who had also grown up in Kuschwantz and been an organist in the

Photo by Lacey Strickler.

Inner City Development Coalition President Danielle Witcher explains the project to a representative of the University of Toledo president's office at the Light the Night event, held the darkest night of the year—December 21, 2008—in the Pickett Academy gymnasium.

big Catholic church. One student's mother currently taught in the local elementary school, and several other students either had grown up or lived for a time in the neighborhood. During Light the Night, when one student was walking around the area, a very old man stopped him and said, "You must be Nathanial Jones." My student—surprised at this correct observation—said, "Yes, but how did you know?" The old man explained that the student's grandfather had lived on his street and his father had grown up there, and the student had even played there as a child. "You look exactly the same now as you did then," the man concluded.

The lessons from fall 2008 centered on identity, common cause, and audience. The collective naming of the group as the Inner City Development Coalition constituted a social transformation because different entities united to become one, linking the dominant-culture social institutions of UT, TPS, and the city of Toledo to the Padua Center, Toledo Block Watch, and churches "to apply the pressure that a social movement can provide" (Anyon 2005, 152). The insight that had been building—that the boundaries between UT student and community members were fluid—began to take hold. At this point, too, Brenda Witcher explained that our main emphasis must not be on communicating about our projects to residents in the neighborhood but rather, communicating as a coalition of residents and students to the elected officials and other powers that be:

> We're over here in this area—this is a black neighborhood over here, and you know they [the city and elected officials] do the least they can do to get away. But when they see other people involved—Caucasians, Arabs—you see them involved in trying to get something going for the local people, and they're going to school. And TU's offering grants for this side to go to school, and other sides. I think that's what woke them up. . . . You bring in other people, different races. . . . We had to take that resource that we had, with this mixed group, to get ahead. Anything that works, use it! (Witcher, Mirzoyants, and Hamer 2009)

It is significant to note that Witcher called the university TU, short for Toledo University, its name until the 1960s. Witcher was not alone. I have seldom heard the university called anything but TU in my four years in the neighborhood, which I take as a sign that UT has not been a relevant part of most of the community's life in the past fifty years. To fix that, as Witcher stated, we must use "anything that works." Thus, our success with Light the Night marked a turning point. Instead of us, university people, and them, community people, we became us, Padua Alliance, working together to influence policies and practices of them, city and school officials, to treat the neighborhood equitably.

The success of Light the Night also led to three significant developments. First, community members and several students continued meeting with the Padua Alliance in January 2009 and wrote a successful grant, "Brighten Up: Ourselves, Our Homes, Our Neighborhoods," to the local Catholic Campaign for Human Development (CCHD) chapter to fund four community organizers to continue working on improving lighting and cleaning up abandoned or absentee-landlord property during the summer. (CCHD funded a second "Brighten Up" proposal in January 2010 to hire a part-time, year-round community organizer.) Second, the affiliation among Pickett Academy, the Padua Center, and UT made it possible to apply for a five-million-dollar U.S. Department of Education grant to involve in-service elementary teachers in graduate coursework concurrently with school parents and guardians in undergraduate classes as a way to open "democratic space" for the free exchange of ideas between the two groups (Hamer et al. 2010). Although this application was denied, proposals to local foundations to provide matching funds were accepted, and the parent/guardian component of

Participants in the Padua Alliance for Education and Empowerment, including University of Toledo graduate students and members from the Padua Center community, travel together to the American Educational Studies Association annual meeting to present two panels on their work.

the project has been implemented and will be discussed later in this chapter.

Third, because connections and trust had developed over the four years of working together, we were able to propose—again to the U.S. Department of Education—a plan to develop a Promise Neighborhoods coalition (Hamer, Kumar, and Jenkins 2010). The Promise Neighborhoods movement, a cornerstone of President Obama's educational plan, is based on the recognition that informal and nonformal education must complement formal education and family and community livelihoods must be supported if children are to thrive in schools (Tough 2008). Although this grant application was also not funded, it gave us a focus and framework for a strong coalition of religious, business, health, cultural, and educational organizations whose scopes span from the neighborhood to the county level. The Kuschwantz/Junction Promise Neighborhoods project has continued without funding and became the framework for our fall 2010 PAR work, prompting organizations and agencies around the city to begin to recognize us as viable partners in their projects and initiatives.

Promise Neighborhood Coalition, Fall 2010

YM (high school student): It is rare about black people [in school] so we really can't get into the material. [In school] you really can't know and understand yourself. (PA2009.JL.01, 19 October 2010)

CM (founder of SETT): In our education, we show them through the Harlem Renaissance, the high cultural part, and many integral people like Langston Hughes and James Weldon Johnson's "Lift Every Voice and Sing.". . . . Children of all cultures—and especially black children—have found an opportunity to feel good about who they are at that particular point, and to realize it doesn't make you any better than anyone, you know, but it doesn't make you any less. (PA2009. LT.01, 9 November 2010)

In the fall of 2010, we branched out from our base at the Padua Center and worked with two neighborhood-based organizations in our Promise Neighborhoods coalition: Your Community Market and Self Expression Teen Theater (SETT). Both were founded by neighborhood residents and leaders inspired by the Civil Rights Movement to promote pride in heritage and self-sufficiency. In the Promise Neighborhoods work, we identified Your Community Market and Blakely's $1.50 Plus store as the lead organizations for addressing children's needs from birth through early childhood. These stores and their indigenous teachers would bring in neighborhood residents with young families and work with various agencies and UT faculty in early childhood education, health education, and literacy. We identified SETT as the lead organization for addressing the needs of middle- and high-school students. SETT with its indigenous leadership would work with TPS, UT faculty in middle- and high-school education, and UT faculty and staff in higher education to support teenagers to stay in school and continue successfully into college.

In September, after our second federal-grant application was rejected, Oscar Shaheer of Your Community Market voiced his desire to have meetings to help educate residents about nutrition and stepped forward to lead that group even without funding. Through the course of the semester and beyond, a series of meetings called "Making Ends Meet" were held monthly, working with the Ohio State University Extension office, UT faculty in health education and environmental studies, and staff in political offices. Some of our fall 2010 graduate students did participant observations of three monthly meetings, collected documentary data, and interviewed Shaheer, his brother Mustafa Shaheer, and other community leaders. We learned, among other things, that the Shaheers' grandfather had farmed in Georgia early in the last century, that the Shaheers' desire to help black farmers had been the guiding force in their opening the store, and that gardening and canning were valuable steps on the road to self-sufficiency.

Also in September 2010, Brother Washington Muhammad, the project coordinator of SETT, expressed willingness to push on with Promise Neighborhoods despite lack of funding. Thus, some fall 2010 students focused on SETT, conducting participant observations during rehearsals (in some cases, participating in drills and skits), organizing a document collection that included skit scripts and publicity from past productions, and interviewing past and current SETT members; they learned through this process that "once a member of SETT, always a member." One document in the collection—a handout entitled "What is SETT?"—explains that it is "a troupe of teen actors who also function as peer educators and counselors," using a "holistic approach" to conquer problems by encouraging teens to "Just Say NO!" and establish healthy lifestyles. SETT presents skits and raps to schoolchildren, peers, and others "to generate thoughtful talk about needs and feelings." The students' observations revealed that a big part of the SETT curriculum is knowledge of African and African American history. We had the opportunity to learn the African American national anthem, "Lift Every Voice and Sing," because SETT members form a circle and sing the anthem, then discuss the group's "rules of engagement," at the beginning of each rehearsal and performance. We also learned the "Serenity Prayer" because at the end of each rehearsal, the group forms a circle again, clears any bad feelings that may have arisen during the time together, and then says the prayer.

Thus, the fall of 2010 brought the PAR process full circle, introducing new organizations with which we could work. These organizations are essentially folk groups, providing, as José Limón (1983) noted, both direct and indirect confrontation to the dominant-culture's hegemony of unhealthy food sold to low-income citizens and unabashedly Eurocentric school curriculum. To the extent that the graduate students have learned the values and behaviors of these groups, they will be able to take that information into their professional lives as educators, administrators, and counselors. If the students continue working with Your Community Market and SETT as part of the same team, they will establish new, alternative organizations. And if the UT students' and faculty members' involvement with the organizations and their members encourages them to become UT students and gain the credentials to be leaders, that will challenge the dominant hegemony even further. In answer to the student interviewer's question, "How can you see the university helping SETT?" Brother Washington summed up his feelings this way:

I see SETT fitting in with the university in a number of ways. There is so much failure among at-risk youth, but we have a high graduation rate. I can see the university partnering with SETT to get a pool of kids that will go to the university and succeed at the university. . . . Our kids graduate at a higher rate than most, and we prepare them for furthering their education. . . . I can see the university looking at our kids and thinking, "Wow! Here's a great program with a great record where we don't have to do a bunch of remedial work with these kids, and they can come to the university and graduate, and they can really go far." (Interview PA 2010.BK.01, 3 November 2010)

Brother Washington's focus on his young students coming from the community into the university paralleled our next step.

Centering the University in the Community

At this point, we turned our attention to bringing adult community members—many of whom had been our research-team partners and had thus been doing university work—into the university, by taking the university further into the community. The need for this move had been apparent since the summer of 2007, when our community partners were doing much of the same work that the graduate students did but not receiving academic credit. On the positive side, community members and graduate students alike were expanding their social networks. However, on the negative side, community members were not getting credentials in the form of university degrees that would boost their earning capacity. In the fall of 2010, we initiated a program entitled Supporting the Parents to Lead the Way.[3] Originally calling the program UT Educational Opportunities (UT-EO), we stated its purpose this way:

> UT-EO provides college education opportunities to low-income parent-guardians of children enrolled in underperforming Toledo Public Schools. UT-EO increases access to higher education by holding classes in those schools, at reduced cost and in a supportive and individualized cohort model. Though the parent-guardians will be the direct beneficiaries of this project, their children will benefit as well as they will have the strongest role models possible for staying in school and pursuing postsecondary education—and when they get to college themselves, as second-generation college students they will be much more likely to succeed. (Hamer, Kumar, Ragland, and Twitchell, 2010, 1)

In the spring of 2011, sixteen students, one the daughter of a neighborhood resident we had worked with in 2007, began university coursework as a cohort meeting at Pickett Academy with the mission—as voiced by those students—of "getting in school, staying in school, and getting a good-paying job." Meeting off campus has at least three advantages. First, it allows us to "start where the individual is the expert and work out from there." The first semester's courses—Diversity in Contemporary Society and Composition I—were selected not only because both are core courses for any undergraduate program at UT but also because the students' existing cultural knowledge could shape and build on these classes, as well as help them contextualize the dominant-cultural content by acquiring vocabulary and authority. Second, meeting off campus is much less expensive, and thus, federal and state student grants will cover expenses so students do not need to take out loans. UT has a program called Workplace Credit, which facilitates coursework at any off-campus site by charging only 78 percent of regular tuition with no additional fees. Furthermore, since it is a cohort program, we were able to pay a writing tutor directly, rather than requiring the students to enroll in the five-credit course, Composition I with Attached Tutoring. Third, the elementary-school students benefit indirectly by being exposed, on a daily basis, to their parents, grandparents, aunts and uncles, and neighbors attending college in their school.

As part of Diversity in Contemporary Society, the students worked with the United Way of Greater Toledo, which has in the past two years intensified work in education with the goal of increasing local graduation rates. Our students contributed to the organization's project documenting parents' ideas about their involvement in schooling. In pairs the students conducted focus sessions with diverse community groups, including two church study groups, a women's support group, a Spanish-speaking mother/child play group, and parent volunteers in an elementary school. They also introduced ideas about using "funds of knowledge" from students' communities as curricular resources in classrooms, based on Luis Moll and his colleagues (1992, 132). One student wrote about his neighbor's "secret to make your tomatoes sweet": "First, take some broken drywall (about three to four pieces) and plant them around the tomato plant. Second, take a banana peel and plant that around the tomato plant. Once the tomatoes are ripened, your taste buds will be the test." Another wrote about her brother teaching her to play the bongos, noting "I can play them very well." Another wrote about her friend, with whom she is embarking on her university education, and said, "We are both in school looking to pursue our career and encourage each other to do what is best." Through this funds-of-knowledge approach, students can begin where they are experts, building on their strengths to succeed in the university.

Conclusions and Next Steps

It is in these democratic spaces, which are in fact characteristic of all FAIE work as folklorists facilitate community members coming into classrooms and students going into communities, that, as Limón suggested, folklore can "offer indirect contestation 'by its presence'" (1983, 35). In other words, simply by putting people who normally live in the dominant-culture world of schools and those who normally live in the nondominant, or subordinate, world outside schools in the same space, we establish conditions to break hegemonic strangleholds and encourage creativity—Dewey's democratic-education ideals. The key, I believe—as with bringing the fiddler to the concert hall—is to transport the "folk" into universities, to recognize and encourage individuals to build on their/our strengths, and to work as collaborators in shaping a new way to do school. Otherwise first-generation college students are less likely to complete a degree program (Choy 2001; Nunez and Cuccaro-Alamin 1998) and thus unlikely to influence institutions. The presence of these groups, which have been historically excluded from higher education for any reason—race, socioeconomic status, culture—challenges hegemonic practices.

If at least part of our work as folklorists is—as I said at the beginning of this chapter—valuing knowledge and expertise of people who have been systematically shut out of full education and employment then I believe one of our roles in educational reform is clear. As Limón suggested, we need to recognize and help others to recognize the relationship between "'economic' base and . . . 'cultural' superstructure"—to see the ways these are "reciprocally intertwined" and how "folklore can . . . offer indirect contestation 'by its presence'" (1983, 50). Educational theorists—particularly those working in social foundations of education—have in the last decade been calling for increased attention to the relationship between families' lack of opportunities outside school and their children's achievement.

Educational sociologists provide the discussion of institutionalized discrimination and the need for social reconstruction that can contextualize the work we do with students and families to help them value their culture: Jean Anyon details the need and opportunity for "a new paradigm of educational policy . . . [that] would transform the political and economic environment that currently stymies most student and educator effort in low-income neighborhoods, as we push toward community involvement" (2005, 13). Mike Rose calls for "an economic discussion of schooling that we ought to hear, but rarely do. This would be a discussion that places individual and school failure in the context of joblessness, health-care and housing security, a diminished tax base, economic policy, and the social safety net" (2009, 27). Clearly Anyon and Rose focus on economic issues; however, a folklorist's appreciation for the connection between economics and culture can help realize the goals they formulate by starting with cultural understanding as a basis for institutional and economic development.

Through our fieldwork methods and deep respect for the cultural expressions and values that exist outside dominant-culture institutions like schools and universities, we can help parents and community leaders organize so they can become key leaders in school success. Traditionally the role of the folklorist in all FAIE efforts has been facilitating understanding between communities' indigenous teachers and schools, and we need to capitalize on that history. Andrew Mott has noted, "There is a desperate shortage of people who are expert at bringing poor people together to build strong organizations and movements for tackling the immense issues they face daily." He calls for developing university programs both to "help people learn how to be effective community change agents" and to prevent these efforts from "suffer[ing] from being isolated, marginalized, and held back from developing the breadth and depth that would maximize their value" (2005, 5). Folklorists working in education have the opportunity, the aptitude, the disposition, and the tools to help administrators and policy makers in dominant-culture schools recognize the value of the strong, self-sustaining organizations already established in socioeconomically disadvantaged groups, as well as the knowledge and skills of the individuals in these groups, and help position these groups and individuals as leaders in educational reform.

Notes

1.   This section incorporates an oral-history collection in process, *Kuschwantz-Junction: Histories of an Integrated Urban Neighborhood in Constant Transition,* which assembles histories collected throughout the coursework described in this chapter. For historic

information on St. Anthony's Parish, see "St. Anthony's: A Memorium, 1882–2005," at http://stanthonytoledo.com For information about Dorr Street during the Civil Rights Movement and urban renewal, see the WGTE documentary *Through Toledo's Eyes*, which chronicles Toledoans' recollections of the Movement as it played out on Dorr Street (http://www.wgte.org).

2. This chapter focuses on Qualitative Research I and the undergraduate cohort classes because they are the central coursework in the overall Padua Alliance project. Other coursework, however, also relates to the Padua Alliance. Each semester for the past two years, approximately two hundred Introduction to Education undergraduates have participated in service learning as the central requirement of their coursework. These placements are at Padua, Pickett, and many other sites we have become familiar with through the Padua Alliance project. Also during these years, we have had a graduate course—Service Learning in Peace Education—in which graduate students help teach the peace-education component of the Padua Possibilities Alternative-to-Suspension Program, an innovative collaboration between the Padua Center and Pickett Academy. Most recently undergraduate and graduate students and faculty in business, health education, and environmental studies have been working—through coursework—at the Padua Center and other local sites. Although some of these collaborations might have occurred without the Padua Alliance, they all started through our connection.

3. Supporting the Parents to Lead the Way is funded in part by grants from the UT College of Education dean's innovation fund of Dr. and Mrs. Thomas E. Brady and from the Toledo Community Foundation, as well as by many units throughout UT. Their support and enthusiasm are gratefully acknowledged.

Conclusion

Learned Lessons, Foreseeable Futures

Paddy Bowman and Lynne Hamer

A BOOK TAKES A WHILE TO COME INTO BEING, and from the vantage point of 2011, seeing what has changed in four years is sobering. We began this book at a more promising time, when Folk Arts in Education (FAIE) programs, professional-development opportunities for teachers and artists, and new curricula and materials were flourishing. We were fresh from exciting education sessions at the 2007 American Folklore Society meeting in Québec City, where Steve Swidler of the University of Nebraska School of Education had the foresight to invite a Utah State University Press editor, John Alley, to a forum, "Making the Intangible Tangible: Uses of Folklife Resources in Educational Settings" (Meister 2007). Gwen Meister chaired the session, which also included Lisa Higgins, Pat Kurtenbach, Maida Owens, Anne Pryor, and Steve Swidler. Alley's enthusiasm for the importance of the work and his surprise at its invisibility as a subfield excited the FAIE presenters, whose essays are now part of this book.

Today that enthusiasm continues despite a lingering financial crisis, a stalled public-education system, and a political environment that seems at the moment intent on cutting arts, culture, and social programs. Such developments potentially stymie the field of FAIE, as well as the work of folklorists in both academic and public sectors. At a time when K–12 educators most need to call upon the local, cultural agencies are cutting folk-arts programs and positions, thus reducing outreach, technical assistance, and resource development. Academic folklore programs have shrunk and, in some cases, even disappeared. Folklorists in state and regional agencies find themselves doing everything but fieldwork or losing their jobs entirely. Many museums and nonprofit folklore organizations are strapped, and some are closing their doors. Once numbering forty-five, the network of state folk-arts coordinators, which Bess Lomax Hawes envisioned and developed while director of the National Endowment for the Arts Folk and Traditional Arts program from 1977 to 1992, is shrinking as state government budgets decline. Concomitantly, since most state budgets are in dire trouble, educators have fewer professional-development opportunities, such as institutes and workshops, and less incentive to accrue in-service and graduate credit because school systems may no longer reward them with higher pay.

As yet the Obama administration's educational policy has not loosened the deadlock wrought by No Child Left Behind (NCLB) and the standards movement, begun as a bipartisan effort led by Bill Clinton before his 1993 inauguration and developed during the George W. Bush years. In "failing schools," elementary teachers may have to teach from a script and students spend art class practicing filling in bubbles for the standardized tests that dominate the school calendar. The trend toward teacher accountability means that such testing will not diminish. The move to create national curriculum standards, plus the emphasis on teacher accountability, may homogenize teacher preparation as colleges of education respond to state educational requirements by developing standardized courses. At the same time, what is offered ostensibly to improve education in these failing schools is not at all democratic and equitable. For example, politically popular programs like Teach for America provide minimal training for temporary teachers who are on their way to other careers in business and law, to work with the most at-risk students in the most neglected of our schools (Veltri 2010).

"School choice" through the burgeoning charter-school movement and expanding voucher programs has succeeded in some areas by introducing competition to entrenched public districts but continues to make second-rate educational options for underprivileged populations more available, instead of providing high-quality education for all, while privatization introduces a strong profit motive incompatible with democratic education (Lubienski 2010). Reading, writing, and mathematics continue to rule, and teaching to the (high-stakes) test governs the curriculum of middle and lower socioeconomic schools, despite evidence that test-driven policies and practices do not improve learning (FairTest 2011; Hursh 2008). In her best-seller subtitled "How Testing and Choice Are Undermining Education," former NCLB proponent and educational historian Diane Ravitch thoroughly recants and writes that "it is the mark of all sentient beings to learn from experience, to pay close attention to how theories work out when put into practice" (2010, 2). Her comment resounds with the call of folklorists working in education for schools to attend to students' and families' experience.

Despite these obstacles, we remain dedicated to the belief that understanding and considering young people and their various, overlapping communities—or folk groups—make for better schooling. At the federal level, the Obama administration is making a hopeful movement toward a community organizing approach to educational reform under the umbrella of Promise Neighborhoods, inspired by the vision of Geoffrey Canada in developing the Harlem Children's Zone (Tough 2008) and supported by research showing the strong relationship between community organizing and school success (Mediratta, Shah, and McAllister 2008).

Advocates and practitioners of multicultural, place-based, ecojustice, and expeditionary education share some of folklorists' perspectives on the importance of engaging with the local and including faces and voices that look and sound like students. As a National Art Education Association monograph notes, "The reality of most classrooms is that students are from many different places and cultures. Dislocation and estrangement often shape their notion of place," and "education in the U.S. neglects the local and ecological in favor of the logic of the standardization and high-stakes testing designed to prepare students for competition in the global economy" (Graham 2009, 2–3).

FAIE materials and methods are ready and waiting to take on these challenges. A folkloristic approach can help overcome feelings of dislocation and disconnection because folklorists define literacy differently from other disciplines, focusing on authenticity, the local, the vernacular, and the deep context of an infinite variety of traditions. A gifted mariachi musician who cannot read music, a scientist who secretly publishes a humorous office blog, a kindergartner who creates YouTube podcasts of her birthday party, and a faculty member who exchanges composting tips with a community gardener are all expert tradition bearers, yet conventional academic standards of literacy and learning would not recognize these examples of creativity and skill.

However, they are exactly the sort of noncanonical texts that educational theorist Cameron McCarthy called for—and lamented the difficulty in implementing—when he identified the need to "ventilate the curriculum" by incorporating heterogeneous learning styles and content into the classroom to create a "critical emancipatory multiculturalism" that would place "relationality and multivocality as the central intellectual forces in the production of knowledge" (1994, 90). Folklorists know that teaching and learning occur throughout the day in every possible setting, with every vocalization and action. Calling upon informal pedagogy—and its centrality in real life—may set folklorists apart from teachers, but folklorists must also investigate and honor the work of professional educators as important tradition bearers coming through the schoolhouse door (Hamer 1999). This attitude remains important because both fields, as the essays in this book reveal, benefit richly from collaboration—and they stand to benefit so much more.

Educational theorists and practitioners espousing an ecojustice framework emphasize teachers and students learning to identify cultural patterns and the ways that they affect human and environmental relationships while turning to Indigenous cultures to learn about sustainable ways of living (Martusewicz, Edmundson, and Lupinacci 2011). C.A. Bowers, one of the founders of ecojustice pedagogy, calls for ecojustice and the salvation of cultural and environmental commons (meaning public holdings where people interact freely) to be the foundation of school and social reform. He charges that "the modern idea of development equates progress with bringing what remains of the cultural and environmental commons under the control of the market forces that have been made even more destructive by the expansion of global competition" (2006, 7). Folklorists' collections of and methods for accessing knowledge that is part of the cultural commons certainly have much to offer this quest.

History educators for the past decade have known that their students see their grandparents as much more reliable sources than their teachers, and their scrapbooks as more authentic history than their textbooks (Rosenzweig and Thelen 2000). Now science educators are also discovering that students learn more science, and learn it better, outside school (Falk and Dierking 2010). Again FAIE materials provide excellent resources that can be implemented widely with relatively inexpensive professional development and even less expensive materials and equipment.

MENC: The National Association for Music Education has begun recognizing the vitality of traditional music as a way to expand music education, exemplified by a recent mariachi education initiative (see http://www.menc.org/gp/menc-s-mariachi-education-site) and outreach to bluegrass music educators. The National Council for the Social Studies emphasizes culture as an essential component of social-studies education. Leadership in the National Art Education Association has long included folklorists such as Kristin Congdon (see chapter 7) as well as scholars who incorporate traditional culture and art forms and address issues of authenticity and representation head-on. Likewise, the National Council of Teachers of English takes culture and authenticity seriously.

After a half century of work and a decade of significant growth, FAIE practitioners will no doubt weather the current storm of cuts. We remain well positioned to contribute to improving democratic schooling practices for all students, but we must perpetually be creative in new ways that work differently in every community and situation—building on our strengths of collaborating with communities while continuing to promote our work as useful in meeting measurable educational standards. Allying with schools of education, school systems, cultural agencies, and organizations that serve young people outside school is more important than ever. (Folklorists and others interested in identifying local and state chapters of national education groups will find a selected list at the end of this chapter.)

We have challenges to overcome in our own practices, most related to making our work visible and accessible. High-quality FAIE resources abound (see the listings in the appendix); however, few FAIE resources make it onto school or public library shelves. Seeking an answer to the question, "Are we just writing for other folklorists?" Paddy Bowman made inquiries. A retired professor of library media sciences examined a significant number of FAIE publications and Web sites and revealed a problem: unless a resource is hardbound, *School Library Journal* will not review it, nor will libraries purchase it (interview with Betty Carter by Paddy Bowman, 15 April 2009, Dallas, Texas). The gorgeous K–12 guide *Quilting Circles - Learning Communities,* by Anne Pryor and Nancy B. Blake (2007), is spiral bound. The Herculean efforts of Marsha MacDowell and LuAnne Kozma to compile *Folk Arts in Education: A Resource Handbook II* (2008) are available in the iconic orange binder—the equivalent of spiral bound—and as a CD-ROM or free download. These excellent FAIE resources, like many others, will thus not make an inroad into many school settings.

Innovative FAIE Web sites? Because of school firewalls, the digital divide, and a crowded school day, they are often inaccessible to teachers and students, and thus also continue to have limited use. For now the best sources for both classic and new FAIE resources remain the Local Learning Web site (http://www.locallearningnetwork.org), the American Folklife Center's Folklife Resources for Educators portal (http://www.loc.gov/folklife/teachers), and the American Folklore Society Folklore and Education Section Web page (http://www.afsnet.org/?page=FolkloreEd) with its annual newsletter featuring reviews of new resources and a roster of annual winners of the Dorothy Howard Folklore and Education Prize. But these resources, along with other notable Web-based publications, are not on the public radar. Here is a lesson learned: before planning a new resource, consulti with school-library media specialists about books, media, and Web sites that they find valuable and accessible.

As folklorists seeking to influence school education, we can learn from an author whose books for young readers *have* found a market among school libraries and classroom teachers. Alan Govenar's first endeavor for students was based on his long relationship with a Dallas folk artist, Osceola Mays. *Osceola: Memories of a Sharecropper's Daughter* (2000) won notable awards in the world of children's literature (but was not reviewed by folklorists). His other books for young readers have earned raves in *School Library Journal* and other educational publications (2006a, 2006b). Likewise, a number of beautiful picture books commissioned by the Vermont Folklife Center and based on oral histories in the Center's archives have won high praise as well as awards (http://www.vermontfolklifecenter.org).

What makes an FAIE guide or Web site both work well and find its way into the hands of educators, students, and the general public? We are still trying to figure that out. The Vermont Folklife Center and Alan Govenar found publishers who market to young readers and produce hardbound, beautifully illustrated and designed books. We have also learned that we must take national and state educational standards into account. Writing toward the standards is not as odious as teaching to the test because folklore fits somewhere in the criteria of all disciplines (see Sidener 1997); creating standards to promote inclusion of important, but marginalized, topics and pedagogies is an approach that educators in social foundations are increasingly taking (for example, Andrzejewski, Baltodano, and Symcox 2009). Conversely, it is useful to place folkloristic approaches and strengths within the dictates of state academic standards. Examining standards is easy since discipline-based education-association Web sites reference national standards (again see the selected list of national education organizations), and states post them on their education-department Web sites. Likewise, holding conversations with teachers of various subjects and grade levels about the standards they need to teach, along with the local resources they have, is valuable.

We propose that folklore colleagues in both academic and public realms make connections with folklorists who work in K–12 education, as well as professional educators. As Lisa Rathje noted in chapter 8, cultural equity relates to educational equity, and as folklorists we are concerned with equality and social justice. Most basically—and of utmost importance—the ways that teachers think of students, their parents, and their communities can dangerously or positively shape and mediate pedagogy. A folkloristic lens helps. Educational reform has been a hot topic for more than fifteen years, but most reform efforts still do not examine school or community culture. Educational reform cannot happen without taking school culture into serious consideration. Folklorists have tools to help educators document and analyze that culture. The Local Learning report, "Our Values and Goals", contains a list of strengths and hallmarks of FAIE projects to help ground people new to the field (http://locallearningnetwork.org/about/our-values-and-goals).

As scholars of local culture and advocates of inclusion, we need to interact with young people and educators to share our scholarship and methods and learn from and with them. The reciprocity of teaching and learning, combined with new media, offers folklorists and educators innovative opportunities. Folklore provides authentic, meaningful content—a primary source that students can both study and create. Engaging young people as cocreators of knowledge, projects, and products through ethnography, technology, and social media holds exciting promise.

The invisibility of the field of folklore in this country hampers all folklorists; educating others about our discipline broadens awareness, support, and audiences for both folklore and the local tradition bearers with whom we work. In the past decade, FAIE practitioners have produced important, engaging resources that elucidate the meaning and power of folklore to nonfolklorists and make creative use of scholarly fieldwork. Folklorists should employ these resources in higher education and public programs. Folklorists in the academy would profit by paying more attention to FAIE practices and resources because FAIE educators find that their teaching and writing improve by working with teachers and young people. Improved teaching better serves undergraduate and graduate students. Public-program folklorists must effectively reach and educate the general public, as well as bureaucrats in state and local agencies. In fact, distilling our work to articulate its depth and value for nonfolklorists is part of every folklorist's job. We invite folklorists as well as educators to call upon the field of FAIE. As we look ahead in this time of economic, political, and social unease, we know that folklore and its approaches to education can benefit educators and their students, as well as their families and communities.

To that end, we offer a final anecdote. Using a Venn diagram of three overlapping circles representing elite, popular (or normative), and folk culture to conclude a graduate education course, Paddy Bowman asked students what would be missing if we knew about and experienced only elite and popular culture, the two realms most visible to the majority of Americans. "Everything," said one student. "Life," said another. "The things that matter most," said a third. Among these things that matter most, we must include our nation's young people, their myriad communities, and their education.

Selected National Education Organizations

The following professional influence curricular and pedagogical decisions and educational policy.

American Association of School Librarians (http://www.ala.org/ala/mgrps/divs/aasl)

American Democracy Project (http://www.aascu.org/programs/adp)

American Educational Research Association (http://www.aera.net)

American Educational Studies Association (http://www.educationalstudies.org)

American Library Association (http://www.ala.org)

Arts Education Partnership (http://www.aep-arts.org)

Association for Supervision and Curriculum Development (http://www.ascd.org)

Kennedy Center Alliance for Arts Education (http://www.kennedy-center.org/education/kcaaen)

Local Learning: The National Network for Folk Arts in Education (http://www.locallearningnetwork.org)

MENC: The National Association for Music Education (http://www.menc.org)

National Art Education Association (http://www.arteducators.org)

National Association for Multicultural Education (http://nameorg.org)

National Council for the Social Studies (http://www.socialstudies.org)

National Council of Teachers of English (http://www.ncte.org)

National Council of Teachers of Mathematics (http://www.nctm.org)

National Guild for Community Arts Education (http://www.nationalguild.org)

National Science Teachers Association (http://www.nsta.org)

National Writing Project (http://www.nwp.org)

Teaching Tolerance (http://www.teachingtolerance.org)

U.S. Department of Education (http://www.ed.gov)

USDOE portal to state education departments and other organizations (http://wdcrobcolp01.ed.gov/Programs/EROD/org_list.cfm)

Works Cited

Abrahams, Roger. 1971. Cultural Differences and the Melting Pot Ideology. *Educational Leadership* 29: 118–21.

Abrahams, Roger, and Rudolph Troike, eds. 1972. *Language and Cultural Diversity in American Education.* Englewood Cliffs, NJ: Prentice-Hall.

American Civil Liberties Union. 2011. School-to-Prison Pipeline. http://www.aclu.org/racial-justice/school-prison-pipeline (accessed 21 April 2011).

Andrzejewski, Julie, Marta Baltodano, and Linda Symcox, eds. 2009. *Social Justice, Peace, and Environmental Education: Transformative Standards.* New York: Routledge.

Anyon, Jean. 2005. *Radical Possibilities: Public Policy, Urban Education, and a New Social Movement.* New York: Routledge.

Anzaldúa, Gloria. 1987. *Borderlands/La Frontera: The New Mestiza.* San Francisco: Aunt Lute Books.

Aristotle. 1976. *The Nicomachean Ethics.* London: Penguin.

Baker, Ronald. 1977. Writing about Folklore: Folklore in the Freshman English Class. *Indiana English Journal* 11 (2): 15–24.

Bakhtin, Mikhail. [1965] 1984. *Rabelais and His World.* Trans. Helene Iswolsky. Bloomington: Indiana University Press.

Bateson, Mary Catherine. 1990. *Composing a Life.* New York: Plume.

Bauer, Dale M. 1998. Indecent Proposals: Teachers in the Movies. *College English* 60 (3): 301–17.

Bauerlein, Mark, with Ellen Grantham. 2008. *National Endowment for the Arts: A History 1965–2008.* Washington, DC: National Endowment for the Arts. http://www.nea.gov/pub/nea-history-1965-2008.pdf (accessed 24 April 2011).

Behar, Ruth. 2003. *Translated Woman.* Boston: Beacon Press.

Belanus, Betty. 1985. *Folklore in the Classroom.* Indianapolis: Indiana Historical Society.

Bettis, Pamela J. 1996. Urban Students, Liminality, and the Postindustrial Context. *Sociology of Education* 69 (2): 105–25.

Bhabba, Homi K. [1989] 2001. The Commitment to Theory. In *The Norton Anthology of Theory and Criticism,* ed. Vincent B. Leitch, 2379–97. New York: W.W. Norton and Company.

Botkin, Benjamin. 1938. The Folk and the Individual: Their Creative Reciprocity. *English Journal* 27: 21–35.

Bowers, C. A. 2006. *Transforming Environmental Education: Making the Renewal of the Cultural and Environmental Commons the Focus of Educational Reform.* Eugene, OR: Ecojustice Press. http://cabowrs.net (accessed 8 November 2006).

Bowman, Paddy. 2006. Standing at the Crossroads of Folklore and Education. *Journal of American Folklore* 119 (471): 66–79.

Bowman, Paddy, and Bartis, Peter. 1994. *A Teacher's Guide to Folklife Resources for K-12 Classrooms.* Washington, DC: The American Folklife Center.

Brenson, Michael. 1995. Healing in Time. In *Culture in Action A Public Art Program of Sculpture Chicago,* edited by Michael Brenson, Eva Olson, and Mary Jane Jacob, 16–49. Seattle: Bay Press.

Britzman, Deborah P. 1992. Structures of Feeling in Curriculum and Teaching. *Theory into Practice* 31 (3): 252–58.

Bronner, Simon J. 2002. *Folk Nation: Folklore in the Creation of American Tradition.* Wilmington, DE: American Visions.

Brower, Aaron M., and Karen Dettinger. 1998. What Is a Learning Community? Towards a Comprehensive Model. *About Campus* (November/December): 15–21.

Bruner, Jerome. 1960. *The Process of Education: A Landmark in Educational Theory.* Cambridge, MA: Harvard University Press.

Brunvand, Jan. 1978. *The Study of American Folklore.* 2nd ed. New York: W. W. Norton and Company.

Bulger, Peggy. 1991. Politics, Principles, and Principals. *Southern Folklore* 48 (1): 13–20.

Butler, Judith. 1990. *Gender Trouble: Feminism and the Subversion of Identity.* New York: Routledge.

Cahnmann-Taylor, Melisa. 2008. Arts-Based Research: Histories and New Directions. In *Arts-Based Research in Education,* ed. Melisa Cahnmann-Taylor and Richard Siegesmund, 3–15.

Cahnmann-Taylor, Melisa, and Richard Siegesmund, eds. 2008. *Arts-Based Research in Education.* New York: Routledge.

Campbell, Anne. 2007. *Louisiana: The History of an American State.* Atlanta: Clairmont Press.

Campbell, Patricia Shehan. 2004. *Teaching Music Globally: Experiencing Music, Expressing Culture.* New York: Oxford University Press.

Cazden, Courtney, and Dell Hymes. 1978. Narrative and Story-Telling Rights: A Folklorist's Clue to a Critique of Education. *Keystone Folklore* 22: 21–36.

Center for Community Engagement. 2006. *Service Learning Curriculum Development Resource Guide for Faculty.* http://www.csulb.edu/divisions/aa/personnel/cce/faculty/documents/ResourceGuideforFaculty0706_000.pdf (accessed 10 January 2011).

Chalmers, F. Graeme. 1996. *Celebrating Pluralism: Art, Education, and Cultural Diversity.* Los Angeles: J. Paul Getty Trust.

Children's Defense Fund. 2007. America's Cradle to Prison Pipeline Report. http://www.childrensdefense.org/child-research-data-publications (accessed 20 April 2011).

Choy, Susan P. 2001. *Students Whose Parents Did Not Go to College: Postsecondary Access, Persistence, and Attainment.* 2001. Washington, DC: U.S. Department of Education, National Center for Education Statistics. http://nces.ed.gov/pubs2001/2001126.pdf (accessed 10 January 2011).

Confucius. 1997. *The Analects.* Trans. Simon Leys. New York: W.W. Norton and Company.

Congdon, Kristin G. 1987. Toward a Theoretical Approach to the Study of Folk Art: A Definition. *Studies in Art Education* 28 (2): 93–106.

———. 2004. *Community Art in Action.* Worcester, MA: Davis Publications.

———. 2006. Folkvine.org: Arts-Based Research on the Web. *Studies in Art Education* 48 (1): 36–51.

Congdon, Kristin G, and Tina Bucuvalas. 2006. *Just Above the Water: Florida Folk Art.* Jackson: University Press of Mississippi.

Congdon, Kristin G., and Natalie Underberg. 2006. Religious Inspiration in Ruby C. Williams' Creative Practices: Presentation and Teaching Approaches in Folkvine. org. *Journal of Cultural Research in Art Education* 24: 7–48.

Cook-Sather, Alison. 2006. Newly Betwixt and Between: Revising Liminality in the Context of a Teacher Preparation Program. *Anthropology and Education Quarterly* 37 (2): 110–27.

Coombs, Philip H., and Manzoor Ahmed. 1974. *Attacking Rural Poverty: How Non-formal Education Can Help.* Baltimore: Johns Hopkins University Press.

Counts, George S. [1932] 1978. *Dare the School Build a New Social Order?* Carbondale: Southern Illinois University Press.

Cremin, Lawrence. 1964. *Transformation of the School: Progressivism in American Education 1876–1957.* New York: Vintage Books.

———. 1972. *American Education: The Colonial Experience, 1607–1783.* New York: Harper Collins.

———. 1976. *Public Education.* New York: Basic Books.

Danielson, Larry. 1976. The Uses of Folk Literature in the English Classroom. *Illinois English Bulletin* 64 (1): 13–21.

Davis, Edwin. 1985. *Louisiana: The Pelican State.* Rev. ed. Baton Rouge: LSU Press.

Davis, Shari, and Benny Ferdman. 1993. *Nourishing the Heart: A Guide to Intergenerational Arts Projects in the Schools.* New York: City Lore, Inc., and Creative Ways.

Delacruz, Elizabeth Manley. 1999. Folk Art as Communal Culture and Art Proper. *Journal of Art Education* 52 (4): 23–24, 33–35.

Delpit, Lisa. [1995] 2006. *Other People's Children: Cultural Conflict in the Classroom.* Updated ed. New York: New Press.

Desai, Dipti. 2005. Places to Go: Challenges to Multicultural Art Education in a Global Economy. *Studies in Art Education* 46 (4): 293–308.

Dewey, John. [1900] 1990. *The School and Society/The Child and the Curriculum.* Chicago: University of Chicago Press.

———. 1916. *Democracy and Education: An Introduction to the Philosophy of Education.* New York: Macmillan.

———. [1929] 1964. American Education and Culture. In *John Dewey on Education: Selected Writings,* ed. R. Archambault, 289–94. New York: Modern Library.

Di Stefano, John. 2002. Moving Images of Home. *Art Journal* 61 (4): 38–51.

Dorson, Richard, and Inta Carpenter. 1978. Can Folklorists and Educators Work Together? *North Carolina Folklore Journal* 26: 3–13.

Dundes, Alan. 1969. Folklore as a Mirror of Culture. *Elementary English* 46: 471–82.

Eisner, Eliot. 1998. *The Kinds of Schools We Need.* Portsmouth, NH: Heinemann.

———. 2002. *The Arts and the Creation of Mind.* New Haven: Yale University Press.

Eleuterio, Susan, in collaboration with staff and master artists of the Missouri Folk Arts program. 2009. *Show-Me Traditions: An Educator's Guide to Teaching Folk Arts and Folklife in Missouri Schools.* Columbia: Missouri Folk Arts Program.

FairTest. 2011. The Case against High-Stakes Testing. http://fairtest.org/k-12/high+stakes (accessed 20 April 2011).

Falk, John, and Lynn Dierking. 2010. The 95 Percent Solution: School Is Not Where Most Americans Learn Most of Their Science. *American Scientist* 98 (6): 486–93.

Farber, Paul, Eugene F. Provenzo, and Gunilla Holm. 1994. *Schooling in the Light of Popular Culture.* New York: State University of New York Press.

Fine, Michelle, Bernadette Anand, Carlton Jordan, and Dana Sherman. 2000. Before the Bleach Gets Us All. In *Construction Sites: Excavating Race, Class, and Gender among*

Urban Youth, ed. Lois Weis and Michelle Fine, 161–79. New York: Teachers College Press.

Florida, Richard. 2002. *The Rise of the Creative Class and How It's Transforming Work, Leisure, Community and Everyday Life.* New York: Basic Books.

Foxfire Fund. 2011. What is "Foxfire"? http://www.foxfire.org (accessed 25 April 2011).

Freedom Writers. 2007. Dir. Richard LaGravenese. Paramount Pictures.

Freire, Paulo and Donald Macedo. 1987. *Literacy: Reading the Word and the World.* New York: Bergin and Garvey.

Freire, Paulo. 2000 [1973]. *Pedagogy of the Oppressed.* 30th Aanniversary Eedition. New York: Continuum Press.

Fryer, Roland G., and Steven D. Levitt. 2004. The Black-White Test Score Gap through Third Grade. Working paper. National Bureau of Economic Research. http://www.economics.harvard.edu/faculty/fryer/files/fryer_levitt_ecls2.pdf (accessed 25 January 2011).

Garza, Carmen Lomas. 2000. *In My Family/En MiFamilia.* San Francisco, CA: Children's Book Press.

Govenar, Alan. 2000. *Osceola: Memories of a Sharecropper's Daughter.* Illus. Shane Evans. New York: Hyperion Books for Children.

———. 2006a. *Extraordinary Ordinary People: Five American Masters of Traditional Arts.* Cambridge, MA: Candlewick Press.

———. 2006b. *Stompin' at the Savoy: The Story of Norma Miller.* Illus. Martin French. Cambridge, MA: Candlewick Press.

Graham, Mark. 2009. Critical Place-Based Art Education: Community, Ecology, and Artmaking. *Translations* 18 (2): 1–4.

Greene, Maxine. 1988. *The Dialectic of Freedom.* New York: Teachers College Press.

———. 2000. Lived Spaces, Shared Spaces, Public Spaces. In *Construction Sites: Excavating Race, Class, and Gender among Urban Youth,* ed. Lois Weis and Michelle Fine, 293–303.

Grider, Sylvia. 1988. *Children's Folklore: A Manual for Teachers.* White Springs, FL: Bureau of Florida Folklife Programs.

———. 1995. Passed Down from Generation to Generation: Folklore and Teaching. *Journal of American Folklore* 108 (428): 178–85.

Groce, Nancy. 1985. *Generation to Generation: The Staten Island Folk Artists in the Schools Project.* New York: Staten Island Council on the Arts.

———. 2000–2001. Broadway's Gypsy Robe. *City Lore Magazine* 8: 14.

Groce, Nancy, with Janis Benincasa. 1987. Folk Artists in Staten Island Schools: Developing a Workable Model for Larger Communities. *New York Folklore* 13: 27–38.

Hamer, Lynne. 1999. A Folkloristic Approach to Understanding Teachers as Storytellers. *International Journal of Qualitative Studies in Education* 12 (4): 363–80.

———. 2000. Folklore in Schools and Multicultural Education: Toward Institutionalizing Noninstitutional Knowledge. *Journal of American Folklore* 113 (447): 44–69.

Hamer, Lynne, Fuad al-Daraweesh, Breck Davis, Laura Hampton, Gregory Johnson, Phyllis Johnson, Tara Meckley-Hill, Anastasia Mirzonyants, David Ragland, Michelle Self, Jean Underfer-Babalis, and Virginia Welsh. 2007. Padua Alliance for Education, Empowerment, and Engagement: Participatory Action Research Meets Qualitative Research Methods. Paper presented at Common Interests-Shared Efforts: A Workshop on Participatory Action Research Tools and Skills, Sofia Quintero Art and Cultural Center, Toledo, OH, 2 June 2007.

Hamer, Lynne, Cynthia Knechtges, Revathy Kumar, and Susanna Hapgood. 2010. Summoning the Village to Raise the Child. Unpublished manuscript. Department of Educational Foundations and Leadership, University of Toledo.

Hamer, Lynne, Revathy Kumar, and Morris Jenkins. 2010. Kuschwantz-Junction Promise Neighborhood Plan. Unpublished manuscript, Department of Educational Foundations and Leadership, University of Toledo.

Hamer, Lynne, Revathy Kumar, David Ragland, and Sarah Twitchell. 2010. Supporting the Parents to Lead the Way: UT Education Opportunities (UT-EO) Pilot Initiative. Unpublished manuscript, Department of Educational Foundations and Leadership, University of Toledo.

Haring, Lee, and Ellen Foreman. 1975. Folklore in the Freshman Writing Course. *College English* 37: 13–21.

Haut, Judith E. 1994. How Can Acting Like a Fieldworker Enrich Pluralistic Education? In *Putting Folklore to Use,* ed. Michael Owen Jones, 45–61. Lexington: University Press of Kentucky.

Heath, Shirley Brice. 1983. *Ways with Words: Language, Life, and Work in Communities and Classrooms.* Cambridge: Cambridge University Press.

Hesse, Maria, and Marybeth Mason. 2005. The Case for Learning Communities. *Community College Journal* 76 (1): 30–35.

Hetland, Lois, Ellen Winner, Shirley Veenema, and Kimberly M. Sheridan. 2007. *Studio Thinking: The Real Benefits of Visual Arts Education.* New York: Teachers College Press.

———. 2007. Making the Case for the Arts: Why Arts Education Is Not a Luxury. In *Studio Thinking: The Real Benefits of Visual Arts Education,* 1–8.

Hirsch, E. D. 1988. *Cultural Literacy: What Every American Needs to Know.* New York: Vintage Books.

hooks, bell. [1990] 2001. Postmodern Blackness. In *The Norton Anthology of Theory and Criticism,* ed. Vincent B. Leitch, 2478–84.

———. 1992. *Black Looks: Race and Representation.* Boston: South End Press.

———. 1994. *Teaching to Transgress: Education as the Practice of Freedom.* New York: Routledge.

———. 2003. *Teaching Community: A Pedagogy of Hope.* New York: Routledge.

Howard, Dorothy. 1950. Folklore in the Schools. *New York Folklore Quarterly* 6 (2): 99–107.

Hufford, Mary. 1979. *A Tree Smells like Peanut Butter: Folk Artists in a City School.* Trenton: New Jersey State Council on the Arts.

Hursh, David. 2008. *High-Stakes Testing and the Decline of Teaching and Learning: The Real Crisis in Education.* Lanham, MD: Rowman & Littlefield Education.

Insight Center for Community and Economic Development (ICCED). 2010. *Lifting as We Climb: Women of Color, Wealth, and America's Future.* Oakland, CA: ICCED.

Jacobs, Jane. [1961] 1992. *Death and Life of American Cities.* New York: Vintage Books.

Jencks, Christopher, and Meredith Phillips, eds. 1998. *The Black-White Test Score Gap.* Washington, DC: Brookings Institution Press.

Johnson, Gregory. 2009. Getting Integrated? A Personal History of Public Schooling. *Pathways* (Literary and Arts Journal of Owens Community College): 80–85.

Khandelwal, Madhulika. 2002. *Becoming American, Being Indian: An Immigrant Community in New York City.* Ithaca: Cornell University Press.

Kierkegaard, Soren. [1843] 1996. *Papers and Journals: A Selection.* Trans. Alastair Hannay. London: Penguin Classics.

Kirshenblatt-Gimblett, Barbara. 1983. An Accessible Aesthetic: The Role of Folk Arts and Folk Artists in the Curriculum. *New York Folklore* 9 (3–4): 9–18. http://www. locallearningnetwork.org/library/the-archive (accessed 21 January 2011).

Kodish, Debora, and Deborah Wei. 2002. Privatization and Folklore. Philadelphia Folklore Project. http://www.folkloreproject.org/folkarts/resources/issues/privatization.php (accessed 25 January 2011).

Kodish, Debora, and Westerman, William. 2011 [1996]. Negotiating Pitfalls and Possibilities: Presenting Folk Arts in the School. *Works in Progress: The Magazine of the Philadelphia Folklore Project 9*, 1/2: 8-11. http://locallearningnetwork.org/library/the-archive (accessed 30 July 2011).

Ladson-Billings, Gloria. [1994] 2009. *The Dreamkeepers: Successful Teachers of African American Students.* 2nd ed. New York: Jossey-Bass.

Lanser, Susan. S. 1993. Burning Dinners: Feminist Subversions of Domesticity. In *Feminist Messages: Coding in Women's Folk Culture,* ed. Joan Newlon Radner, 36–53. Chicago: University of Illinois Press.

Lawless, Elaine J. 2001. *Women Escaping Violence: Empowerment through Narrative.* Columbia: University of Missouri Press.

Limón, José. 1983. Western Marxism and Folklore: A Critical Introduction. *Journal of American Folklore* 96 (379): 34–52.

Lindahl, Carl, Maida Owens, and Renee Harvison. 1997. *Swapping Stories: Folktales from Louisiana.* Jackson: University Press of Mississippi.

Lippard, Lucy. 1997. *The Lure of the Local: Senses of Place in a Multicentered Society.* New York: New Press.

Local Learning. 2010. About Folklore and Folk Arts. http://locallearningnetwork.org/about/about-folk-arts-and-folklore (accessed 20 April 2011).

Long, Lucy. 1999. *To Dance Irish: An Educational Resource Guide.* Bowling Green, OH: Department of Popular Culture, Bowling Green State University.

Lorde, Audre. 1981. The Master's Tools Will Never Dismantle the Master's House. In *This Bridge Called My Back: Writings by Radical Women of Color,* ed. Cherrie Moranga and Gloria Anzuldúa, 98–101. New York: Kitchen Table Women of Color Press.

Lowenthal, David. 1985. *The Past Is a Foreign Country.* Cambridge: Cambridge University Press.

Lubienski, Christopher. 2010. *The Charter School Experiment: Expectations, Evidence, and Implications.* Cambridge, MA: Harvard University Press.

MacDowell, Marsha, ed. 1987. *Folk Arts in Education: A Resource Handbook.* East Lansing: Michigan State University Museum.

MacDowell, Marsha, and LuAnne Kozma, eds. 2008. *Folk Arts in Education: A Resource Handbook II.* East Lansing: Michigan State University Museum.

McCarthy, Cameron. 1994. Multicultural Discourses and Curriculum Reform: A Critical Perspective. *Educational Theory* 44: 81–98.

McCarthy, Cameron, and Greg Dimitriadis. 2000. Governmentality and the Sociology of Education: Media, Educational Policy and the Politics of Resentment. *British Journal of Sociology of Education* 21 (2): 169–85.

McFee, June King. 1966. *Preparation for Art.* Belmont, CA: Wadsworth Publishing Company.

McIntyre, Alice. 2000. *Inner-City Kids: Adolescents Confront Life and Violence in an Urban Community.* New York: New York University Press.

Magnuson, Katherine, and Greg J. Duncan. 2006. The Role of Family Socioeconomic Resources in the Black-White Test Score Gap among Young Children. Conference paper presented as part of the Harvard Graduate School of Education Achievement Gap Initiative. http://agi.harvard.edu/Search/SearchAllPapers.php (accessed 25 January 2011).

Martin, Renee. 1991. A Model for Studying the Effects of Social Policy on Education. *Equity and Excellence in Education* 25 (2): 53–56.

Martusewicz, Rebecca, Jeff Edmundson, and John Lupinacci. 2011. *EcoJustice Education: Toward Diverse, Democratic and Sustainable Communities.* New York: Routledge.

Mascia-Lees, Frances E., Patricia Sharpe, and Colleen Ballerino Cohen. 1989. The Postmodernist Turn in Anthropology: Cautions from a Feminist Perspective. *Signs: Journal of Women in Culture and Society* 15 (1): 7–33.

Mediratta, Kavitha, Seema Shah, and Sara McAllister. 2008. *Organized Communities, Stronger Schools: A Preview of Research Findings.* Providence: Annenberg Institute.

Meister, Gwen, Chair. 2007. Making the Intangible Tangible: Uses of Folklife Resources in Educational Settings. Forum at the American Folklore Society Annual Meeting, Quebec City, October 19, 2007.

Missouri Department of Elementary and Secondary Education. 1996. Show-Me Standards. http://dese.mo.gov/standards (accessed 12 December 2010).

Missouri Secretary of State. Why Is Missouri Called the Show-Me State? Missouri History. http://www.sos.mo.gov/archives/history/slogan.asp (accessed 15 January 2011).

Moffett, James, and B. J. Wagner. 1983. *Student-Centered Language Arts and Reading K–12: A Handbook for Teachers.* Boston: Houghton Mifflin.

Moll, Luis, Cathy Amanti, Deborah Neff, and Norma Gonzalez. 1992. Funds of Knowledge for Teaching: Using a Qualitative Approach to Connect Homes and Classrooms. *Theory into Practice* 31 (2): 132–41.

Mondloch, Kate. 2007. Be Here (and There) Now: The Spatial Dynamics of Screen-Reliant Installation Art. *Art Journal* 66 (3): 20–33.

Moonsammy, Rita. 1991. From Majority to Maturity: The Development of Folk Art in Education Programs. *Southern Folklore* 48 (1): 21–29.

———. 1992. *Passing It On: Folk Artists and Education in Cumberland County, New Jersey.* Trenton: New Jersey State Council on the Arts.

Mott, Andrew. 2005. *University Education for Community Change: A Vital Strategy for Progress on Poverty, Race and Community Building.* Washington, DC: Community Building Project.

National Endowment for the Arts (NEA). 2007. *National Heritage Fellowships 1982–2007.* Washington, DC: NEA. Accompanying DVD-ROM includes *Masters of Traditional Arts Education Guide,* by Paddy Bowman, Betty Carter, and Alan Govenar.

Nunez, Anne-Marie, and Stephanie Cuccaro-Alamin. 1998. *First Generation Students: Undergraduates Whose Parents Never Enrolled in Postsecondary Education.* Washington, DC: U.S. Department of Education, National Center for Education Statistics.

Nusz, Nancy J. 1991. Folklife in Education: Introduction and Selected Bibliography. *Southern Folklore* 48 (1): 5–12.

Oakes, Jeannie, and Martin Lipton. 2003. *Teaching to Change the World.* Boston: McGraw-Hill.

Oliver, Melvin, and Thomas Shapiro. 2006. *Black Wealth/White Wealth: A New Perspective on Racial Inequality.* 2nd ed. New York: Routledge.

Orfield, Gary, and John T. Yun. 1999. *Resegregation in American Schools.* Cambridge, MA: Harvard University Civil Rights Project.

Payne, Charles. 2008. *So Much Reform, So Little Change: The Persistence of Failure in Urban Schools.* Cambridge, MA: Harvard Education Press.

Pryor, Anne. 2004. Deep Ethnography: Culture at the Core of Curriculum. *Language Arts* 81 (5): 396–405.

Pryor, Anne, and Nancy B. Blake, eds. 2007. *Quilting Circles - Learning Communities: Arts, Community, and Curriculum Guide.* Madison: University of Wisconsin School of Education and Wisconsin Arts Board.

Puckett, John. 1989. *Foxfire Reconsidered.* Carbondale: University of Illinois Press.

Ravitch, Diane. 2010. *The Death and Life of the Great American School System: How Testing and Choice Are Undermining Education.* New York: Basic Books.

Remer, Jane. 2003. Artist-Educators in Context: A Brief History of Artists in K–12 American Public Schooling. *Teaching Artist Journal* 1 (2): 69–79.

Ritchhart, Ron, Patricia Palmer, Mark Church, and Shari Tishman. 2006. Thinking Routines: Establishing Patterns of Thinking in the Classroom. Paper presented at the American Educational Research Association conference. http://www.pz.harvard.edu/Research/AERA06ThinkingRoutines.pdf (accessed 25 January 2011).

Robertson, Judith P. 1997. Fantasy's Confines: Popular Culture and the Education of the Female Primary School Teacher. *Canadian Journal of Education/Revue Canadienne de l'éducation* 22 (2): 123–43.

Roland, Craig. 1995. The Use of Journals to Promote Reflective Thinking in Prospective Art Teachers. In *Preservice Art Education: Issues and Practices,* ed. Lynn Galbraith, 119–34. Reston, VA: National Art Education Association.

Rose, Michael. 2009. *Why School? Reclaiming Education for All of Us.* New York: New Press.

Rosenberg, Jan. 2004. Reflections on Folklife and Education: Is There a Unified History of Folklore and Education? *AFS Folklore and Education Section Newsletter.* http://www.afsnet.org/sections/education/Spring2004 (accessed 10 April 2011).

———. 2011. From "Me" to "We": Folklore and Education in the Work of Three Early Twentieth Century Educators. Unpublished manuscript, Heritage Education Resources, Inc., Bloomington, Indiana.

Rosenzweig, Roy, and David Thelen. 2000. *The Presence of the Past: Popular Uses of History in American Life.* New York: Columbia University Press.

Rugg, Harold, and Ann Shumaker. 1928. *The Child-Centered School: An Appraisal of the New Education.* Yonkers-on-Hudson, NY: World Book.

Ryan, William. 1976. *Blaming the Victim.* 2nd ed. New York: Vintage Books.

Sandell, Renee. 2009. Using Form + Theme + Context (FTC) for Rebalancing 21st Century Art Education. *Studies in Art Education* 50 (3): 287–99.

Sanjek, Roger. 1990. *Fieldnotes.* Ithaca, NY: Cornell University Press.

Saper, Craig. 2008. Toward a Visceral Scholarship Online: Folkvine.org and Hypermedia Ethnography. *Journal of e-Media Studies* 1 (1). http://journals.dartmouth.edu/cgi-bin/WebObjects/Journals.woa/xmlpage/4/issue (accessed 10 January 2011).

Schaff, Leo. 2009. Clara's Song: Writing Songs from Interviews. *CARTS* 10: 20–21. http://locallearningnetwork.org/library/articles (accessed 24 April 2011).

Shakur, Tupac. 2000.. *The Rose that Grew from Concrete.* Audio CD. Interscope Records

Sidener, Diane. 1997. *Standards for Folklife Education: Integrating Language Arts, Social Studies, Arts, and Science through Student Traditions and Culture.* Immaculata, PA: Pennsylvania Folklife Education Committee.

Simons, Elizabeth Radin. 1990. *Student Worlds, Student Words: Teaching Writing through Folklore.* Portsmouth, NH: Heinemann.

Smith, Gregory A. 2002. Place-Based Education: Learning to Be Where We Are. *Phi Delta Kappan* 83 (8): 584–94.

Smith, Gregory A., and David Sobel. 2010. *Place- and Community-Based Education in Schools*. New York: Routledge.

Spring, Joel. 2009. *Deculturalization and the Struggle for Equality: A Brief History of the Education of Dominated Cultures in the United States*. 6th ed. Boston: McGraw-Hill.

Stekert, Ellen. 1969. Folklore: A Vehicle for Teaching Objective Analysis and Cultural Awareness. In *Perspectives on Folklore and Education*, 4–7. Folklore Forum Bibliographic and Special Series 2. Bloomington: Folklore Institute, Indiana University Press.

Sunstein, Bonnie, and Elizabeth Chiseri-Strater. 2002. *Field Working: Reading and Writing Research*. 2nd ed. Boston: Bedford/St. Martin's.

Szwed, John. 2010. *Alan Lomax, the Man Who Recorded the World: A Biography*. New York: Viking.

Take the Lead. 2006. Dir. Liz Friedlander. New Line Cinema.

Tishman, Shari, and Patricia Palmer. 2006. *Artful Thinking: Stronger Thinking and Learning through the Power of Art*. Cambridge, MA: Project Zero, Harvard Graduate School of Education.

Tough, Paul. 2008. *Whatever It Takes: Geoffrey Canada's Quest to Change Harlem and America*. Boston: Houghton Mifflin.

Trier, James D. 2001. The Cinematic Representation of the Personal and Professional Lives of Teachers. *Teacher Education Quarterly* 28 (3): 127–42. http://findarticles.com/p/articles/mi_qa3960/is_200107/ai_n8978277/pg_2 (accessed 25 January 2011).

Trinh T. Mihn-Ha. 1989. *Woman, Native, Other*. Bloomington: Indiana University Press.

Tyack, David. 1974. *The One Best System: A History of American Urban Education*. Cambridge, MA: Harvard University Press.

Umphrey, Michael. 2007. *The Power of Community-Centered Education: Teaching as a Craft of Place*. Lanham, MD: Rowman & Littlefield Education.

Underberg, Natalie, and Kristin G. Congdon. 2007. Folkvine.org: Ethnographic Storytelling in Folk Art Web Design. *Visual Anthropology Review* 23 (2): 151–61.

Veltri, Barbara Torre. 2010. *Learning on Other People's Kids: Becoming a Teach for America Teacher*. Charlotte, NC: Information Age Publishers.

Wagler, Mark. 2000. Kid-to-Kid Cultural Dialogue in the Center of the Social Studies. In *Social Studies and Technology: Classroom Action Research 1999–2000*, 61–96. Madison, WI: Madison Metropolitan School District.

———. 2002. The Inquiry Approach and Publishing. In *Publishing with Students*, ed. Chris Weber, 120–29. Portsmouth, NH: Heinemann.

———. 2006. Teaching the World We Live In: Collecting and Telling Ethnographic Stories. In *The Storytelling Classroom: Applications across the Curriculum*, ed. Sherry Norfolk, Jane Stenson, and Diane Williams, 109–13. Westport, CT: Libraries Unlimited.

Wagler, Mark, and Michael Beeth. 2002. Communities of Teacher Inquiry. In *Science: A Chapter of the Curriculum Handbook*, edited by Steven Jay Cross, 27–45. Alexandria, VA: Association for Supervision and Curriculum Development.

Wagler, Mark, Ruth Olson, and Anne Pryor. 2004. *Kids' Guide to Local Culture*. Madison, WI: Madison Children's Museum.

Walton, Shana. 2004a. Lessons in Folklife and Technology for English Language Arts (LiFT-ELA) grant application submitted by Tulane University Deep South Regional Humanities Center to the Louisiana Board of Regents' Louisiana Systematic Initiatives Program (LaSIP).

————. 2004b. High Stakes Testing and New Orleans Public Schools. Paper presented at the American Anthropological Association annual meeting, San Francisco, 19 November 2004.

Watzup. Life Unpredictable. 2007. Unpublished script from The Art of Many Voices project, written by high-school students from William Penn High School, Harrisburg, PA.

Weis, Lois, and Michelle Fine, eds. 2000. *Construction Sites: Excavating Race, Class, and Gender among Urban Youth.*

Wells, Robert W. 1968. *Fire at Peshtigo.* Englewood Cliffs, NJ: Prentice-Hall, Inc.

Williams, Raymond. 1958. *Culture and Society 1780–1950.* New York: Columbia University Press.

Wilson, Bruce L., and H. Dickson Corbett. 2001. *Listening to Urban Kids: School Reform and the Teachers They Want.* Albany: State University of New York Press.

Winner, Ellen, and Lois Hetland. 2000. The Arts in Education: Evaluating the Evidence for a Causal Link. *Journal of Aesthetic Education* 34 (3–4): 3–10. http://www.jstor.org/stable/3333636 (accessed 25 January 2011).

Witcher, Brenda, Anastasia Mirzoyants, and Lynne Hamer. 2009. Starting a Successful PAR: Assets & Needs from Community Members' Points of View. Radical Possibilities in the Graduate Classroom. Paper presented at the American Educational Studies Association annual meeting, 5 November 2009, Pittsburgh, Pennsylvania.

Woodson, Carter G. [1933] 2011. *The Mis-education of the Negro.* New York: Tribeca Books.

Appendix

Selected Folk Arts in Education Resources

Bibliography

Many publications that academic and public-sector folklorists produce are highly useful for K–12 educators and students. This list represents some of the resources that the editors use often, and each entry will lead the reader to additional excellent resources as well.

Astroth, Kirk A. 2004. *Spurrin' the Words: 4-H Cowboy Poetry Project.* Bozeman: Montana 4-H Center for Youth Development.

Belanus, Betty. 1985. *Folklore in the Classroom.* Indianapolis: Indiana Historical Society.

Bowman, Paddy. 2004. "Oh, that's just folklore": Valuing the Ordinary as an Extraordinary Teaching Tool. *Language Arts* 81 (5): 385–95.

Bowman, Paddy, and Amanda Dargan, eds. *CARTS.* A newsletter copublished by Local Learning and City Lore since 1996. Find excerpts of back issues in the Archive of the Library section at http://www.locallearningnetwork.org

Bowman, Paddy, Alan Govenar, and Betty Carter. 2007. *Masters of Traditional Arts Education Guide.* PDF on the National Endowment for the Arts *National Heritage Fellowships 1982–2007* DVD-ROM, produced by Documentary Arts. Order free at http://www.nea.gov/pub/pubFolk.php

Campbell, Patricia Shehan. 1998. *Songs in Their Heads: Music and Its Meaning in Children's Lives.* New York: Oxford University Press.

Congdon, Kristin G. 2001. *Uncle Monday and Other Florida Tales.* Illus. Kitty Kitson Petterson. Jackson: University of Mississippi Press.

Eleuterio, Susan, in collaboration with staff and master artists of the Missouri Folk Arts Program. 2009. *Show-Me Traditions: An Educator's Guide to Teaching Folk Arts and Folklife in Missouri Schools.* Columbia: Missouri Folk Arts Program.

MacDowell, Marsha, and LuAnne Kozma, eds. 2008. *Folk Arts in Education: A Resource Handbook II.* Lansing: Michigan State University Museum. Order hard copy or CD-ROM or download at http://www.folkartsineducation.org

Moonsammy, Rita Zorn. 1992. *Passing It On: Folk Artists and Education in Cumberland County, New Jersey.* Trenton: New Jersey State Council on the Arts. Find an excerpt at http://locallearningnetwork.org/library/the-archive.

Pryor, Anne. 2004. Deep Ethnography: Culture at the Core of Curriculum. *Language Arts* 81 (5): 396–405.

Pryor, Anne, and Nancy B. Blake, eds. 2007. *Quilting Circles – Learning Communities: Arts, Community, and Curriculum Guide.* Madison: University of Wisconsin School of Education and Wisconsin Arts Board.

Simons, Elizabeth Radin. 1990. *Student Worlds, Student Words: Teaching Writing through Folklore.* Portsmouth, NH: Heinemann.

Sunstein, Bonnie, and Elizabeth Chiseri-Strater. 2002. *Field Working: Reading and Writing Research.* 2nd ed. Boston: Bedford/St. Martin's.

Toelken, Barre. 1996. *The Dynamics of Folklore.* Logan: Utah State University Press.

Wagler, Mark, Ruth Olson, and Anne Pryor. 2004. *Teacher's Guide to Local Culture* and *Kids' Guide to Local Culture.* Madison: Madison Children's Museum and Center for the Study of Upper Midwestern Culture. Download at http://csumc.wisc.edu/ wtlc/?q=resources. [Note: This is the correct order. I may have done this wrong in Works Cited, I think I put Pryor second, she's third.]

Webography

> *These Web sites represent only some exemplary folk-arts-in-education online resources. Many more may be found in Regional Resources at http://www.LocalLearningNetwork.org and in Folklife Resources for Educators on the Web site of the American Folklife Center at the Library of Congress, online at http://www.loc.gov/ folklife. Also see an extensive annotated webography by Gregory Hansen in* Folklore and the Internet: Vernacular Expression in a Digital World, *ed. Trevor J. Blank, 213–30. Logan: Utah State University Press, 2009.*

Alaska Native Knowledge Network at http://www.ankn.uaf.edu publishes model lesson plans and the groundbreaking *Culturally Responsive* education standards.

American Folklife Center at the Library of Congress at http://www.loc.gov/folklife has many digital collections useful in the classroom plus Folklife Resources for Educators, a portal to many free online curriculum guides.

American Folklore Society (AFS) Folklore and Education Section at http://www.afsnet.org publishes an annual newsletter for members, who may sign up for ten dollars without having to join AFS.

Bullfrog Jumped in the Classroom, available at http://www.alabamafolklife.org/content/ bullfrog-classroom, provides audio excerpts of children's songs recorded in 1947 in an online guide by Paddy Bowman and Marsha Weiner for prekindergarten through grade three.

Center for the Study of Upper Midwestern Culture at http://csumc.wisc.edu (see chapter 3) supports the Wisconsin Teachers of Local Culture network and projects that demonstrate how deeply students can reflect about culture and themselves, including a section on cultural tours.

City Lore at http://www.citylore.org provides professional development for teachers and artists as well as resources and residencies.

Crossroads of the Heart: Creativity and Tradition in Mississippi at http://www.arts.state.
  ms.us/crossroads frames the state's traditions in multimedia portals, including a
  teacher's guide.

Culture in Context: A Tapestry in Expression at http://www.njn.net/artsculture/cultureincon-
  text features many New Jersey folk artists and art forms organized around the themes
  of home, work, and community.

Digital Traditions at http://www.digitaltraditions.net profiles South Carolina folk artists
  from the McKissick Museum Folklife Resource Center and provides the downloadable
  education guides *Dave: I Made This Jar, Jubilation: African American Celebrations in
  the Southeast,* and *Row upon Row: Sea Grass Baskets of the South Carolina Lowcountry.*

Documentary Arts at http://www.docarts.com produces many resources useful to educators, including education guides and award-winning children's books by Documentary Arts director Alan Govenar.

Folkstreams at http://www.folkstreams.net streams American folk culture documentaries
  and offers users extensive background materials for each film. Paddy Bowman created the Educators Portal, which includes lessons and worksheets for high-school and
  college students, and the Generations Portal, which provides scaffolding for public
  screenings and discussions.

Folkvine at http://www.folkvine.org (see chapter 7) gives users video, audio, and text
  options to explore folk artists of Florida, including bobble-head dolls that represent
  real-life scholars of the state's traditional culture, a virtual board game for elementary
  students, and theoretical constructs for not only K–12 audiences but also higher-
  education students and faculty.

Iowa Folklife: Our People, Communities, and Traditions is an award-winning multimedia
  guide with intergenerational components for each lesson. Volume one is available at
  http://www.uni.edu/iowaonline/folklife, and volume two is at http://www.uni.edu/
  iowaonline/folklife_v2

Local Learning at http://www.locallearningnetwork.org (see chapter 1) advocates for inclusion of folk arts and artists nationwide and provides virtual-artist residencies with
  NEA National Heritage Fellows, a library of useful articles for teachers, links to
  regional resources, and tools to engage young people in fieldwork and folklore.

Louisiana Voices: An Educator's Guide to Exploring Our Communities and Traditions at http://
  www.louisianavoices.org (see chapter 2) includes all the background, lesson plans,
  worksheets, and rubrics that teachers and students need to integrate the study of
  folklore and documentation of local folklife and tradition bearers across curricula.
  This comprehensive interdisciplinary guide also features essays, photos, video, and
  audio and is in the public domain and adaptable for any region.

Michigan Folkpatterns at http://www.museum.msu.edu/s-program/folkpattern supports a
  long-term, statewide 4-H folk-arts and education program.

Missouri Folk Arts Program at http://maa.missouri.edu/mfap (see chapter 5) plans to publish an online edition of *Show-Me Traditions: An Educator's Guide to Teaching Folk
  Arts and Folklife in Missouri Schools.*

Museum of International Folk Art at http://www.moifa.org features online curricula,
  including information on children's clothing around the world, New Mexico
  National Heritage fellows, shadow puppets, and Hispanic folk arts.

National Museum of the American Indian at http://www.nmai.si.edu features virtual exhibits and guides on its Web site.

Nebraska By Heart at http://www.nefolklife.org/byheart (see chapter 6) is a multidisciplinary site for students to explore traditional arts and folklife in the state.

Nevada Arts Council Folklife Program at http://www.nevadaculture.org provides resources for educators and students, including an online folk artist roster and the *Folk Arts Education Guide*.

North Country Folklore at http://www.northcountryfolklore.org is the educational Web site of Traditional Arts in Upstate New York and offers several ways for users to explore the region: music, special places, foodways, and oral traditions.

Smithsonian Center for Folklife and Cultural Heritage at http://www.folklife.si.edu provides online curriculum and interviewing guides and links to Smithsonian Folkways recordings and lesson plans for various musical genres around the globe.

South Georgia Folklife Collection at http://www.valdosta.edu/library/find/arch/folklife features online exhibits and the education guide *Folkwriting*.

Vermont Folklife Center at http://www.vermontfolklifecenter.org supports education through a series of award-winning children's books based on stories in the Center's archive and the Discovering Community project at http://www.discoveringcommunity.org, which provides training and resources to educators.

Wisconsin Folks at www.wisconsinfolks.org (see chapter 3) teaches students about folk art and artists of that state in a lively fashion and provides examples of many genres and artists from fish decoys to dance.

Index